Praise for
Gathering Strength:
Conversations with Afghan Women

"Kelsey masterfully weaves the comments of Afghan women from different backgrounds and fields into a narrative comparable to Studs Terkel's oral histories."

Steve Maginnis, *IndieReader*

"This beautifully conceived and written book is likely one of the most important to be published in recent years…should be required reading for us all."

Grady Harp, Amazon Hall of Fame Reviewer

"Few books can match the depth of social and cultural exploration found in Gathering Strength. [The book] allows for great insight into the lives of these women through their own words [with] fearlessness in the face of adversity that truly sings off the pages."

Christine Zibas, *Helium*

"I so appreciate Peggy Kelsey for introducing me to these fine women. Through great interviewing, commentary, and exquisite photography, Gathering Strength makes me feel as though I know each of these women personally."

Barbara Glass, *The Senior Voice*

Gathering Strength

Gathering Strength:
Conversations with Afghan Women

Peggy Kelsey

Pomegranate Grove Press • Austin, Texas

Second Pomegranate Grove Printing 2013

Ten percent of the proceeds from the sale of *Gathering Strength: Conversations with Afghan Women* will be donated to an Afghan organization that works with women and children.

Permissions

Grateful acknowledgement is made to the following for permission to reprint:
Dr. MS Noury: two poems titled *Love*, by Rabia Balkh translated by Dr. MS Noury
Ketab Corporation: *The Sin*, by Forugh Farrokhzad. Translated by Ahmad Karimi Hakak in *Remembering the Flight: A Parallel Text in English and Persian*
Ismail Salami: *The Captive* by Forugh Farrokhzad, translated by Ismail Salami
Afghan Women's Writing Project: Excerpted from *Recipe for a Protest* by Shakila. First published on the Afghan Women's Writing Project blog: http://awwproject.org/2010/04/recipe-for-a-protest/
Map of Afghanistan courtesy of University of Texas Libraries
Jacquelyn Davidson: pictures of Tajwar Kakar taken in 1968:

Author photograph by Jane Steig Parsons
Afghan History Timeline by MG Wizard and P Kelsey

Printed in the United States

Pomegranate Grove Press Speaker's bureau can bring authors to your live events. For more information or to book an event, contact the Pomegranate Grove Speaker's Bureau at 1-512-799-5915 or visit our website at http://www.pomgrovepress.com

Library of Congress Cataloging in Publication Data

ISBN-10: 0985750200

ISBN-13: 978-0-9857502-0-6

Includes bibliographical references and an index.

1. Women—Afghanistan—social conditions—21st century. 2. Afghanistan—social conditions—21st century. 3. Afghanistan—history—1979-2012. 4. Afghanistan—personal narratives. 5. Muslim Women. 6. Women Social Reformers—Afghanistan—biography. I. Kelsey, Peggy. II Title.

Cover photo: Sahraa Karimi, Afghan filmmaker

Title Page: Round Islamic decoration with a historic symbolic meaning. The circle represents the Earth, the leaves symbolize nature and harmony. The star shape radiates equally from every corner and represents the center and expansion of Islam and its unity. Islamic Ornament created by Anicka / FreeVectors.net

To Bill

For my daughters, Petra and Danielle

And the women of Afghanistan

"To be hopeful in bad times is not just foolishly romantic. It is based on the fact that human history is a history not only of cruelty, but also of compassion, sacrifice, courage, kindness. What we choose to emphasize in this complex history will determine our lives. If we see only the worst, it destroys our capacity to do something. If we remember those times and places (and there are so many) where people have behaved magnificently, this gives us the energy to act, and at least the possibility of sending this spinning top of a world in a different direction. And if we do act, in however small a way, we don't have to wait for some grand utopian future. The future is an infinite succession of presents, and to live now as we think human beings should live, in defiance of all that is bad around us, is itself a marvelous victory."
-Howard Zinn, patriot, historian, and author

Table of Contents

A few women drive in Kabul.

Preface

In the Western world, the media has led us to think of Afghan women as an homogenous group with one outlook and one set of generally horrific experiences. In fact, the country, its population and perspectives, are quite diverse. Afghanistan can be divided into three very different zones: the capital of Kabul, provincial cities, and the rural areas.[1] Thirty-three years of war and interventions have affected each of these areas differently and continue to do so. War has ravaged different areas at different times, while others remained relatively peaceful. Four major and three minor ethnic groups and two major languages divide Afghan women's experiences. Despite this diversity, they have much in common with each other and with women around the world.

I traveled to Afghanistan in 2003 and 2010 to photograph and interview women. I wanted to look beyond media stereotypes, to explore how Afghan women see and experience their world, and to learn about the strategies they use to surmount tragedy and challenges. At some point, the project began to take shape as a book.

What the women say in the interviews may not always be correct according to history. What was said to me may differ from reality for many reasons. Each interviewee sees events through the lens of her personal history, biases, history of her ethnic group, circumstances, economic conditions, and personal psychology. I tried to confirm statements of fact when I could.

Another factor to consider is ephemeral memory. For example, when I interviewed Tajwar Kakar in 2003, 18 years after her imprisonment, she said she had been tortured for a week. She told Doris Lessing,[2] who interviewed her in

1985, that she had been tortured for a month. I believe that in this case, Tajwar's memory of the length of her ordeal was compressed by time and that the earlier interview was more accurate. Women in prison often suffer from post-traumatic stress disorder (PTSD) and other mental issues stemming from the abuse they suffer before, and sometimes during, incarceration. A woman may also have private reasons for not being entirely objective or truthful.

Dari,[3] a dialect of the Western Iranian languages group, and Pashtu, a dialect of the Eastern Iranian languages group, are Afghanistan's two national languages. They both use the same Arabic alphabet, with some additional letters. What are known to English speakers as "short vowels" aren't normally written, but only vocalized. When words are transcribed into, for example, English, there is no consensus on vowels used. As a result, *Bamyan* is also spelled *Bamiyan* or *Bamian*; *jerga* can be spelled *jirga*; *mujahidin* as *mujahideen* or *mujahadeen*; and *Band-e Amir* as *Band-i Amir*. I have striven for consistency as being most conducive to readibility and comprehension.

One slight exception is in spelling of names. Some women with the same name spelled it differently, as in Suraia, Soraya, and Soroya. Some names I never saw written, and in those cases opted for spellings different from other women with the same name. I also included an initial or other identifier if needed. For example, two young women in the Sports chapter, interviewed at their Taekwondo school, share first names with women I met elsewhere. I appended "TKD" to the dojo students' names to distinguish them from others.

Language conveys culture even outside of words used. In the flow of Dari, ideas may be stated, restated, and then summarized in each paragraph in a slow-paced effort to communicate. This can be frustrating for Westerners accustomed to "getting to the point," so I have edited the women's words for redundancy, while making sure to stay true to their intent and meaning.

At times, the language barrier created issues. My knowledge of Dari is limited and of Pashtu nonexistent. Interviews were conducted with and/or translated by non-native-English-speaking Afghan women, leaving room for imperfection. One humorous example occurred when I was talking with a woman who had been ill-treated by her in-laws, with whom she lived. She was quiet, soft-spoken, and seemed depressed. When I asked her how she got through her hard times, she replied that her "passion" helped her. Passion? I wasn't seeing an ounce of passion. A bit later, another woman in the house replied to my question the same way and added that Islam had taught her passion. It suddenly dawned on me that the translator was thinking of the word "patience," and she confirmed this.

As between any two languages, words that seemed to have similar definitions might have very different connotations. For example, the Dari word *mobareza*, meaning "struggling or trying not to give up," is often translated as "fight." When a woman told me that when someone opposed her she "would fight with him," her words seemed bellicose if not outright dangerous. Yet I found this usage to be very common, and mostly preserved it here.

Tajwar and others always referred to the Soviet troops as Russians. However, many soldiers were from the Union of Soviet Socialist Republics' (USSR) 14 other states. After one of my talks, a Kazakh man corrected me on this matter. His father had fought in Afghanistan and was very proud of his service. It bothered him that people only credited Russians with serving in Afghanistan.

The term "warlord" appears frequently throughout the book. Although the term has become an epithet used to discredit those one doesn't like, the Afghan women and I use the word according to the dictionary: "A military commander exercising civil power in a region, whether in nominal allegiance to the national government or in defiance of it."[4] Warlords operate with impunity in the areas they control.

The Arabic word for God, *Allah,* is used to refer to God throughout the Arabic-speaking world, among Christians and Jews as well as Muslims. In Persian and Dari, Muslims mostly say *Khoda* except when they are praying; then they say *Allah*.

⊱━◈꘡◈◈꘡◈━⊰

Identifying my interviewees without endangering them is an issue I struggled with from the beginning. It would be ironic and tragic if my efforts to help Afghan women actually made their lives worse. While I understand and respect the fears some women and/or their families expressed about being seen in a book, I don't think this book will put anyone in any more danger than they already face. Most women I met used both first and last names with me, but I've chosen not to use last names except for women who are public figures. The book is written in English, and its price will limit its distribution in Afghanistan. The woman pictured on the cover, Sahraa, is currently living in Slovakia.

⊱━◈꘡◈◈꘡◈━⊰

Shakilla S., one of my translators, once said to me, "Women are women, Eastern or Western. If the children grow good, the country will grow good. If the children grow bad, the country will grow bad. The effect of all this is up to the women. We must help women in this situation."

I have endeavored to present a balanced picture of Afghanistan and the thoughts of a wide variety of women there. Still, there are vast areas of the country and a few ethnic groups, such as the Kuchi, that I have yet to visit. Women who were thoroughly sequestered offered no point of contact and I avoided regions of active conflict.

While I strived to present a balanced and fair view based on my knowledge and experience, I am the product of a Westernized education, upbringing, and worldview. I acknowledge that the lens through which I view the world has left its imprint on this book despite the efforts I have made to see beyond it.

Guide to reading this book

Conversations in this book take place in different imaginary rooms set aside for certain broad topics, and the women in each room speak to that topic. Dialogues flow according to themes that evolved as I revisited their stories. Compared to mass media reports, *Gathering Strength* presents a more nuanced, expanded view of Afghan women, and by extension of women everywhere. I interviewed a cross-section of Afghans from the capital, Kabul; some provincial cities; and some villages. Women from different age groups, income and educational levels, social classes, and ethnicities shared their concerns. The conversational format allows me to show many issues and perspectives within and among groups of women. My own story is a bridge that may enable readers to see the world through my eyes, and then those of my respondents.

Because of the number and variety of women and the situations in which I interviewed them, the book has a complex format. For the most part, the women in each chapter are introduced at its beginning, and the conversation begins with the last woman introduced and flows to the others. I play two roles in each chapter. The first role entails posing questions to help guide the interview. In the second role, I work to help clarify the answers and provide additional context to help the reader better synthesize the information. My questions appear in italics, my commentary in plain text.

Some women appear more than once in the book. To easily find other chapters where each woman speaks, I've listed in bold typeface the first names of all my interviewees in the Index.

The book has two glossaries. The first includes definitions for Dari, Pashtu, Arabic, and a few other words. These are italicized in the text and definitions are provided there or in endnotes if used only once, or in the Glossary of Terms if used more often.

The second glossary lists many of the prominent and obscure individuals, locations, and organizations mentioned by women with whom I spoke, with an often-bewildering array of acronyms. Those mentioned only once are described in endnotes for the chapters where they appear. Those mentioned more than once appear in boldface when first mentioned and are included in the Glossary of People, Places, and Organizations. Each group's internet link, at time of publication, is provided where available.

In Focus sections highlight women who made one or two important points in our conversations that didn't fit well into other chapters. In two longer chapters, I interviewed individual women whose years of involvement in Afghans' struggles have given them a great deal to say.

The annotated Bibliography consists of books that I've read and recommend to others. Authors whose names are in bold typeface in the endnotes are included in the Bibliography.

To help readers keep the women in each chapter in mind, panels of small photos on the left hand side of each two-page spread identify women in that chapter.

Shaded tabs along the outer page margins highlight the glossaries and other Appendices.

Welcome, now, to my "salon." Like a fly on the wall, you will observe Afghan women engaging in virtual conversations with each other and with me. Although separated by time and space, groups of women come together to share their stories and perspectives on social activism, creating their arts, doing business, living as refugees, practicing Islam, playing sports, looking to the future, and much more. Their remarks may surprise you.

A luncheon gathering at the home of Muslimat in Kunduz.

Sana

Every afternoon, 15-year-old Sana hobbled into my room at the **School of Leadership, Afghanistan** (SOLA) guest house on her crutches, to tell me about her day. A whirlwind of energy and delight, she talked a mile a minute, her face expressing all of the drama in any story she shared. She had a beautiful singing voice and was very proud of her part in a promotional video for **Solace for the Children**.

Everyone looked at me. They said, "She's disabled and she's coming outside!" In Afghanistan, disabled girls don't go outside, not even to go to school or take courses.

Sana was born in Kabul and went to Pakistan when she was very young. At nine, she was diagnosed with polio, and suddenly lost her ability to walk. When she and her family returned to Afghanistan, she got crutches from the **Red Crescent** and resumed her studies. One winter afternoon, Ted Achilles, SOLA's founder, saw her fall, get up, fall again, and get up again, and he invited the determined young woman into his program. Since then she has traveled to the US with Solace for the Children for life-saving operations. She returned to the US in 2011 for more operations and a year of university preparation. Now she is studying at the American University of Afghanistan.

Peggy: *What is it like for a disabled person in Afghanistan?*

Sana: It is very sad and lonely to be disabled here. When I first couldn't walk with my legs, I walked with my hands, but I was always left at home when my family went out to weddings or parties. I stayed home and talked with the walls; I talked with spoons; I talked with anything.

When we came back to Afghanistan, my mother took me to the Red Crescent and they gave me some crutches. My family agreed that I could go to school and I was so excited! I went to class and sat in an empty chair. Then the teacher called me to the front of the room and told me that since I was disabled I didn't need to come to school. I cried, but she wouldn't let me stay. My brother said I could come to school, so I went back the next day, and she sent me home again. I kept going back every day, and finally the teacher took me to the principal's office. I told the principal that if she didn't want me in school, then I would go to the Ministry of Education. She said that I should be allowed to come.

After a year, I decided to take an English course. It was very hard because it would take me an hour to go from my house to the street where I could catch the bus. At the bus stop, it was very crowded and people pushed me. When it was winter, I kept falling on the ice. When I would fall, it hurt and I would cry, and small boys would laugh at me and throw stones. But I kept going and I was top of my class.

Peggy: *Are there any schools or organizations to help disabled people in Kabul?*

Sana: There is the Community Center for the Disabled (CCD),[1] but I don't know of any others besides the Red Crescent.

Peggy: Those with physical or mental disabilities, especially women, children, and the elderly, face negative social stigmas that often result in their being hidden away at home. A dozen or so organizations provide services, but due to lack of funding they only reach a small percentage of those who need assistance.

When somebody tells you that you can't do something, how do you react?

Sana: I say, "Okay; I'm disabled, but that doesn't stop me." I don't show that I'm feeling sad or angry, I just tell myself, "I'm going to school." I hide my feelings and just pretend everything is fine.

When people laugh at me, I don't show my face [my feelings]. When they throw stones at me or push me down, I don't show my face. I just go home and cry. I don't show it to my family, either, because maybe they will tell me I can't go to school. So I've learned to cover up my feelings.

Peggy: *What are your hopes for the future?*

Sana: I want to study politics. I want to help the women who beg in the streets and kids who are working and not going to school. I want to help disabled girls who have to stay at home.

Peggy: *What else would you like to say?*

Sana: I want my people to help disabled girls and poor women. A lot of girls burn themselves because they were married to old men. I saw with my own eyes a seven-year-old girl who was married to a 40-year-old man. Helping these girls gives me hope.

Rural Afghanistan is made up of long river valleys such as this one. This poses challenges for those wanting to establish health clinics or schools in these areas and reach a significant number of people.

The Hindu Kush Mountains as seen from the Panshir Valley.

3000 - 2000 BCE. Earliest known urban centers rise at Mundigak (near present day Kandahar) and at Deh Morasi Ghundai.

2000-1500. Kabul City thought to have been founded.

628. Zoroaster introduces monotheism (this date varies widely).

331. Alexander the Great arrives in Afghanistan.

Common Era (CE) begins. Year Zero.

50 - 200 CE. Kushan Empire.
c 150. Buddha statues carved at Bamyan.

642. Muslim forces capture Herat.

c 914. Rabia Balkhi, first female Muslim poet.

13th century. Queen Goharshad commissions Mussala Complex.
1207. Poet Rumi born.
1219 - 1221. Genghis Khan invades.
1273. Marco Polo crosses Afghanistan.

1501 - 1722. Safavid Empire rules Iran and Western Afghanistan.
1526 - 1707. Moghul Empire rules today's Eastern Afghanistan.

1708. Mirwais Hotak drives the Persians from Kandahar.
Mid - 1700s. Ahmad Shah Abdali, unites Afghanistan.

1839 - 1842. First Anglo-Afghan War.
1878 - 1880. Second Anglo-Afghan War.
July 18, 1880. Malalai carries flag against British troops.

1917 - 1921. World War I.
May 1919 - August 1919. Third Anglo-Afghan War.

1943 - 1945. World War II.

1959. Women enroll at Kabul University and enter the workforce.

July 17, 1973. Soviet-backed Daoud overthrows King Zahir Shah.
December 27, 1979. USSR invades Afghanistan.

1989. Soviet Army leaves Afghanistan, Najibulla regime continues.

April, 1992. Mujahidin government established.
July, 1992. Civil war erupts between warring mujahidin.
Spring, 1994, Talibs rescue girls from warlord. The Taliban is born.
September, 1996. The Taliban seizes Kabul.

September 11, 2001. World Trade Center in New York attacked.
October 7, 2001. US and Allies begin air strikes against Taliban.
2002. Hamid Karzai elected President.

History and Geography

Before beginning the women's stories, this brief review of some highlights of Afghan history is intended to provide a contextual framework for their modern-day accounts. Many Americans may be familiar with recent Afghan history, but not its roots. For Afghans, both ancient and modern history inform their world view.

The history of Afghanistan is indeed a "his"-tory in that the historical record largely concerns men's actions and achievements. Much of the record is a history of invasion, conquest, resistance, feuds, and war. However, a few shining female examples stand out.

The first is Rabia Balkhi,[1] a legendary poet who lived in the 10th century CE. Of royal birth, she fell in love with her brother's slave. When her brother found out, he imprisoned her in a bathroom and cut her throat. She wrote her final poems on the bathroom wall with her own blood. The poems seen here and many others describe an idealized romance with love itself that permeates the Afghan character even today.

Another notable woman in Afghan history, Queen Goharshad, lived in Herat and commissioned a mosque and university complex there in the 13th century. During the Second Anglo-Afghan War (1878-1880), a commoner, Malalai of Maiwand, won fame by taking up the Afghan flag and leading discouraged soldiers back into battle.[2]

Rabia Qozdari, also known as Rabia Balkhi after the place of her birth, was the first female poet of the Islamic world. She was bilingual and wrote her poems in Arabic and Persian.

Two Poems by Rabia Balkhi

Love

I am caught in love's web so deceitful
None of my endeavors turn fruitful.
I knew not when I rode the high-blooded steed
The harder I pulled its reins the less it would heed.
Love is an ocean with such a vast space
No wise man can swim it in any place.
A true lover should be faithful till the end
And face life's reprobated trend.
When you see things hideous, fancy them neat;
Eat poison but taste sugar sweet.

Love

Your love caused me to be imprisoned again
My effort to keep this love as a secret was in vain
Love is a sea with the shores you cannot see
And a wise [one] can never swim in such a sea.

Afghanistan's location between Eastern and Western worlds, as well as Central and South Asia, factors into its turbulent history; both as an object of conquest and a buffer between rival empires and nations. In newsrooms, stories about the country are routed to the South Asia desk, to be grouped with India and Pakistan. Afghans are not Arabs, but descended from Aryans (the ancient peoples of India), Turkish tribes, and Central Asians. The ancestors of the Hazara are said to have come from the Xinjiang region of northwestern China and to be descendants of Genghis Khan and his followers.[3]

Pashtuns make up more than half the population. Tajiks, the same ethnicity as people of the independent nation and former Soviet state of Tajikistan, make up about one quarter, and the Hazaras and Uzbeks are each nine percent. Relatives of the Uzbeks inhabit the independent nation and former Soviet state of Uzbekistan.

Successive waves of invaders – Persians, Greeks, Huns, Turks, and Russians – have rolled across what is now known as Afghanistan throughout history, and its borders have fluctuated with such invasions.[4] For convenience, I will refer to the modern area of Afghanistan as "Afghanistan" when describing its earlier history, although it did not gain its national identity until the mid-1700s.

In 628 BCE, Zoroaster[5] introduced monotheism in Bactria (Balkh), an area in today's northern Afghanistan. Alexander the Great conquered and ruled Afghanistan from 330-323 BCE. When Alexander's armies moved on, some Greeks stayed behind to administer the territory. However, the Afghans were not subdued, and bloody revolts became commonplace. The city of Kandahar is named after a form of Alexander's Greek name, "Iskandar."

Nomadic Kushans wrested control of Bactria from the Greeks in about 135 BCE, but adopted local customs and kept the Greek alphabet and coins. Buddhism was introduced around this time as well. In Bamyan, two giant Buddha statues, one 115 feet tall, and the second 180 feet, were carved between the second and third centuries CE. Arab Muslims captured the western city of Herat in 642 CE, and by 870 CE had conquered the rest of Afghanistan. It wasn't until the 11th century, though, that the region completed its conversion to Islam.

After Mohammad died in 632 CE, Islam split into Sunni and Shia factions with the Sunnis more numerous throughout the Islamic world. Persia, our modern-day Iran, (which then included the western part of Afghanistan) under the Safavid empire formally adopted Shiism in 1501. Currently, 10-20% of Afghans are Shia.

Genghis Khan led Mongol invasions from 1219 to 1221, scorching the earth in various regions of Afghanistan including Bamyan, Herat, and Balkh.

Many Afghans are proud to claim the mystical Sufi poet, Mowlana Jalal ad-Din Mohammad ar Rumi[6] (1207-1273) as one of their own. Known in the West as "Rumi" – actually a reference to the Turkish area where he lived and wrote – in Afghanistan he is sometimes called Al Balkhi, for his birthplace. At age nine, Rumi fled Balkh with his father because of the political and religious climate, and rumors of the coming Mongol invaders.

The Mogul Empire (1526-1707) was founded by Babur, a Turkicized prince descended from Genghis Khan. In its prime, the Empire controlled the eastern half of Afghanistan and most of India. Later, Moguls coming back westward from India brought an all-encompassing garment for women that eventually evolved into the modern-day *burqa*.[7]

By the early 1700s, the Persian Safavid empire (1501-1722) controlled much of western Afghanistan. In 1708, Mirwais Hotak (also called Mirwais Neeka and considered Afghanistan's Grandfather) led Kandahari warriors to wrest control from the declining Persians and establish himself as prince of most of today's southwestern Afghanistan.

In the mid-1700s, Ahmad Shah Durrani, aka Ahmad Shah Abdali, Ahmad Shah Baba, and the "Father of Afghanistan," gave birth to his country by conquering cities from Mashhad (in present day Iran) to Herat to Kabul, and down to Lahore (Pakistan) and Delhi (India). He used the fortunes he amassed to bind rival chiefs to his cause by giving them large shares of land and booty. His country became known as Yagestan, which means "Land of the Unruly." It was also called Khohistan, the "Land of Mountains," and later Afghanistan, the "Land of Afghans."

In 1813, the Russians and British began playing what Rudyard Kipling would call the "Great Game." The Russians, ruled by Catherine the Great of the Romanov dynasty, were expanding their empire southward. The British, concerned that the Russians would also expand into Persia (now Iran), thereby coming within striking distance of the British Indian Raj, the so-called "Jewel in the Crown of the British Empire," pushed northward. This struggle for control was not a war. "Occasional battles broke out, and a few massacres, an atrocity here and there, but the Great Game consisted mostly of plotting, pushing, conspiring, maneuvering, manipulating, politicking, bribing and corrupting people in the region mentioned."[8]

To balance the competing influences of the British, Soviets, and Germans in Afghanistan, King Habibullah Khan maintained a policy of neutrality during World War I, as did his successor, **Zahir Shah**, during World War II. Zahir Shah also signed a non-aggression treaty with Turkey, Iran, and Iraq in 1937.

⚬❖◉❖◆❖◉❖⚬

Afghanistan's current borders encompass about a quarter million square miles, 12-15% of it suitable for farming. Its western border abuts Iran. Its northern boundary follows the Amu Darya River, also known as the Oxus, opposite Turkmenistan, Uzbekistan, and Tajikistan. The Wakhan Corridor, a "panhandle" extending to the east, dates from 1873, when Great Britain and the Russian Empire established it as a buffer between their opposing spheres. The corridor is roughly 140 miles (227 kilometers) east-to-west and between 10 and 40 miles (16-32 km) north-to-south. China lies along its eastern edge. South and east of Afghanistan is Pakistan, itself part of British-dominated India until 1947.

Afghanistan lies between the 38th and 27th parallels, as does the land between Washington, DC, and Key West, Florida, but altitude determines its climate to a greater extent. Kabul, at roughly 6000 feet (1829 meters) above sea level, has hot dry summers and cold snowy winters. In Kandahar and Herat, at elevations hovering around 3000 feet (914 m), average summer temperatures are over 100° F (38° C). Mazar-e Sharif, the lowest of the large provincial cities at 1240 feet

(378 m), averages 102° F (39° C) in July. In Bamyan, not the coldest place in Afghanistan, winter temperatures have been recorded as low as -22° F (-30° C).

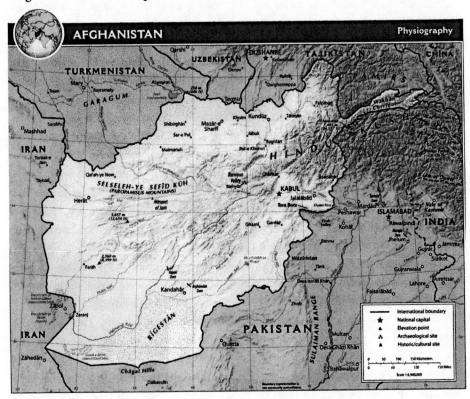

Before the series of wars that began in 1979, forests covered about 4.5% of Afghanistan, mostly in the east and southeast. By 2010, those forests of evergreens, oaks, poplars, hazelnuts, almonds, and pistachios had declined to 2.0%. The northern plains, with the country's most fertile soil and rich crops of grain and fruit, fed the region and the nation before the wars.[9] Ancient underground canals, or *kariz*, provide irrigation in the southwestern deserts for melons, wheat, grapes, and orchards of pomegranates and apricots. Dug by ancient peoples, *karizha* are cooperatively maintained by surrounding villages.

The steppes of the Wakhan Corridor are home to several endangered species,[10] including snow leopards and the Argali sheep, more widely known in the West as Marco Polo Sheep, named by Europeans for the Great Explorer, who described them after he crossed into the country in 1273.[11] In 2008, breeding grounds of the rare large-billed reed warbler were discovered in the Corridor by researchers of the World Conservation Society.[12]

The 1950s and 1960s were a golden era for urban Afghan women. Photographs from that era[13] show women with knee length skirts and uncovered heads, female professionals, as well as men and women talking together in public and going to movie theaters. Some women I interviewed remember these times.

By the mid-1950s, the Soviet-American rivalry known as the Cold War was in full swing and the US and the USSR were playing their own version of the "Great Game," as each tried to win the hearts and minds of the Afghan people. For example, both superpowers constructed road systems. In the mid-1960s, the Soviets built the mile-long Salang Tunnel at an altitude of over 10,000 feet (3048 m). The tunnel eliminated about 125 miles (201 km) from the very dangerous mountainous route between the Soviet border and Kabul. Soviet roads mostly connected their own border towns in the north with Kabul. American-built roads connected Kabul to Pakistan in the south and Iran in the west. The Soviets built a nitrogen fertilizer plant, an automobile repair facility, assorted factories, and a gas pipeline from the Afghan Shibarghan fields in the north to the Soviet border, and both sides were working to improve agriculture.

The US contracted with the Morrison-Knudsen[14] company and the Afghan government to build the ill-fated Helmand Valley Project. Their plan was to "kindle economic development and bolster the Afghan-US bilateral relationship"[15] by building two dams to control the flow of the Helmand River. They also built hydro-powered electrical plants and a system of canals to distribute water for agriculture.

Because of skyrocketing costs, the planned intensive ground water surveys were scrapped and the project rushed to completion. As a result, the two dams caused underground water to rise, bringing underground salt to the surface,[16] ruining the already poor soil for farming. From 1946 through 1963, the project consumed 19% of the Afghan government's budget, drained brains from other parts of the country, and slowed down economic growth overall. Its failure soured US-Afghan relations.

The USSR began to gain more political influence, and on July 17, 1973, while King Zahir Shah was in Italy, his cousin **Daoud Khan** seized power with Soviet backing and declared himself President and Prime Minister of the Democratic Republic of Afghanistan.

The land reforms that followed (taking land from the rich and powerful and distributing it among the poor) along with modernization (forcing women out from under their *burqas*, forcing girls and boys to leave their villages to attend schools in the provincial cities) precipitated revolts and clashes throughout the country. The Marxists' professed atheism added fuel to the fire and contributed to conservative backlash. What had been intended to help the poor was badly implemented, and the feudal order remained strong enough that people followed tribal leaders into rebellion against the government.

The Cold War competition dominated American foreign policy, and six months before the Soviet invasion, the US began covertly urging the *mujahidin* to rebel, intending to provoke the Soviets to invade and give them their own version of our Vietnam war.[17]

Kabulis and other educated people around the country, many of whom had jobs under the Soviet-backed regimes, supported the communists because they saw the programs addressing what they viewed as backwardness and inequities in their own society.[18] But the Afghan communists, especially in Kabul, split into competing factions that imprisoned and murdered each other along with their rivals' families and supporters. Between 1978 and 1992, several successive Soviet-backed presidents were assassinated at the behest of their successors. When the *mujahidin* took over Kabul in 1992, the last president standing, **Mohammad Najibullah**, fled to sanctuary in the UN compound. He lived there until 1996. The Taliban killed him that same year when they took Kabul.

To keep the Cold War cold, the Americans needed their support for the anti-communist partisans to be surreptitious. Once the Soviets invaded, American collaboration with Pakistan to arm the *mujahidin* began in earnest.[19] Commander **Gulbuddin Hekmatyar**, a fanatical *Islamist* and one of the world's largest heroin dealers, received the lion's share of US money and weapons.[20] Others of the strongest and most repressive warlords received funding as well, leaving moderate tribal leaders to fend for themselves.

Between one and two million Afghans were killed and thousands more imprisoned during the horrific Soviet occupation from 1979 to 1989. Soviet bombing raids demolished entire villages in retaliation for being, or based on the supposition of being, *mujahidin* hideouts. Most of the destruction occurred in rural areas and provincial cities.

In 1989, the Soviet Army withdrew and the US cut off military aid to its erstwhile Afghan allies. This left a power vacuum. *Mujahidin* who had worked together to fight the Soviets now went at each other's throats over control of the country. A power-sharing agreement was reached, but soon fell apart, engulfing the country in civil war.

This war was concentrated in Kabul. The capital sits on a flat plain surrounded by hills. In effect, **Burhanuddin Rabbani** would station himself on one hill, Hekmatyar on another, and they would fire rockets at each other over the city. The majority of the missiles landed randomly in Kabul, but Hekmatyar also purposely targeted areas populated by Afghans who had worked for the Soviets. In addition, groups of fighters roamed the city, killing each other and anyone who got in their way. Women were routinely captured and raped or forced into marriage.

One story[21] about the origins of the Taliban tells of an incident near Kandahar. Neighbors told **Mullah Omar**[22], at the time a village *mullah* who ran a *madrassa*, that a nearby militia commander had abducted and raped two teenage girls. He led 30 *talibs* in an attack on the warlord's base and captured a large supply of arms in addition to freeing the girls. A few months later, they rescued a young boy who was being fought over by two lusty commanders. However, their role of protecting women and children against evil-doers was short-lived.

In 1994, chaos reigned throughout the country while *mujahidin* rockets fell mostly on Kabul. By the end of that year, factions led by rival warlords had divided Kandahar. They stripped the city of anything of value, including copper wire and machinery; they stole anything that could be sold. The warlords seized homes and farms, robbed merchants, and kidnapped girls and boys to use for sex. Checkpoints operated by various factions, as well as independent bandits, lined the roads to shake down travelers.

This anarchy, and especially the roadblocks, became intolerable to the transport cartel that brought goods between foreign markets and those in Kandahar and Herat. The cartel paid Mullah Omar to rid them of the bandit plague that was shaking down truckers and other travelers. As a result, Mullah Omar's Taliban attacked Hekmatyar's base in the border town of Spin Baldak in October, 1994, and transferred control of that important truckstop to the cartel.

A medical supply convoy from Pakistan was robbed by other militia commanders later that month. Pakistan invited the Taliban to come to the rescue. After defeating the hijackers, the Taliban moved on to Kandahar, and within two days won control of the entire city. Among their spoils were tanks, transport helicopters, and several MIG aircraft left over from the Soviet occupation. The local people were very grateful to the "Robin Hoods" who rescued them from the feuding warlords' rapacious grip. By December, 1994, 12,000 Afghan and Pakistani students had joined the Taliban, and within three months they had taken control in 12 of Afghanistan's 31 provinces and seized the attention of the world.[23]

Who were these *talibs*? In the beginning they were all children of the *jihad*. Some had lost their entire families and been invited to the *madrassas*[24] to study. Others had been born in refugee camps along the border. *Madrassa* representatives came to the camps, offering free schooling and room and board to young boys, pleasing parents whose sons then had a chance at education, while they had one less mouth to feed. From a very young age, *talibs* were sequestered from women and taught the *Quran* and Islamic law by fundamentalist teachers. Students learned that women are a temptation, a distraction from service to God. In many schools, boys were "educated" without having ever studied math, science, geography, or history. As a result, even as adults, their thinking was simplistic and puritanical, and they had no acquired trades or skills except for those who had learned how to fight.

The Taliban enjoyed popular support in the beginning. They brought peace and security to the war-drained citizens and imposed what they saw as the true Islam. In 1994, the people in the places they controlled were relieved to have the fighting end and order restored. Once the Taliban had captured a city, they left "good Muslims" behind to enforce their rules and moved on. They made decisions by consensus, sometimes after long debates. By 1996, however, as they neared their goal of controlling the entire country, they became increasingly dictatorial and inaccessible. As Mullah Omar's power grew, he became more introverted and secretive, and his organization more ruthless and autocratic, like the communists, warlords, and *mujahidin* before them.

For the next several years, the Taliban fought different *mujahidin* commanders across the country. In September, 1996, the Taliban took Kabul. Eight months later, Pakistan recognized the Taliban government, even though it was still struggling to control parts of Afghanistan. In fact, while the Taliban were in power, they never controlled the entire nation. At their peak, only about 80-90% of Afghanistan was under their purview. Some areas never stopped fighting against them, especially where the **Northern Alliance** held sway.

When the Taliban took over Kabul, all girls' schools were shut down and female teachers at boys' schools were fired, resulting in the closure of many boys' schools for lack of instructors. Men were given a mere six weeks to grow full beards. All festivities were restricted, including weddings and even Islamic feasts. Repressive, brutally enforced edicts were issued, banning women from most civic and public life and restricting them personally by disallowing the use of fashionable clothes, makeup, and even noisy shoes. The only country to stand up against the Taliban at that time was Iran.[25]

Afghanistan's annual production of opium from 1992-1995 ranged between 2000-3400 metric tons, according to the UN Drugs Control Program (UNDCP). By 1996, when the Taliban controlled most of the country, it was projected to be 2200 metric tons. It rose by 400 tons in 1997 and reached 4600 metric tons by 1999.[26]

Initially, the Taliban proclaimed Islamic approval for opium poppy (*Papaver somniferum*) production, rationalizing that it was used by infidel foreigners and not by Muslim Afghans. Following this logic, they then banned marijuana (*Cannabis sativa*) cultivation; marijuana-derived hashish was a traditional intoxicant. Such intoxication, along with other festivities, was no longer permitted in the belief that it would distract Muslims from God. The 20% tax the Taliban levied on opium dealers helped fund their own expansion. By the end of 1997, opium-filled cargo planes were heading for Arabian Gulf ports. When Pakistan cracked down on heroin production on their side of the border, the labs moved into Afghanistan.[27]

Once the Taliban controlled Kabul, they hungered for international recognition. Mullah Omar petitioned the UN and the US for recognition of the Taliban government in exchange for ending poppy cultivation. He was ignored.

The Northern Alliance held Afghanistan's seat at the UN General Assembly. In a bid to strengthen their own claim of legitimacy, in July, 2000, the Taliban began to vigorously enforce a poppy ban. Pressure from Saudi Arabia and the United Arab Emirates, both heavy Taliban supporters, played a critical role as well in the decision to stop poppy cultivation.

The ban was amazingly successful. Within one season and with no outside help, opium production fell by 99%. Close local monitoring and eradication, as well as threats and the actual public punishment of both farmers and village elders who allowed poppy cultivation, all worked together to stop production.

However, only poppy cultivation was banned. Due to a glut on the market, the price of opium had dropped so low that huge amounts were stockpiled, awaiting the better price that was quickly generated by the ban. The Taliban taxed the transport of opium, not production, so trafficking continued to provide the bulk of their income.

The Taliban were also interested in making money from a proposed oil pipeline to run from Turkmenistan down the western edge of Afghanistan, through Pakistan, and on to the Arabian Gulf. Unocal, a California oil company, and an Argentine company, Bridas, competed for the concession. Unocal had the advantage because US and international recognition of the Taliban government, necessary for pipeline funding, would accompany its contract. US President Bill Clinton was about to grant that recognition until American feminists, moved by Afghan activists speaking out in America about the Taliban's harshly misogynistic rule, cut him short.

However, the Taliban didn't become America's enemy until late 1997, when al Qaeda leader Osama bin Laden met with the Taliban leadership and persuaded them of his world view. In 1998, the Taliban expressed a willingness to expel bin Laden in exchange for US recognition, but by 1999 that window had closed.

On October 7, 2001, the US and the "Coalition of the Willing" began to drive the majority of the Taliban into Pakistan, partly in retaliation for the infamous 9-11 attacks on the World Trade Center and US Pentagon. The allies oversaw the establishment of a new civilian government. However, fighting continued in the southwest, and slowly the Taliban has re-infiltrated the country and is making a comeback. They are not the unified group they once were. In addition to new factions within the Taliban, independent but allied groups such as the **Haqqani Network** have gained prominence.

On December 5, 2001, **Hamid Karzai** became the US-backed president of the Afghan Transitional Administration. Karzai was welcomed by many Afghans because he didn't have blood on his hands from the civil war. Urbane, fluent in six languages, and well-educated, he came from a prominent **Pashtun** family. His popularity eroded as he brought human rights-abusing former warlords into the government, was unable to control increasingly widespread corruption, and began to backpedal on women's issues. He won two popular elections, although the second was contested due to irregularities. Karzai is still president as this book is being readied for publication in the summer of 2012.

When the history of twenty-first century Afghanistan is written, women will be seen to play a much bigger role. But perhaps the most important Afghan heroes will be the many unheralded mothers who bring up their children to respect women and value their importance.

An old-city street in Taloqan, the provincial capital of Takhar Province.

Peggy's Story

The Afghan Women's Project came about by accident. Fourteen Afghan women visited Austin, Texas, on a US State Department-funded tour to get a first-hand look at American civil institutions. I was invited to a reception for them.

Alan Pogue's[1] photographic gallery, housed in a century-old Victorian converted girls' school, hosted the gathering. Alan had visited Afghan refugee camps and his dignified, elegant, black-and-white portraits evoked gut-wrenching awareness of the refugees' trauma and misery.

But the actual Afghan women at the event made an even stronger impression on me. They were so different from the media's portrayal of Afghans as helpless victims. Some appeared gentle and delicate; others, feisty and strong. Some seemed energetic and extroverted; others, tired and shy. At one point Alan stood on his grand staircase and talked about some of the images. I turned and saw one of the Afghan women quietly crying. Others had tears rolling down their cheeks as they recalled events and re-experienced their grief.

The uniformly somber images, the diversity of the women, and their tears struck me like lightning. I suddenly wanted to go to Afghanistan and bring back a broader, more complete picture of Afghan women. Rather than simply raising awareness of tragedies, my goal would be to capture women's struggles and successes through their own eyes. Alan's portraits portrayed a truth, an important one, but only part of a reality that also encompasses many other sides of life. As a professional photographer who had lived in the Middle East, and has connections in Afghanistan, I saw I could provide a more complete picture of their lives.

As a child growing up in the south and mid-west I never intended to travel outside the United States. I saw my country as a huge, beautiful, diverse "world" that could take a lifetime to explore. As for the rest of the world, I didn't know much about it except that it was scary out there.

Only as an adult have I learned to appreciate that my "normal" middle class upbringing was quite uncommon. My father, a Korean War veteran, spent his career climbing the ladder of a wood preserving company. Each promotion took us to a new part of the US and taught me to adapt to new surroundings. My mother seemed content as a housewife, raising their three daughters, until the day I came home from my sixth grade science class and shared a "fact" I'd just learned. She told me it was untrue, and began to think that she, with her science-oriented home economics degree, could do a better job than my teacher. And she did; she became a middle school science teacher and later a high school guidance counselor.

I grew up a tomboy, inhaling TV adventures such as "Rin Tin Tin," "Lassie," and "My Friend Flicka," featuring kids going outside their normal boundaries, solving mysteries, and outwitting bad guys to save the day. These kids (and their amazing animals!) did things their own way and became heroes.

Yet my actual life was prosaic. I was an obedient teenager. I started college in 1969 at Ohio's Miami University and, not knowing what else I wanted to do, studied to be a teacher like my mother.

When a social work professor lectured in one of my classes, I realized for the first time that what excited me about teaching was the one-on-one relationship with young people, and that I'd be more likely to find that in social work. At the end of my sophomore year I transferred to the social work program at Kent State and began summer school. Not incidentally, Kent State was only 35 miles from Cleveland and my boyfriend, Thom.

In mid-summer, two students came into my class to talk about that fall's exchange program to Iran. Two days later, Thom broke up with me. Heartbroken, I looked at him and spat, "Well, then, I'll just go study in Iran!"

I'd only wanted to make him jealous and regret his decision. But Thom was a serious yoga student. "Do you know how close that is to India? You *have* to go." Suddenly, I was considering it....

That weekend I drove home and sat at the kitchen table with my parents, who were footing my college bills. "I've got something to tell you and something to ask you." They sucked in their breaths, bracing for the worst. "Thom and I have broken up." Huge exhalations; they were obviously delighted and relieved.

"And?"

"I want to go study in Iran." Then I launched into my spiel. After conferring, they agreed. Looking back, I can see that they were calculating that 35 miles separated Kent State from Cleveland, where Thom lived, while 6000 miles separated Cleveland from Iran. Also, the exchange was a university program and therefore should be relatively safe.

As I was leaving the next morning to return to school, my mother gave me a look of exasperation and asked, "Why can't you go someplace normal like Europe?"

Iran in 1971 was not ruled by religious *mullahs* as it is today. Swiss-educated Mohammad Reza Shah Pahlavi[2] sat on the "Peacock Throne," continuing his father's policy of modernization and secularization. Iran sided with the US in the Cold War and, because it was producing and selling huge amounts of oil, was the second-largest buyer of American weapons. Socially conservative Muslims, the majority, were generally invisible to Americans. A semi-Westernized middle class was emerging in the cities. Blue jeans were all the rage.

Pahlavi University, the site of our program, was in Shiraz, the provincial "City of Roses." Elaborate rose gardens enhanced the beautiful architecture of centuries-old shrines. Roses lined modern boulevards. I loved Vakil, the cool, musty, multi-vaulted bazaar. It was built in the mid-1700s, but to my small-town eyes it seemed ancient. Small shops lined the bustling streets. Sheep quarters hung in butcher shops next to photo studios covered with movie-star-style portraits next to vegetable sellers whose produce spilled out onto the sidewalks.

We lived in '60s-style dorms, concrete boxes not much different from those at Kent State. The Iranian girls – in the Middle East and in Afghanistan, a girl is not called a woman until she marries – in my dorm were friendly but cliquish and I was an object of their curiosity. We'd sometimes sip tea while they asked me questions and practiced their English. I didn't become close to any of them. In part, I found it hard to relate to girls so sheltered they had never even spoken with the boys with whom they were "in love." They reminded me of American pre-teens "in love" with pop singers. I'm sure I was just as alien to them.

A professor and I visited a nearby village during one school break. Strolling down a street lined with mud-brick walls, we came upon a store so small that the shopkeeper could reach any item without taking a step. The open upper portion of a Dutch door let customers view his goods. The elderly proprietor asked what we wanted from the half-dozen dusty cans on his shelves.

"How do you survive with so few items to sell?" my professor asked.

The man looked to the ceiling for a moment and replied, "I survive by the grace of *Allah*."

That hit me hard. Growing up, we commonly prayed for good test grades or to thank God for our not-fully-appreciated abundance. This was the first time I'd encountered anyone who depended on God for his very subsistence. This man appeared so simple and pure in his deeply held beliefs; how, I thought, could he be consigned to Hell, as the religion in which I was raised professed? This experience led me to believe that *all* religions lead to God and that we are not judged by what we believe, but how we lovingly live whatever beliefs we have.

The school year neared its end and the question of what to do for the summer arose. Should I go back to Ohio? I was already in the Middle East; when, if ever, would I be able to return? I'd earned enough teaching English during the school year to fund an on-the-cheap excursion. I'd traveled with friends in different parts of Iran and knew enough Farsi to get around. India beckoned. I preferred to travel alone, so I wrapped myself in a *chador* and headed out.

The decrepit, rickety bus chugged through the dusty mud-brick villages and rocky deserts of southern Iran. Despite my blue eyes and blue jeans, I was treated respectfully throughout the journey across Iran and Pakistan; I'm sure in large part because of the *chador*. No one knew what to make of me; with my Islamic covering, I didn't fit any stereotypes.

I rode trains from the Pakistani border at Zahedan and I vividly recall Quetta, a city in the **Pashtun** heartland approximately 75 miles (121 k) south of the Afghan border. Rough wooden houses perched on cement blocks lined the tracks. Men wearing large turbans and baggy *shalwar kameez*, with rifles slung over their shoulders, stood around chatting. The place had the feel of the American "Wild West."

Northern India was a blur of colorful saris, fantastical architecture, and bearded, turbaned men who smelled of *ghee*. I was enthralled. I rode trains around the edges of India for a month-and-a-half until I reached Bombay (now Mumbai), where I was to meet my new boyfriend, Jamshid, an Indian medical student on summer break from his college in Iran.

After I'd been at my boyfriend's house for two weeks, his brother arrived from a trip with his buddies to Afghanistan. The brother was the only one to return; the rest had been brutally murdered right in front of him. I didn't feel it appropriate to ask what exactly had led to that fate. I had already bought my train ticket and was scheduled to depart two days later for that suddenly-scary country. Everyone tried to talk me out of going, but I refused to change my plan. I hadn't yet seen Afghanistan, and I'd heard from other travelers that it was a whole different world.

But their pleadings had an effect. I stayed in Kabul less than a week and didn't venture far from the beaten path. Kabuli women's dress surprised me, especially having just come from India, where female legs were always covered. In Kabul, women walked down the street in fashionable, knee-length, Western-style dresses. Bare-headed women strolled tree-lined sidewalks in high heels and fancy hairstyles. Others cloaked themselves in huge scarves, concealing the knee-length dresses they wore over baggy pants, but leaving their faces bare.

Here and there, goldenrod yellow, olive green, or medium brown phantoms floated among the women. I'd never seen nor heard of *burqas* before and found it hard to imagine that a person walked beneath each flowing tent. These were traditional *burqas*, made of heavy cotton, not the nylon used today. They went to the ground all the way around, unlike their modern counterparts that have a shorter panel in front. When they went out, traditional women wore high-waisted homespun pants called *duloq* over the pants worn at home. I learned later that during this period, some Kabuli women held parliamentary and ministerial positions, worked as scientists, pharmacists, and teachers and ran their own businesses.[3]

When I left Kabul, I took the direct bus to Herat traveling through the desert via Kandahar rather than the three-day mountain route through the north. I generally felt safe the entire time.

Herat lies on an ancient trade route near Afghanistan's border with Iran. Centuries-old elegant mosques, shrines, and a citadel dating back to Alexander the Great are well-visited even now by Heratis as well as a sprinkling of Afghan and foreign tourists. Queen Goharshad,[4] an artist in her own right, established the Musalla Complex, a 15th century mosque and university whose ruined columns tower over Herat today. A lover of knowledge, she commissioned the educational center's construction.

Legend has it that because the university she created was only for men and she also wanted women to study, she decreed that 200 women of her court should each marry a student, so that they, too, would have access to the extensive libraries.

8>◆IOI◆ ◆IOI◆◆<8

A few years after that first foray to Afghanistan, degrees in hand, I left Ohio to seek my destiny in Washington, DC. I found it in the form of Bill Kelsey, a missionary kid who'd grown up in Jordan. Within nine months of meeting, we became engaged and set off on our around-the-world-on-the-cheap pre-wedding honeymoon.

In Japan, we marveled that a five-foot stack of beer cases in the alley behind our hostel was still intact upon our return later that night. In lively night markets in Taiwan we saw aphrodisiac salesmen cut the gall bladders out of living snakes, pour the bile into shot-glasses of sorghum whisky, and offer the concoction to passers-by. Electricity was just being installed in the Philippine village where we stayed, and I considered the life changes and unintended consequences it would bring. Bali was the "exotic east" on steroids. I pondered the wealth of a society that charred dozens of ducks to accompany a funeral procession. The snake temple in Malaysia hypnotized me, as well as the many snakes lounging around, and I delighted in being able to safely photograph them at close range.

Thailand presented our biggest challenge when, walking among northern hill tribes' villages, Bill came down with typhoid fever. All the way uphill, I had seen the villages as cute and enchanting, almost a primeval Garden of Eden. Our first host said he was planning to move out of the mountains down to the road. As someone healthy and well-educated, I privately mourned the loss of his "pure and idyllic" life.

When Bill fell sick two days later, we hurriedly retraced our steps dragging ourselves back to civilization and a hospital. Now those same villages looked squalid, dirty, and poor, and I began to understand our former host's fervent desire to be close to a road with access to medical care, schools, and other vital services.

Bill soon recovered and we eventually made it to Jordan and were married by my father-in-law. We spent our official honeymoon with my parents traveling in Jerusalem and the Galilee.

We worked in Bahrain and Yemen before returning to the US. Yemen in the late 1970s had the highest number of researchers and foreign aid workers per square foot of any nation in the world, due to its strategic location across from the Horn of Africa. One could encounter North and South Koreans, mainland and Taiwanese Chinese, and Soviets and Americans engaged in aid and development, espionage, or anthropological research.

I had studied Arabic while in Jordan and found work with **Save the Children** in Yemen. I felt close to local friends there but during one conversation was put in my place. I had said that the Soviet people I'd encountered were stone-faced and unfriendly, always keeping to themselves, "so different from us." My Yemeni friend corrected me, saying that Soviets and Americans were like peas in the same pod while Yemenis, being very traditional and Muslim, were from an entirely different garden.

Bill and I realized that to have meaningful careers overseas, we needed concrete skills besides language facility. We returned to the US.

My childhood dream had been to live on a "ranchette" near an interesting city. In 1980 Bill and I bought ten acres near Austin, Texas. We began building a small house, doing the work ourselves, and started a magazine distribution business. We weren't ready to give up the simple life of our Yemen experience. As soon as the walls were up and the roof was on, we moved into the shell and tended our goats, pigeons, chickens, and a few years later, our daughters. By the 1990s the house was nearly finished. We'd saved enough money for Bill to pursue his dream of flying airplanes and for me to follow my long-buried interest, photography.

Ever since our trip around the world, we'd talked of giving our kids the experience of living in another culture. In 1997, Bill got a job as a bush pilot for **Airserv**, in Quelimane, Mozambique, a city with a quarter-million people but that felt like a small town. I closed my portrait-and-wedding photography business, packed up our 11- and 13-year-old daughters, and followed.

In Quelimane, I loved going around with my friend Keika, a Japanese photographer whose husband worked for the United Nations (UN). We had a routine for our bicycle jaunts out beyond the paved roads. When we'd spot something interesting, one of us would make a big show of slowly taking out her camera, leisurely focusing and refocusing, setting up everything just exactly right, while the children who inevitably appeared mugged in front of the camera. Meanwhile, the other one was quickly grabbing the shots she wanted.

I had homeschooled the girls for a year-and-a-half when they begged to go to a boarding school in South Africa like the children of other aid workers. Sending my daughters off to school gave me freedom to take my own excursions.

One trip took me down the Zambezi River to visit Mary Livingstone's[5] grave. I hired a boat in Caia and the captain, his assistant, and I motored three hours downstream to Chupanga, where the colonial cemetery lay. I eagerly jumped onto land to begin exploring but the captain and a man on the dock shouted at me. "Stop!"

"Landmines," they explained. I was suddenly reminded that Mozambique's eleven-year war of independence from Portugal and the ensuing fifteen-year civil war had ended only seven years earlier. So I carefully followed the guide's steps to Mary's picturesquely overgrown grave. Just as I was pulling out my camera, another man came running down the hill to say that I first had to go with him to get official permission. We marched uphill, where the governor and I had tea and a nice chat. I returned to the gravesite with the required permission just in time to see workers clearing up after extensive pruning. To my chagrin, all of the charm had been clipped away.

In 2000, we moved our family back to Texas, this time inside Austin. I resumed my photography business while keeping my eyes open for something more meaningful.

That "something" happened the evening of Alan Pogue's photography exhibit. Creating the Afghan Women's Project was like having a baby. I had the conception. It took nine months to develop the vision, raise funds, make connections to meet women in Afghanistan, and attend to the many details. The project would have collapsed many times without Bill's encouragement and support. My life coach also held my feet to the fire. Joia's[6] most important question came at a time when I was losing sight of my vision. "OK," she asked, "What if you *don't* go?"

People think I must be brave to visit Afghanistan, a land of violence and war. Certain areas were very dangerous, and I avoided them. Others were quite safe. Years of world travel in developing countries have given me a good sense of how to dress and carry myself in traditional societies and what to do if things go wrong.

I was terrified, however, when I stood before a sympathetic group of American Sufis on a ranch outside Austin to ask for money for my project! At the time, I wasn't sure I could pull it off. When I began my speech, my quivering voice and shaking legs pained the audience so much that someone spoke up to tell me that this was a very accepting group and I could relax! Getting through that speech and not running away shamefacedly afterwards required much more courage than I ever needed in Afghanistan.

To prepare for my trip, I contacted friends who might have connections or be interested in supporting my endeavor, as well as aid agencies working in the area. Offers of help and rejections took me on a dizzying roller coaster ride until I finally learned not to get attached to any particular possibility and just trust that my overall efforts would bear the needed fruit. Inspired by the courageous and dedicated **Revolutionary Association of Women of Afghanistan** (RAWA) members I'd encountered on the internet, I contacted them for interviews, too.

As in pregnancy, the gestation finally came to an end, and in August, 2003, I set off for Kabul.

Airserv, the company Bill had worked for in Mozambique, put me up in their crew house in Kabul in exchange for photographs of their flight operation. They also flew me around the country on their scheduled flights when space was available. My situation was nearly ideal. I had the companionship of Westerners and access to an office with "safe" electricity; that is, without random spikes that could fry my computer. I also had access to a printer and could share photographs of the women I met with them.

Kabul was relatively safe at that time. People I met were grateful the US had driven out the Taliban, despite innocent Afghans having been killed in the process. I felt at ease, although remaining alert while walking alone and taking taxis.

Pictures I'd seen on American TV suggested that Kabul was a moonscape-like, ruined hellhole. It wasn't. Yes, thousands of random civil war rockets had left piles of rubble and destroyed entire neighborhoods, but the TV and newspaper cameras hadn't shown areas where life continued as usual. Some buildings were untouched, or only pocked with bullet holes. Even in damaged areas, buildings with their upper floors destroyed housed shops below that were open for business. Squatters had bricked in parts of broken building shells for shelter. People walked around the scars of war on sidewalks lined with vendors as they made their way to bustling markets. Life carried on.

My first few interviews went sufficiently well, but I was less satisfied with my photographs. I was slowly getting my feet on the ground and developing my shooting technique. After a week, RAWA still hadn't gotten back in touch with me to visit their projects. Making other contacts to find interview subjects was going slowly, in part due to erratic phone service. I only had two weeks left and I felt devastated.

Had I come halfway around the world, and accepted the financial support of my friends, only to do something mediocre? I cried. I prayed. I meditated. Within thirty minutes RAWA called. I got through to other groups who were happy to introduce me to interview subjects. The idea for my signature shooting technique came to me, allowing me to get natural images, slices of the moment. I learned that getting a visa extension and changing my flight would be easy.

Before I left Texas I'd feared I wouldn't find anyone willing to talk with me and be photographed. The opposite turned out to be true; many women were eager to share their experiences and didn't mind having their pictures taken. I began to see that especially for uneducated, impoverished women, having a Westerner come all the way to Afghanistan to listen to them and acknowledge their pain and difficulties could be empowering, affirming, and healing.

The powerful need to tell one's story was brought home shortly before I left the country. I had just completed two interviews at a literacy and tailoring school. As I was leaving our interview room, I saw fifteen women sitting against the wall, each waiting patiently, hoping to be heard. Unfortunately, I was unable to stay longer.

❧ ━◆◦◇◦◆◦◇◦◆━ ❧

The visa extension allowed me to visit Taloqan, a city of 64,000 people located 150 miles north of Kabul. The director of an aid agency had invited me to stay in the agency's spacious compound on the edge of town. After breakfast the morning after I arrived, I set off alone looking for interesting pictures. But as soon as I slipped out the gate, the guard[7] came running after me, saying that I *must* have an escort in case I got lost. Well, Taloqan is a small town and I have a good sense of direction. But I understood that when staying with Afghans, whether an organization or a private family, they assumed responsibility for me and it would be rude, impolitic, and – who knows – possibly dangerous to go wandering alone. So as I walked the guard trailed behind, and I must admit I felt secure having someone watch my back while my eyes were glued to the viewfinder.

The modern areas of this provincial capital had two-story buildings filled with shops selling gadgets from China and Pakistan. Private cars and taxis shared the road with brightly-decorated horse-drawn taxis, donkey carts, men or kids on donkeys, hand-carts, and pedestrians.

But the vegetable market with its rows of rickety wooden carts filled with fruits and vegetables and the outdoor grain market seemed right out of a Rudyard Kipling novel. I only felt discomfort there, a place of *no* women. Watching grain being weighed and sold, it was easy to imagine that I was observing life centuries ago. The use of plastic grain bags rather than hemp sacks was the only apparent anachronism. Although I only peered in from the road, I could see the merchants' brows furrowing and eyes narrowing, as if telling me that I didn't belong in this male enclave. So we moved on.

✽◆IO◆✦IO◆◆✽

Returning to Texas six weeks later, I created a photo exhibit that included a short biography and an excerpt from each woman's interview to hang beside her portrait. Slide show presentations to civic groups, churches, and universities soon followed, enabling me to share the women's stories as well as my own perspective on what I had seen.

The process of carrying out the Afghan Women's Project changed me in profound ways. I'd become more confident, developed strategies for dealing with my personal shortcomings, found information and resources to help me define my mission and purpose, and learned to craft statements to solidify my vision. I wanted to share what I'd learned, so I began giving workshops to encourage and help others with their creative endeavors.

A few years later I began to feel Afghanistan calling me to return. This time, in 2010, I entered the country on a tour with **Global Exchange**[8] so I could gain access to women I might not have met otherwise. These dedicated leaders showed me a side of Afghanistan that seldom made mainstream news.

When the Global Exchange tour ended, I stayed with the **School of Leadership, Afghanistan** (SOLA). Here I met a wide range of delightful young people, all of them seriously dedicated to helping rebuild their country. They lifted me out of the discouraged mindset I'd developed from focusing on political and military developments.

Afghan youth, like people everywhere, run the gamut from selfish to idealistic. But the SOLA students and others inspired me with the possibility that through their hard work and dedication, their nation may one day enjoy competent leadership and relative justice. It won't happen before the next election; it will likely take until these youths are middle-aged and current leaders have retired or died. But if these young people stay true to their dreams, then I believe their hopes might just be realized.

In the seven years since my last visit, Kabul had changed. In 2003, I felt safe walking for miles along city streets. In 2010, I was warned not to walk anywhere. In 2003, I'd hailed taxis off the street. In 2010, I was told to use only certain vetted taxi companies that would pick me up at my door in unmarked cars. Traffic in 2010 was heavier and slower, the air even more polluted, and the city an armed camp.

Guards in towers above fortress-like walls looked down on traffic and pedestrians. Sandbags lined the street-side walls of important buildings. Blast-proof fifteen-foot molded concrete barriers along the streets protected ministries. Short barriers protruded into roads, forcing drivers to weave slowly around them. Afghan National Police with loaded AK-47s were everywhere. Female guards patted me down and searched my bags anytime I entered a public building. A few times every week I'd see a convoy of Allied military vehicles, but I never saw those soldiers walking around. I was surprised by how quickly I got used to such an armed environment.

One highlight of my trip was a visit to Bamyan. After Kabul, I was in heaven there in the central highlands. I walked miles every day through crisp clean air to interview women or get internet access at the university. There were few taxis. I hired a guide to tour the caves in the Buddha-cliff[9] and learned that they were all hand-dug. Bright remnants of beautiful frescos have survived over two thousand years in some of these caves. I saw one soldier, a UN guard, the entire nine days I was there.

Bamyan is a small city in the Afghan central highlands, also called the Hazarajat; or the place of Hazaras. Bamyam is also the name of the province. The Hazaras are mostly Shia Muslims, while the rest of Afghanistan's population is mostly Sunni. Bamyan City is home to more than 61,000 people and lies about 150 miles (241 km) north of Kabul. In 2010, a journey on the more secure of the two routes from the capital took about eight hours. Now, on a newly-paved road, travel time has been cut in half. Tourism has and will continue to aid in bringing resources to Bamyan and tourists to nearby Band-e Amir National Park.

The city's mile-long bazaar meanders alongside the Bamyan River. Small shops, kabob stands, and a few two-story hotels flank the street. Between the rear of the shops and the river containment wall, rows of vendors sell vegetables amid makeshift stalls full of cheap Chinese goods.

Beyond the bazaar, the road crosses the Bamyan River at an angle and intersects a branch of the famed Silk Road.[10] A line of cliffs parallels the road as it heads east toward Kabul and west, in front of Bamyan Hospital, to the Buddha grottoes, and then out of town towards magnificent Band-e Amir.

A mixture of ruins, mud brick houses, and a few cement buildings lies in the triangle formed by the bazaar and river, the Buddha wall, and a connecting road.

A midwife training center, where I interviewed Kobra (found in the Women's Health Workers chapter), is located there. A wall of inhabited caves stretches well beyond the World Heritage "Buddha section" in both directions. Suburbs containing government offices and modern housing continue to spring up around the edges of the city. Now that Bamyan has electricity every evening, television satellite receivers occasionally appear on top of mud-brick houses. The internet is non-existent, except in offices or the university.

From Bamyan I rode five hours over gravel roads to Yakolang to visit the **Leprosy Control** (LEPCO) clinic where people with tuberculosis and leprosy stay until cured. I sat in the sun with some of the women and watched one embroider a large curtain while we tried to communicate with my broken Dari. From there I went to Band-e Amir, where I spent four days hiking in the clean air and staying with a village family. At 8000 feet (2438 m) above sea level, I found fossilized brain coral lying on the cliffs above an amazingly deep-blue lake. Each evening I shared the day's photos, letting my hosts see their everyday environment through my eyes.

⊗►◄►◄►◄⊗

My purpose for this book is to break open stereotypes. I want to expose readers to stories that challenge assumptions. I hope to help you see Afghanistan, her people, and their issues in a more nuanced light.

Biased, one-dimensional information in the mass media, from across the political and philosophical spectrum, guides people to view the world according to particular agendas. Important issues are conflated, leading people to form simplistic ideas about possible solutions. I long to see positive efforts in Afghanistan that will still be effective after 50 or even 100 years. This will only happen if participants take into account deeper issues behind the problems, and if reforms are directed by Afghans in a distinctly Afghan way.

Why do I focus so much effort on women? Men have most of the power in Afghanistan. It's critical for young boys to grow up seeing women as human beings, as contributors to the family and society, as partners. Women, who will bring up the next generation, must first have that vision of themselves and their gender before they can pass it on to their sons and daughters. Through the portraits, conversations, and stories here, I hope to encourage that vision.

1/The Artists

The artist's life is one of self-expression and discovery. Afghan artists have customarily faced a mixed reception. Performance artists such as singers have traditionally been looked down on, while poets, architects, and non-representational visual artists like tile designers and painters have garnered respect. Even so, women announcers and singers performed on Radio Afghanistan as early as 1957, and in 2003 Radio Sahar,[1] a woman-run radio station, began broadcasting in Herat.

Afghan women artists face serious issues, ranging from the lack of a supportive artistic community to familial misunderstanding and apprehensions, to societal disapproval, to occasional anonymous death threats. But even in this environment of nosy neighbors, conservative relatives, and traditional customs, some women artists feel compelled to stand up to or otherwise work their way around these limitations in order to express themselves.

For many Western artists, and I especially speak for myself, the battles are with my own internal censor and my strong ethic of "work and responsibility" before "pleasure and art." The issue here is one of selfishness. By "selfishness" I mean knowing and honoring my own vision and sense of self; the sense and ability to be "true to one's self." Self-worth is not the narcissistic interpretation of "it's all about me." Artists need a certain amount of selfishness in order to create art. We need to know who we are, what we like and dislike, and what we want and don't want. Being accused of selfishness is a mild criticism in the individualistic West, but a strong condemnation in the communal cultures of the East. Finding and claiming an individual identity is often a struggle.

Afghan women are normally immersed in rich, complex family lives with children, relatives, and girlfriends, plus endless rounds of housework, all vying for their attention. If a woman lives with parents-in-law, as many do, finding personal time is even more difficult.

A woman who tries to carve out her own space is often looked on as selfish and odd. Afghan artists face many internal as well as external struggles unique to their culture. Each challenge takes courage to confront and creativity to work around.

As Afghans struggle to recover from decades of war, art has been relegated to the sidelines. Nevertheless, art plays an important role in helping artists as well as audiences find a way into the future. Young artists are especially important as they bring into being their visions for a new society.

Saghar
Painter

In Kabul in 2003, a friend offered me access to the Herat applications for the US Fulbright Scholarship Program. I was planning to spend time there and looking to round out my selection of subjects. I chose to interview Saghar because she was an artist. Her well-written Fulbright essay, in English, led me to think I wouldn't need a translator. When I met Saghar, however, I realized that her English wasn't good enough for me to do an adequate interview. She had hired a scribe to write her essay. Considered cheating in the West, it would be traditional and logical in a country where illiteracy is high. I offered to call off the interview but she wouldn't hear of it. Since Saghar didn't know any women who could translate, her husband, who wanted to be present, eventually found a male friend who could, and the four of us sat down for the interview.

I became interested in drawing when I was eight years old in primary school. I made some little drawings in my notebooks and people said that they were good. But no one taught me any art until I reached the university. This is my last year.

Saghar has lived her entire life in Herat, a conservative, historic trading center near the border with Iran. Her school was shut down in 1994 when the Taliban controlled the city, so her parents hired a private tutor. Her college entrance scores were high enough to qualify for the Herat University law school. She chose to study art instead. She was married in 2001 and as of 2003 had one son.

Mariam

Photographer/Translator

I loved Mariam. We both enjoy travel and photography. I felt sorry to leave Afghanistan because it would have been fun to be friends and hang out with her. I could easily imagine adventures we could have had and photographs we could have taken… We did go on one photo excursion to the Kabul bird market – more on that later.

My father was a big hand behind my success. He always believed in me and encouraged me.

Mariam was born in Kabul and lived there until she was nine. Sometimes when she was a little girl, she and her older brother worked with her father in his shop, making tin wood-burning heaters. When the civil war came, her family escaped to Pakistan where she finished school. When the Taliban fell, the family returned to Kabul, where she found employment as a public relations assistant. Several years ago she went to the Netherlands for training, and later to India for two months to study photography. Now she travels all over Afghanistan with foreigners as a freelance photographer and translator and is the marketing manager for a printing company.

Setara

Writer

I first read Setara's writings on the **Afghan Women's Writing Project** (AWWP) blog. I was impressed not only by her articulate, thoughtful, picturesque poetry and sometimes humorous prose, but also the strength of her character as she speaks out for her beliefs and ideas. In person, she was calm. I sensed a pillar of strength residing within her. Her eyes glowed when she spoke of her favorite poets. **Note:** Setara is an alias. Her true identity has been withheld from publication at her request for her and her family's security.

Setara came from an educated family as did both her parents. When the Taliban came she was in seventh grade. Even at that young age she had dreams of being a university professor. For the next five years she studied at home under her father's tutelage, but was still very frustrated at not being able to attend school like her brothers. Ironically, they had little interest in academics. After the Taliban left, she resumed her public school studies and in June, 2010, she graduated from Kabul University with a Bachelor of Arts in Persian literature.

My dream and desire is to get my Master's and PhD degrees so I can become a professor at the university and work for women.

Sahraa Karimi
Filmmaker

During our interview, I felt very close to Sahraa. We are alike in many ways. We both feel the need to spend time alone, to create, and to do things in our own way. That is easily understood and respected here in the West, but Afghanistan is a very communal society, and group identity and approval by the family is paramount. This way of being keeps society stable and protects it from change. It keeps the group safe, but also inhibits individual blossoming. Afghans who break out of these boundaries are more courageous than we may imagine.

My main subjects in high school were mathematics and physics. But when I went to the University, I don't know, somehow I went into art and studied film directing.

Sahraa was born in Mashhad, Iran, a modern university town near the Afghan border. When she was 13, her father died and she and her mother moved to Tehran, Iran's capital. After high school, Sahraa went to a university in Slovakia and earned a PhD in film directing. In 2009, she came to Afghanistan, got married, and began teaching at Kabul University. In 2011, to pursue her passion for film making in an environment more conducive to her creative self-expression, she returned to Slovakia. In order to fund her artistic endeavors, she accepted a university teaching job at VMSU, a Slovakian branch of the University of Edinburgh. Her latest film, *Nasima: a Refugee Girl's Everyday Memories*, won the Slovakian Academy Award.

Elaha

Singer

My translator and I arrived at Elaha's small, gray house in mid-afternoon. She led us through her sparse courtyard; up a dark, cramped staircase; into a vibrant peacock-blue room with orange trim. Red and gold *toshaks* and matching pillows lined the walls in lieu of couches and chairs. We pulled back the heavy curtains to have enough light for photography. Elaha reminded me of a little bird, nervous, self-conscious, and fragile.

Despite being a refugee from Afghanistan, Elaha grew up a leader among her Iranian classmates. At about age 12, she fell in love with painting and created some modern works in oil and graphite. When her family returned to Kunduz, a provincial capital in northern Afghanistan, she worked as a journalist on a radio program about women.

Later her family moved to Kabul, where she studied music at a private school for five years. She studied many kinds of music but chose to perform pop/rock because she can best express her feelings through that musical style. Her break came when she appeared on the television show *Afghan Star*,

The biggest consequence of being on television was that now some people loved me and some people hated me. Before, no one knew me so I didn't have this experience.

a program like *American Idol*. She sang occasionally on Ayna, an Afghan TV channel, gave a performance at The Women's Garden[2] on International Women's Day, and also a concert in Mazar-e Sharif for Now Ruz, the Afghan New Year.[3]

Because of her appearances on TV and the resulting family conflict, she, her sister, and her brother moved out of their parents' house to live on their own, where I met her in 2010. A year later, she went to India for further study.

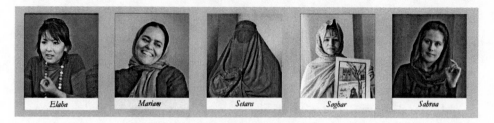

Elaba   Mariam   Setara   Saghar   Sabraa

Peggy: *What is it like for you to be onstage, singing a song that you love to a huge audience listening with rapt attention? What is that like?*

Elaha: Most of my songs are sad. When I try to sing a happy song, somehow it seems to contain tragedy or sadness. When I'm onstage, I try to express my feelings very strongly. Some people make fun of that; some people like it. Some just listen to the tune and others to the poetry. There are also people who resonate with the feelings in the song and the way I sing it. The most important thing is that I can express myself and share my experience. But my interpretation of the songs is related to the audience; every listener finds him or herself in my song. So it's not just about me. The audience is also part of my singing and they interpret my songs however they like. I take something from the culture and transfer it to the audience. Their interpretation of my art is not related to me personally, but it has a very clear relationship with their own personal and historical experience.

Peggy: *Do you write your own songs?*

Elaha: No, but I love the poetry of **Forugh Farrokhzad**[4] and Siavash Kasrai and I often sing their poems.

Poems by Forugh Farrokhzad

Afghans and Iranians share similar languages (Farsi and Dari) and the love of poetry. Both Setara and Elaha mentioned Forugh Farrokhzad, a modern Iranian poet, as their favorite.

The Captive is about the poet having to give up her son should she divorce.

The Captive

I want you, yet I know that never
can I embrace you to my heart's content.
you are that clear and bright sky.
I, in this corner of the cage, am a captive bird.

from behind the cold and dark bars
directing toward you my rueful look of astonishment,
I am thinking that a hand might come
and I might suddenly spread my wings in your direction.

I am thinking that in a moment of neglect
I might fly from this silent prison,
laugh in the eyes of the man who is my jailer
and beside you begin life anew.

I am thinking these things, yet I know
that I can not, dare not leave this prison.
even if the jailer would wish it,
no breath or breeze remains for my flight.

from behind the bars, every bright morning
the look of a child smile in my face;
when I begin a song of joy,
his lips come toward me with a kiss.

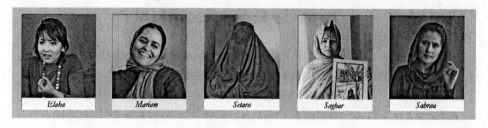

Elaha   Mariam   Setara   Saghar   Sahraa

O sky, if I want one day
to fly from this silent prison,
what shall I say to the weeping child's eyes:
forget about me, for I am captive bird?

I am that candle which illumines a ruins
with the burning of her heart.
If I want to choose silent darkness,
I will bring a nest to ruin.

The Sin

I sinned, a sin all filled with pleasure
wrapped in an embrace, warm and fiery.
I sinned in a pair of arms
that were vibrant, virile, violent.

In that dim and quiet place of seclusion
I looked into his eyes brimming with mystery
my heart throbbed in my chest all too excited
by the desire glowing in his eyes.

In that dim and quiet place of seclusion
as I sat next to him all scattered inside
his lips poured lust on my lips
and I left behind the sorrows of my heart.

Peggy: *What do you think is the greatest enabler of your success as a singer?*

Elaha: The most important ingredient of my success is a commitment to good morality. Many people think that if a woman sings on TV, she is a prostitute. It's important for me to be an example that this is not the case.

Peggy: *Sahraa, what do you want to accomplish with your films?*

Sahraa: I want to find my identity as a woman, not as a refugee girl. Growing up in Iran, the shadow of being a refugee girl from Afghanistan was a limitation that made me want to improve myself. It gave me a challenge. That's one reason I moved to Slovakia. Only by living in another culture could I find the identity I had lost in Iran. It's very important that people start to search inside themselves. Everyone's way of searching is different. For photographers it's to take photos; for writers it's writing; for me as a filmmaker, it's to make films. I find that filmmaking is a kind of questioning, a way of finding my identity that they stole from me.

Identity, for me, is to show myself as I am, not how society thinks I should be nor how they want me to be, but how I really am, including all my mistakes. We are all human beings and we all have different sides. Identity means that I say what is on my mind. I don't censor myself. It is very hard to be like this in Afghan society. In Slovakian society I could say what I wanted. Maybe they wouldn't agree with me or like me, but at least I had the power to speak my truth. Here, we don't have this power.

Here people judge you. Afghan society in Iran did the same and I hated it. To avoid this judgment I decided to live somewhere else. I wanted to be free to speak without worrying that if I say something, maybe I will hurt someone or maybe somebody won't like me. Through art, and especially film, I can speak out. Film helped me overcome my shyness about my face and body and to speak about what this body likes and doesn't like.

But when I began to really think for myself, I started to make mistakes. These mistakes brought me back. Sometimes it was very painful, but I'm happy that I did these things because they helped me find myself.

Peggy: *Saghar, tell me about your painting.* (Seen in her portrait.)

Saghar: This painting is one of my first ones. I wanted to show the world the Afghan people's misery. You see that both of these doors are closed. Rich people live behind that beautiful door, poor ones behind the other. But it doesn't make a difference to that boy in the foreground, sitting under the tree in the snow. Neither one is helping him. You see these animals, the crow and the wolf? The

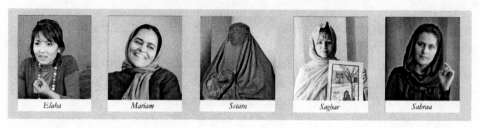

Elaha   Mariam   Setara   Saghar   Sahraa

animals have feelings for the boy, but the people in the houses don't. There is no humanitarianism here.

Peggy: *What do you think about art and its importance in society?*

Saghar: Here in Afghanistan, unfortunately, people do not pay attention to art. Because of the lack of education they never think about it. But personally, art helps me a lot.

Peggy: *Will you ever be able to show or sell these pictures of people and monuments that you have here?*

Saghar: No, no one appreciates this kind of art. I also paint geometric designs on colored vases that my husband sells in his pharmacy. The other paintings will stay in my house or I may give some to my relatives.

Peggy: *How will you use your art after you graduate?*

Saghar: I'm interested in teaching, but here, if students want to be teachers, they have to choose that when they begin their studies. It's too late for me now. After I graduate, I will just paint here at home and raise my son.

Peggy: *Mariam, what drew you to photography?*

Mariam: Some people say that they've always wanted to be a photographer, but not me. I was working in public information for the **Danish Committee for Aid to Afghan Refugees** (DACAAR), writing an article about cultivating saffron. It needed an illustration, so someone lent me a camera and I took some pictures. They loved them. Those pictures led me to take a course at Aina Photo Agency here in Kabul. I also had to learn English. During that program I took a picture of a laughing *mullah* and the instructor was so pleased that he helped me sell the photo to a magazine. That's how I got the idea that I should try to become a photographer.

But now in Afghanistan people don't appreciate photography. If they ask you what you're doing and if you say you're a photographer, they don't understand, and they say, "Photography???" It's a question mark in their minds.

Sahraa: This film I made, *Women Behind the Wheel*, wasn't perfect but it was very open. It portrayed how I saw Afghan society at the time. When I came here from Slovakia and started to live with my in-laws inside Afghan society, I began to communicate with a different kind of people. I saw that the truth of the film was much more painful than this picture showed. A lot of women have a very bad life inside their family. From the outside you can't see it; they have nice clothes, they have children, they are busy with things to do, but they are always being there for other people and they never think about themselves.

You can see lots of girls who are very modern, who wear stylish clothes, who laugh in the street. But if you talk with them, you can see that they still don't have their power. They don't have the ability to say what they want because they are still afraid. For that, I want intellectual people to stand up and speak their minds. I think they would have a lot to say.

Everybody's story is very important. For me, as a woman in Afghan society living inside Afghan culture, there are a lot of things I should tell but I can't. Our society is not very open and it doesn't give me the opportunity to tell these things. Here, culture and everything should be moral. Your behavior, your way of thinking, your way of life, everything should be moral. Because of that, I think the story of the Afghan girl and the Afghan woman has a very specific color, a dark color. For me as a filmmaker, it's important to show this color in a true way, and through these women tell the story.

Everyone thinks that women here don't have rights; that they don't have the right to speak. Okay, that's true. But there is something more important. Afghan women don't have a chance to know what they think. They always live for their family, their husband, or their children. It's their way of life. You can never tell them that this is not the right way. They believe that it's right; they're proud of it. When you're proud of something, you can never get away from it. When you're proud as a daughter, you should be with your mother because society says so, but you can't be a "good" daughter and a "good" wife, and also be good for yourself.

Peggy: The things Sahraa points out about Afghanistan are also true here in America in certain subcultures.

What about film directing excites you?

Sahraa: Filmmaking is a way of thinking. It's a way I can express my thoughts, opinions, and ideas about society, myself, women, and people. I can communicate my agreement and disagreement with what I portray. Most important for me is that it's a way of thinking about the world in general. Filmmaking is about more than technique or technical issues; it's how I view my culture, how I criticize my culture, how I see. To make films and especially to direct films is my life's commitment.

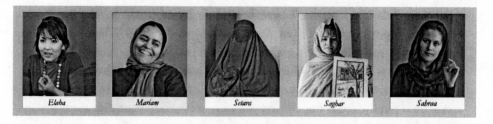

Elaha   Mariam   Setara   Saghar   Sabraa

Peggy: *What advice do you have for someone who wants to be a photographer?*

Mariam: Not only for being a photographer, but if a woman wants to do something but doesn't have much courage, or if she feels weak or not capable, I say, "You have abilities you can use to help people. Whatever skill you have, you have to look for it, you have to seek it out. Then you can go ahead."

Peggy: *What do you like most about photojournalism?*

Mariam: Through taking pictures, I'm getting to know about women's personal lives, the way they're living, and how they overcome their difficulties. We have a lot of problems in Afghanistan, especially in the rural areas. I remember my time in Bamyan Province. When I talked with a woman in a small village I saw how difficult their lives are, especially in the winter. The roads are completely blocked and if a woman is pregnant, she might die. There is no nearby clinic so if something goes wrong, nobody can help them. And there's no school for the children.

It makes me wonder... Security is good. There is no fighting like in the south; this area is completely safe and calm. The air is clean; the landscape, beautiful; and the need, so great. Why aren't there more projects to help these people? Women's development is mostly in the cities. I'm fine with that; I can work there. But just once think about those people in the very remote areas. Where are the development projects for them?

Peggy: *Have you experienced people reading something you've written and saying that it changed their lives or changed their thinking?*

Setara: Yes. When I write in Farsi, I only share it with my close friends. When I read them my poems the first time they told me, "Please continue writing, Setara."

Otherwise no one knows I'm a writer. I'm sure that if people knew they wouldn't like it. They think that whenever a woman writes, there is a fault, especially with the reality. I've experienced this. Whenever a woman writes, people think she should be at odds with society and therefore lose something. As in the case of Forugh Farrokhzad, her outspoken writing caused her to lose the respect of her family and friends. She lost one thing and gained something else. This is how people see all women writers.

But for my English writings... on the AWWP blog, readers make comments and those comments change my writing, change me, and change the way I think. They write things like, "Wonderful, excellent, amazing." When I see that my writing has readers, it encourages me to continue. My English writings are improving. I really came to trust myself only after people remarked on my writings. Now, I'm one of the most active writers. When I write in English, I feel that I can express most of my feelings, and I can share my experiences and pain with others. Now, 44 of my writings are on the web. On March 8, 2009, at an event in California, a well-known Hollywood actress read my poems. I was so proud and it encouraged me very much.

Peggy: *Do you ever translate your Farsi writings into English or is it too different?*

Setara: The feelings come in English and I automatically write them in English, or my feelings come in Farsi and I write them in that language. Someday when I get time, I will translate them, but I am very busy right now.

I want to start a small group of women writers. We can be a good example for Afghan women and help bring positive changes. We can learn from each other so that we will stand on each other's shoulders.

Peggy: I asked Saghar, the painter, if there was a student art association or any association of female artists in Herat but she said, "No." I suggested that while she was still in school might be a good time for her and some of her classmates to start one so they could encourage and support each other throughout their careers. I started a photography group while in photo school that continues to provide resources, camaraderie, information, and support. Connecting with other artists raises my spirits and can help me overcome artist's block.

When I returned to Herat in 2010 the phone system had changed, and I couldn't contact Saghar.

Mariam: My freedom to come and go did not happen easily. When my director first asked me to travel to Herat to translate for them, I told her that I could never get permission. So she came home with me to talk with my father. In the end he laughed and said, "Since you have come to my house, I cannot reject you, so I will let her go." Everything went smoothly. Shortly afterwards, she wanted me to return to Herat but this time my father said, "I let you go the first time and now

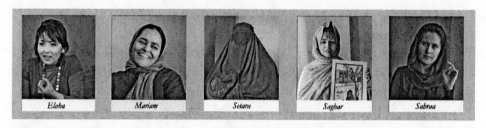

| Elaha | Mariam | Setara | Saghar | Sabraa |

you come asking me again. No, it's not possible." So, I cried and tried to convince him, and over the weeks kept asking him until he finally agreed.

I told him, "I was born in war and I will die in war. I can't wait for a better situation."

He laughed and said, "I wish you were a son."

I said to him, "Look, my Father, if anybody outside our house sees me and my attitude and the way I talk with people, they don't look at me as a girl, they think of me as a man." So this is how I became able to go outside of Kabul and even outside the country. I went alone to the Netherlands and to India for training. Now he allows me to work on projects that require me to be away for even three weeks at a time. Here in Kabul, sometimes I have to work late at the print shop. He just asks that I call to let him know I'm OK.

It's not a crime to travel alone or come home after dark, but it has many problems. Maybe your father or brother doesn't agree. Even your mother and your sister might feel that because you're a woman you are weak. If you go, and something happens, everybody will talk about you, every relative will say bad things about you *and* your parents for letting you go.

Peggy: *What is the most difficult challenge in your career and how do you deal with it?*

Mariam: Aside from my father, society is also a problem for me. A career in photography is not known or respected. Normal people laugh at me and ask why am I spending my time learning these things? It sounds crazy to them. But I always explain that I get paid for it and many people want to hire me. They come to accept it just by my talking with them.

Peggy: *What are some of the issues you are facing in your life?*

Mariam: One of my brothers is sick and can't work. He has a daughter and son but he's not able to support them. I have to do something to help them and to help my mother. My other brother is only in seventh grade and the government schools are not places where he can learn well, so I put him in a private school. Every three months I have to pay $400, big money in Afghanistan. But anyway, I have to make it.

Peggy: Mariam's story belies what we are led to believe about Afghan men's intractability. I interviewed many determined women who wanted something badly enough to stand up to their fathers or brothers to make their case. Very often they received the permission they sought. In some instances it happened after a person from the outside, sometimes an Afghan woman in authority, or in this case Mariam's foreign female boss, made the effort to go to their house, drink tea, and make a plea on the woman's behalf. It might take more than the proverbial "three cups of tea," but men can many times be convinced if a way can be shown that will ease their deeper concerns. Of course this takes time, but that doesn't make it impossible.

Traveling alone and returning home after dark pose real risks for Afghan women. People are curious about their neighbors' business, and if someone happens to notice that a woman is coming home alone after dark, rumors can spread that she is out misbehaving. "After all, why else would a woman be out after dark?" These sorts of rumors can lead to difficulty in finding the girl a husband, or in extreme cases, to her conviction for adultery. This is a little less of a concern for Mariam's family because they don't have conservative family members living with or near them. However, if anything were to go wrong, her reputation as a respectable girl could be in jeopardy.

One significant detail: Mariam's dad wasn't letting her go off on pleasure trips with girlfriends. She was going to work. Her liberation and travel would earn needed money for the family, specifically for her brother's schooling. Their children's earnings are the main social security Afghan parents have. When women contribute to the household income, not only are they more respected, but they receive more freedom as well. People think photography is a crazy thing to pursue until Mariam tells them that she earns money doing it. Afghan photographers earning a living with photography bring legitimacy and respect to the whole profession.

Sahraa: I married a man that I never knew before. It was totally my choice. Sometimes I think I'm very stupid. I take a lot of risks in life. But in this marriage I started to notice society more and more. My husband is totally different from me. He doesn't talk about art, he doesn't even like art. In his eyes, everything is political. But being married to him is another kind of searching. It's another experience. I'm sure that I'm not going to divorce him, because every day I learn something new about him that teaches me something new about myself. Through him, I started to really notice society. If I want to speak about and criticize this culture, then I need to know about it from experience, from the inside. I live with my parents-in-law. They're totally religious, traditional people. They always pray. I don't pray, and I come like this, in blue jeans. I don't limit anybody in my house, I am just myself. I create a question in their minds.

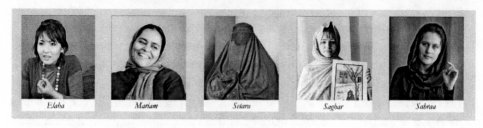

Elaha   Mariam   Setara   Saghar   Sahraa

Peggy: *It seems that even though your parents-in-law are very traditional, they don't try to control you much.*

Sahraa: My PhD is important to them. They always say, "You are a very educated woman, so you know what you do." But I also have very good support from my husband. This is a key point. So when my husband agrees with something that they don't like, they go along with it, but it's very hard.

For example, last week I appeared on Tolo TV. We were all watching it together after supper. When they saw their bride on TV, it was like I had dropped a bomb. They felt ashamed and my father-in-law didn't speak with me for two days. He's a very good person, though. Yesterday we were at home alone and got a chance to talk. So I asked him, "Why are you so angry with me?" I am the first bride who has spoken with him so openly. He started to tell me that it was shameful that I spoke about cinema on TV. I said, "Okay then, what should I talk about? Cinema is what I studied; this is my work."

He replied, "I don't have a problem with you being on television because I know that not every woman who appears on TV is a prostitute. You can speak on TV but don't speak about cinema." It's good that he improved a little. At least, he said I can be on TV. He is from this country and thousands of people think like he does. Also, thousands of women are like me, they have talent and want to be filmmakers. Unfortunately, they don't have the opportunity to go abroad, to transform their thinking, to come back to Afghanistan and be a rebel. I don't want to be a rebel, really. I want a very normal way to change certain things. Even if this change is very small, it's still change.

I'm only 27 so it would be very egotistical to think I can change his mind. It would be selfish really. So I don't try to change him, but to show him another way and help him be more open-minded. For example, my brother-in-law's wife wears a *burqa*. I don't. They don't speak with men, but I do. I listen to opera and sing it in the house. My brother-in-law keeps saying, "Why doesn't she wear a *burqa*?" and my father-in-law just answers, "That's how she is." But now I cover myself up more [with a hooded long-sleeved cloak] when I go out because it's good not to provoke or embarrass them. I respect them very much, but I don't want to play the role of someone I never knew. I was a good daughter, but my father died. So now, for whom should I be a good daughter?

Peggy: I talked with Sahraa again in May, 2012 when she was in California, presenting her films at the Berkeley Iranian Film Festival.

What did your mother have to say about your marrying your husband?

Sahraa: She and my family didn't want me to marry him because they know me and could see how different we are. But they didn't pressure me.

Peggy: *Are you still married even though you live in Slovakia?*

Sahraa: Yes, and when I go back to Afghanistan I stay with my family. I accept and love them and they feel the same towards me. We get along fine. Before I married I told my husband that I am a filmmaker and that is the most important thing for me. He doesn't mind that I travel a lot and he doesn't want to live in Slovakia.

Peggy: *Is there resentment or jealousy between you and your* burqa-*wearing sister-in-law?*

Sahraa: No, I love her and we get along well. I have convinced her not to wear the *burqa* and her husband has agreed. The problem is that people in Afghanistan don't think with their minds, they think with their eyes. What they see others do is what they think is right. Wearing a *burqa* was a habit for her, but when I pointed out that it's not necessary in Islam, they changed their minds. All of my in-laws are very tolerant and we respect each other.

Peggy: *What projects are you working on now?*

Sahraa: I just finished a film on the life of Suraia Perlika. (See the chapter on Suraia in this book.)

Peggy: *How was it when you were a little girl growing up? Did your parents encourage your art?*

Elaha: My parents loved their daughters and always encouraged us to be politicians, business women, or engineers, but not singers. They didn't hate art, but they were concerned about how society would accept me as a singer. So they were against me becoming a singer.

Peggy: *So how did you fight against that, because now you are a singer?*

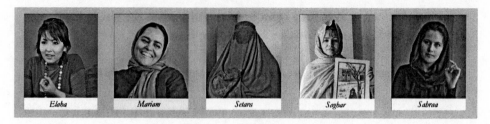

Elaha   Mariam   Setara   Saghar   Sabraa

Elaha: Even now my parents don't like me to sing. I love my parents but that doesn't mean that their ideas are always right. They have to accept me and I have to accept them. Traditionally in Afghanistan, singers have never had a good reputation. This makes it much harder for me. This attitude puts a lot of pressure on my family, especially my parents. Before I sang onstage, my parents had a good relationship with my entire extended family. But my conservative uncle had a big fight with my mother when I was singing on *Afghan Star*. Now he and his family have stopped socializing with us and they won't come to our house. They accuse my parents of changing their culture. I have to be careful now because some people don't like me because I'm a singer.

Peggy: *Even without all this repression from society, it's hard enough to be an artist. I'm wondering where you find the strength to stand up to this.*

Elaha: First of all I have self-confidence. When I was young, my parents always encouraged me and they believed that I could achieve something great. I have always been a leader among my friends, so that gives me confidence, too. Believing in myself, my talent, and skill is the most important thing.

Our society has suffered a lot and our generation has different ideas from our parents' generation. We have to sacrifice in order to bring the changes we want to see.

Peggy: *When you encounter people trying to stop you or condemn you, what is your response?*

Elaha: It depends. If somebody tries to put me down I will ignore them. This way I can make them feel that they didn't touch me. Other times I will try to give them my reasons.

Peggy: *What is the best part of your life so far?*

Setara: The best part of my life is my education, my struggles for my education, and the conflicts I face. Whatever I see I find interesting and it becomes the best part of my life. Most Afghan women are far from education. If they try to continue, they have to hide it in the kitchen while they stay at home and raise their children. I'm not going to be like those women. I'm going to change my life and think differently. I'm going to experience the things that are my right. I have to show my sisters, my friends, my family, and Afghan women all over the world that we can change if we have a chance.

Peggy: *During those five years under the Taliban, did you have poetry, were you interested in literature?*

Setara: Yes, I studied poetry, but I was not writing at that time, only following my English classes at home with my father. Sometimes I took courses like knitting, and I can make many nice things now.

Peggy: *So during the Taliban, were there things that helped you deal with depression and sadness?*

Setara: There was nothing because I was not writing, just studying. I had my poetry books and my diary notebooks, and whatever poems were my favorites. I spent my time trying to memorize them. I lived the way the scholars and the classic poets lived, in a sort of monastery. Now when I write, it is my healing. If I don't think that I'm a writer and if I can't write, then for me there is nothing. I have to express myself.

Peggy: This impulse and even compulsion to express is the driver of the "artistic soul." Sometimes what comes out is beautiful; sometimes ugly, but it is *the* truth as seen or felt by that person in that moment. *The* truth can be different in another moment, and that also can demand expression.

When something happens to you that you don't like, how do you react to that?

Setara: Afghan women and girls hide everything inside. They feel a mountain of pain and have no way to struggle against it. I am the same as others, but now whatever I see I write about. Positive or negative, it doesn't matter. If I limit myself and write only about positive things, I can't write. I'm not going to hide anything in my writing. Whenever you try to hide something, you cannot present reality.

Peggy: *How did your art help you get through difficult times?*

Saghar: In those [Taliban] times we could do nothing. We couldn't go out. We couldn't visit our friends. My only choice was to work inside my home and leave

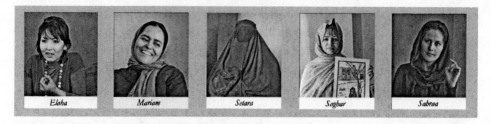

Elaha   Mariam   Setara   Saghar   Sabraa

everything else to the almighty Allah. When I felt bad and when I was suffering, I painted. It helped me forget my isolated condition. Do you see this [7 foot tall] painting of an ancient pillar? I painted it from a picture I had. By painting it, I was able to bring something from outside into my house.

Peggy: In order to create my own art, I need a conducive space. I need quiet. I need the space of mind to let my spirit soar beyond my physical surroundings. I need to be in the "right" mood. When I'm down, I just don't feel like being creative. If I do work during those times, my art reflects that and the result is mediocre, half-hearted, and forced. Harnessing anger to make art is another story. Depression, however, is much more prevalent in Afghanistan, one consequence of a cultural norm that seeks to protect loved ones from unpleasantness.

Listening to Saghar, I wondered if I could have created anything under the circumstances she endured. The truth is, at that time, during the Taliban she wasn't being very creative either. Her simply-drawn children's faces featuring huge sad eyes were a worthwhile exercise. They did express her feelings, but they were copies of pictures popular in the 1960s that she found in books. We didn't discuss it, but perhaps painting those faces had also been a small rebellion. Had the Taliban discovered her paintings of living beings, or her books of images, they would have been destroyed and she would have been punished.

One day back in Austin I attended a lecture by my friend Jen O'Neal about her work in Uganda. She told us stories of women who had sustained or been forced to perpetrate horrific atrocities. Although those women she met certainly had residual emotional effects as a result, she told me that they were generally not depressed. They had access to their emotions, both positive and negative.

I thought about this in comparison to the Afghan women I'd met. I realized that there was a key difference between the two groups.

In 2003, I asked women in Welayat prison[5] how they supported each other. A few told me that when a new woman came into their room, they encouraged her to tell her story and they cried together. Their mutual tears helped them bond as each woman in the group took on some of the storyteller's pain. By connecting with their own similar stories, they could begin to heal their traumas. These women in the prison were strangers who had already fallen from respectability by being jailed. They didn't feel the need to protect each other's reputations or dignity as they might have with relatives or the still-respectable. When I asked women outside of prison how they most often dealt with the difficulties they faced, many said that they hid their troubles so as not to add to the burdens of their loved ones. Silence is a prescription for isolation and depression.

Whether Ugandans or Afghans, those who move forward are actively engaged in creating better lives for their children and/or the wider society. They heal more quickly and have access to the most joy. In Setara's case, she moves forward and finds healing by sharing in her writing the experiences of Afghan women.

Who helped you get through your hard times?

Mariam: My cousin. When the *mujahidin* came to Kabul [1992], my uncle, who had already gone to Pakistan, advised us to join him. So my father closed up his wood heater shop and we set off. We lived in Pakistan for 11 years while my brothers, sisters, and I studied. My father sold tea and cold drinks in the bus station because he couldn't get a job. He was the only one supporting us – seven children, my mother, his mother-in-law, and grandmother.

When we first went to Pakistan, I was very weak in studying. On the first day of school they put my younger sister in fifth grade and me into second, even though I'm older. How can it be possible for me to be in second grade and my younger sister in fifth? It's not fair! I refused to go to school for one year because of this.

But one day my cousin told me, "Right now you have a lot of time, so what does it matter if you go into the second grade? If you study, you will soon be promoted to the fifth and then sixth. You can be in the top grade if you want. If you don't go to school, you will spend your life doing hard work and sitting in the corner. You won't have any talent; you won't have anything. If you don't get educated, one day your brothers and sisters will tell you that you are only good for washing their shoes." That hit me hard. Then she took my hand and led me to school saying, "I'm not going to let you just sit at home and do housework."

Peggy: *What gives you hope for Afghanistan?*

Setara: The struggle and hard work of the young generation, both women and men, give me great hope. When I see how hard they're working at the university, how they're trying to build their personalities in both their personal and social lives, I'm optimistic that that there will be something good in our future. I grew up in war, conflicts, rockets, and fire; everything that was in Kabul. I can remember

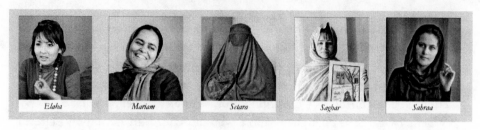

| Elaha | Mariam | Setara | Saghar | Sahraa |

that time, and even now I continue to experience the bomb blasts and suicide attacks. At that time I just watched. Now I write about it.

Peggy: *What do you see for your future?*

Elaha: I don't have any idea because I've never felt like I belonged to this country. I've always seen myself as an outsider. Perhaps it's because I was raised in Iran... My life is so different from others' here and that's why I never feel like I'm an Afghan. I feel like I'm in Neverland and that I am not of this world. I grew up in Iran, but I'm not an Iranian either. In some ways I feel very alone and there are a lot of young people who feel the same way.

Peggy: After her interview, Elaha offered to perform for me. She called a guitarist friend to accompany her and then took me down to her tiny practice room. As she sang, I watched her lose herself in her music.

Afterwards, she led me into her bedroom. It was a small, neat, well-lit room with a single bed in the corner and a desk on the far side. The black walls had been stamped with chalky, white handprints from the lower corner at the foot of her bed up to the ceiling above her pillow. The fingers reminded me of the feathers of a bird taking wing, flying out of a black prison. In the far corner, opposite her desk, hung a noose, a hangman's noose. She stood under it, tilted her head, stuck out her tongue and asked me to photograph her.

I was taken aback by this artistic expression of what many Afghans live with and the fact that she wanted to share it with the world: that death is always nearby, an option should things get too bad. Although their lives may look fine from the outside, the artist's life-path can be one of danger and loneliness.

Sahraa: I must tell you, we are a lost generation. All of us, because of our society, lived our lives for our mothers, fathers, or family and then when we started to live for ourselves, it was a little late. We must respect everybody, our in-laws, our parents, our elders, but we must also start to realize what we ourselves want, because our life is very short.

The Bird Market

Peggy: Mariam and I took a photo excursion into Kabul's bird market and surrounding neighborhood. What a gutsy woman she is! Our one option was to go on a Friday, the only day of the week when her print shop was closed. By the time we got to the bird market, the narrow alley was filled elbow-to-elbow with men. Not one other woman was in sight. Both sides of the cramped passageway were lined with cages on top of cages, each filled with pigeons, parakeets, *kabks* (Chukar partridge, a bird used for fighting), and more. Above the birds, empty baskets and cages precariously lined the edges of the roofs. Mariam plowed right in, with me in her wake. We'd walk a bit and then step up into a shop doorway, stepping out of the river of men streaming by to get our shots. Yes, I was a little nervous entering into this commotion, but felt safe enough following Mariam. The whole time I was never harassed nor touched inappropriately. I also couldn't understand what anyone around me was saying.

At one point, Mariam turned to me and said, "Let's go. Now." She turned on her heel and I followed her back the way we'd come, the river of men parting to let us pass. I could tell that someone had said something that made her realize that we weren't welcome there; that it wasn't safe to continue deeper into the male bastion of this market. We left that confined, crowded alley and turned onto a wide street. Only a few other women were walking about and even they were cloaked in *burqas* or enormous scarves.

On our way to the market, I had felt pretty safe walking on this same street, bustling with the every-day activities of vendors and their customers. Now I was nervous. Warnings to foreigners not to walk on the streets flooded my mind. My actual level of safety hadn't changed, but my level of fear had. Mariam and I continued the few more blocks to her house without incident. We sat comfortably in her living room while her mother and sisters served us a delicious lunch of qaboli rice[6], a parsley and tomato salad, and yogurt accompanied by a plate of fresh hot peppers.

The bird market in central Kabul.

2/Islam

In its history and prehistory, Afghanistan has been home to various religions. Zoroaster is credited with establishing the world's first monotheistic religion. Buddhists came as early as the sixth century BCE, and lived throughout the country. Hindus, Jains, and Jews were already part of the demography when Alexander the Great arrived in 330 BCE. He and his entourage introduced pagan Greek beliefs, but the Greeks and Macedonians coexisted with the locals and sometimes adopted their religions. In the first few centuries of the Common Era, Christianity entered the mix. Sufism developed between the twelfth and fourteenth centuries.

As noted earlier, Arab Sunni Muslims conquered Herat between 642 and 683 CE and gained control over the rest of Afghanistan by 870. The Safavid Empire that ruled Iran and western Afghanistan officially adopted the Shia version of Islam in the sixteenth century. According to the Pew Research Center,[1] the *Shia* presently constitute 10-20 percent of the Afghan population and are mostly, but not only, ethnic Hazaras.

During the years of Muslim expansion, newly conquered peoples were given the choice to subject themselves to the new empire or die; once they accepted the authority of their new rulers, they were given the choice to convert to Islam or not as they wished. Those choosing not to convert had to pay a "protective tax"[2] and were excluded from military draft. Those who did convert were ordered to pay a "Muslim tax" and were subject to compulsory military service. There were benefits and risks associated with conversion, but it wasn't mandatory.[3]

One result of this rich and complex religious past is that historically, Afghans were very tolerant of different faiths and of variations within Islam. This acceptance faded with the introduction of the communist regimes, leading up to the 1979 Soviet invasion. In general, during any political, economic or social unrest, populations become more rigid and uncompromising in their beliefs. Additionally, the tactic of pitting one group against another was practiced during all of the Afghan wars.

Today, Afghanistan's official name is the Islamic Republic of Afghanistan. It is a crime for an Afghan to profess or convert to a religion other than Islam. Media portrayal of fundamentalist extremist beliefs and those of the Taliban lead outsiders to believe that all Afghans, or at least all Afghan men, hold similar views. In reality, many Afghan men want their wives and daughters to be educated and to participate in society. Much of the dogma espoused by those opposing these ideals is based on *Pashtunwali*, the traditional "code of honor" of the Pashtun people, and other very patriarchal traditions, rather than on the actual tenets of Islam. As with any religious text, there are liberal and conservative interpretations of what is written in the *Quran*.

The majority view in the West is that Islam subjugates women. However, the Afghan women I met stated the opposite: that Islam gives them their rights. Historically this is true, since Islam was the first monotheistic religion to give women property and inheritance rights. While their percentages of property and inheritance seem disproportionately small to modern Western eyes, those rights were given in the context of a traditional society where no one lived independently. Before Afghan society's fabric was rent by war, both women and men had their own roles, rights, and responsibilities; everyone had a place.

The women in this chapter tell of their experiences with Islam and their beliefs about it. Rather than wishing they were not subject to Islam, they wish that all Afghans would practice it.

Several women in this chapter are introduced more fully in later chapters; others appear only here. Because most of their remarks are brief, I've omitted introductions except for Hajai Gulalai.

Hajai Gulalai

Haji and *Hajai* are terms of respect for men and women, respectively, who make the *hajj*, a ritual-filled pilgrimage to Mecca required of every devout Muslim who can make the journey.

I met Hajai Gulalai in the middle class, former Soviet apartment complex of Macrorayan in Kabul. Overstuffed furniture filled the room where we talked. Prints of idealized natural scenes hung on the walls in ornate gilt frames. Even though we swept back the heavy curtains, the room remained dark.

Hajai Gulalai came from an educated family. Although they lived in the conservative town of Jalalabad and belonged to a prominent Pashtun tribe, her father made sure that all of his daughters were educated. Gulalai graduated from Jalalabad High School and taught the Pashtu language at Kabul's Aisha Durrani High School for 20 years. She married, as a second wife, while she was a teacher. She stopped teaching when the civil war became too dangerous, and she and her family fled to Pakistan. She now lives with her husband, two sons, the older son's wife, and their daughters, her granddaughters.

When I went on the hajj, *we walked around the* **Ka'aba**. *God said that this is His house and we can come here to apologize and be forgiven.*

Peggy: *What are your best memories from your youth?*

Hajai Gulalai: The best memory of my life was going on the *hajj*. I went last year with my youngest son because my husband was sick at the time and I had to go with a *maharam*. On that trip, I kept comparing the Arab countries with Afghanistan and I felt like I was in heaven.

Peggy: *Tell me about the* hajj. *What did you do and what was it like?*

Hajai Gulalai: First, we put on the traditional white clothes and made seven trips around the **Ka'aba** seven times. Each seven times counts as one set and between the sets, we gave offerings or prayed. If someone is really old and can't walk, one time counts as a whole set. If someone is young and strong, they can go around as many times as they please. We took a break in our hotel, and after 2 pm we walked around it more.

The next day, we went to Mount Arafat and walked for seven or eight hours in the areas where our Prophet lived and experienced his miracles. The next day we went to the Ebo Stone[4] and sacrificed a goat.

Peggy: *Of all of your* hajj *experiences, what was the most important and meaningful?*

Hajai Gulalai: This experience made me believe in God more. I'd read stories about the Prophet, but when I went there, the truth of God was given to my body and mind. I learned a lot about Islam and my faith became stronger. The historical places that we visited from Mohammed's life gave me a real experience of Islam and a different view of my religion. The other best part was to feel forgiven and to forgive.

Peggy: *What hope do you have for the future of your life and for Afghanistan?*

Hajai Gulalai: I have a vision of peace and freedom for the future of Afghanistan. God should take the Taliban away from us. I want Afghanistan to develop in peace. It is especially hard for the parents who stayed in Afghanistan and whose children went abroad. Those children should come back so they can live together.

Peggy: *What do you have to say to people in the West?*

Hajai Gulalai: I'm very thankful for the United States and other countries that are helping Afghanistan. What hurts me the most is that sometimes people just walk in the streets of the provinces, and the foreign soldiers capture them, put them in prison, and hurt them. Foreigners should not inflict violence against Afghans because they cannot understand them. They cannot know who is bad and who is not.

Peggy: *What is the most important part of Islam for you?*

Rabia: For me, Islam is about serving humanity and helping people, because God says he can forgive anything you do to him. For example, if you pray to me instead of Him, He can forgive it, but if you do something to his creatures, He will not forgive you. If you hurt someone, God will not forgive you, but if you help someone, God appreciates it. That's why I think I have to help people. In that way, God will be very satisfied with me. I have to serve my family, myself, my people, and the world.

Sahera Sharif: Islam is a social religion; it's about how to build a good community. It is good, broad, and covers everything in our lives. Unfortunately, when there are rules that affect men and women equally, the men in our society only address the rules toward women.

Hajai Gulalai: Honesty and not lying. Not harassing or punishing anyone without good reason. Offering prayers five times a day, and keeping God in front of you all the time. I know that God is here and whatever I do, He will see all of it. The day is coming when we will die and will see God face-to-face.

Belgheis: I think it's important to look for common ideas among all religions because there are many. It's important for me to be kind to other people. We should work together, form good relationships, and not just think about ourselves. I think it's very good to be concerned about society.

However, now we see some very bad events, especially in Iran, that are actually not part of real Islam. My father is a *mullah*; he studied Islam, but he doesn't like the Iranian government and the form of Islam that governs [there] and mixes politics, economics, and business with Islam.

It's difficult to know what Islam says, because during different periods it changed and each time it has taken the color of that time and place. I can't say that I'm a real Muslim because there are some things that I disagree with, but I try to follow the aspects I like.

I'm satisfied because I have my prayers and all day, I have the time to be quiet and contemplate. Everyone needs some moments like this. All day we work and worry and keep busy. In our solitary times we can try to connect with peace, quiet, and kindness. That makes me happy and relaxed.

Meena: I believe in praying five times a day, and for me, *hijab* is very important. But I think that being clean in your heart makes the biggest difference, whether or not you keep the *hijab*. A really good Muslim woman would have a clean heart, be a kind person, and be honest with her family, her community, and everyone.

Peggy: *What is the most important part of Islam for women?*

Setara: As a woman, I like my *hijab* and I feel very comfortable in it. The *burqa* is not *hijab*. This is also in my poem.[5] Additionally, under Islam, women cannot be forced to marry someone. Many women are forced here, but it's not part of Islam.

Shakilla S: Islam appreciates mothers and helps women. They say that under the foot of women is heaven, which means that women must go to heaven because they give milk to their children.

Saleha: There are many laws in Islam that support women. For example, since breastfeeding is not a duty or a responsibility, women can ask to be paid for doing it. A woman can ask for payment even for breastfeeding her own children. There are many things like this in Islam that support women.

Ramzia: If the men obey Islam, it has very good points for women. When a woman has a baby or when she breastfeeds, the husband should hire a woman to work for her. And during this time her husband shouldn't shout at her.

Peggy: *How long does that last?*

Ramzia: Usually it lasts for two years. Afghan men don't like this and don't do it, however. For 40 days a new mother should rest and get strong. She should eat good food like chicken and meat. The new mother must have good food three times a day, sometimes four. She also should stay in the house. If they work in the government, they give them three months' holiday.

Shakila: Islam requires both men and women to take responsibilities. Islam supports women and families, but in some ways it doesn't. Both men and women are required to take care of their children, but in different ways. This is good because life is about sharing and it gives them a shared responsibility.

However, I don't like the part that says a man can take away their children if he and his wife separate, even if he is the one to initiate the separation. The women have no choice in this and it doesn't depend on their situation or what anyone wants. It's just the rule. But there are many interpretations about these kinds of things.

Suraya: Women and men have equal rights, but the rights are not the same. They cannot be the same. Women have a right to study, learn, and teach. For example, the Prophet Mohammad's wife, Aisha, was very bright and a good teacher to the men. That shows me that if you are qualified, you can do anything; you can even teach the men. Everything that Mohammad did was an example for us. When some of the people and *mullahs* don't let girls have an education, it is not from Islam. Also, in Islam, you don't have the right to beat women.

Batool: I think Islam gives men and women equal rights, but it's not practiced. There is a sentence in the *Quran* that says a man can beat his wife, but it should not be painful. What does that mean? The *mullah* says, "Yes, you can beat them," but I think it's our misunderstanding of Islam. Although Islam has many things that I don't accept as a Muslim, my problems with it revolve around the misunderstanding of Islam, and how the *mullahs* misuse their power.

Anisa: I think that in teaching Islam, there should be more emphasis on showing the reason rather than just following blindly. It doesn't matter what you are: open-minded, in the middle, or close-minded; whatever you do it's going to look bad to one of them, so we should make our own decisions.

Dr. Yacoobi: Islam is a democratic religion. It provides women with many rights. It provides kindness, equality, and a fair share. However, people are taking away those rights in the name of Islam. I feel that if women can read, write, and think critically, then they can ask questions and nobody can abuse them because they will be able to respond logically with what is right and what is wrong.

Additionally, Islam is not against education for girls. People who say that are ignorant. My father was illiterate but he allowed me to get an education, and he wasn't unusual.

Peggy: *What part of your belief in Islam has helped you the most?*

When I asked this question, Siebewal flew into a rage. She showered my translator with a torrent of anger while I sat and wondered how I'd offended her.

Siebewal: [*Crying and angry.*] In Afghanistan, all people are Islamic. But all during the fighting, the people who made a problem for me, who killed and injured my family, and who stole from me all claimed to be Islamic. If we really are Muslims, then we would never kill, steal, or do things against others. Afghanistan is an Islamic country, but there are no Muslims here!

Shakila: Islam encourages my commitment to my family. We each have a responsibility to the other. Because I have this commitment, because it's part of my belief and part of my life, I can really enjoy life in Afghanistan. When I improve myself and have a commitment to other people in my life, I can help them improve, too.

Ramzia: All parts of Islam help me, but prayer helps the most. If I'm angry, sad, or nervous, praying and reading the *Quran* soothes and calms me a lot.

Anisa: First, the *Quran* itself helps me whenever I recite it. That's what I do during my morning prayer and before I go to bed. It helps me calm down after a busy day.

When I was in the United States, wearing the scarf was a big deal and everybody would ask me about it. I got used to it and after a month, I knew all the questions they would ask. It made me find out the answers. When I returned, I went to the *mullah* I had known in Iran and asked him all the questions others had asked me. He thought it was very strange that I was asking questions and that America had changed me; he thought I was doubting my beliefs. I stopped asking him, but I kept reading books. There are many religious people like him who think it's wrong to question.

I like the tradition of wearing the scarf, though, because it's something the *Quran* asks us to do, and it makes us different from others. Our Prophet Mohammed wanted us to differentiate ourselves from the rest. I like that. I love everything about the *Quran*.

Zakiya N: I think it's important to respect one's parents. Children today don't respect their parents as much and are more concerned about their own lives.

Suraya: Honesty. Whatever I do, I think, "God is watching me." You cannot hide anything from God.

I also believe that all humans are the same. Only God is higher than us. I do not like people who don't respect a cleaning person or a servant. At work I respect the cleaner as much as I respect the director, because I respect someone on the basis of their behavior, not position. For example, I don't like a person if they are fine to me but do wrong to someone else. Having good manners and good relations with people means a lot to me.

Peggy: *How did you learn about Islam and how has your thinking about it changed?*

Saleha: When I was very young, I attended religion classes but they never taught us the reasons behind what we were learning. In high school, I met some teachers who demonstrated those religious values. Now, I apply those principles in my life and have experienced that they are really true.

My religious beliefs haven't really changed much. When I was younger I only thought about them; but now I've discovered them for myself. I've found that sometimes the obligations and limitations of Islam are good, but it depends on how they are carried out. For example, I think that the requirement that nine-year-old girls should fast during Ramadan is cruel. It's important to be a nice person, so those duties should be carried out in a nice way.

Anisa: After our third year living in Iran, I went to a week-long summer program that taught us about the *Quran* and other things in our religion. We were all nine and ten years old, and there were a lot of activities for us. I enjoyed it.

Peggy: *There are* Quran *schools and camps for girls as well?*

Anisa: Yes. When I was in Iran, there were many.

Peggy: *Was it a good experience for you?*

Anisa: Yes, it really was, because it helped me understand a lot more. My younger sister didn't get to go because we were already in Afghanistan by the time she was old enough. I kept all my materials and my books, so I taught her and we did the activities together. When our relatives wanted private time inside the house, I would go outside with her and teach her.

Peggy: *When I heard other Afghan people talk about Iran, they said the Iranians taught by forcing students to memorize things without understanding them. They said that if students asked questions, they'd be beaten. Was that your experience?*

Anisa: There are very poor schools that punish the students like that. In those places, they would hit the students on their hands with rulers, but that didn't happen at our school. I really liked how they taught us. From the beginning, they trained our brains for memorization. We practiced study skills for six hours every day. We have a saying that if you lay the first brick in a house crooked, the walls will go up crooked and the house will not last.

Zakiya N: When children are young they usually follow their families' thoughts on religion. After that, they need something to help them understand it deeply. In my own case, I don't believe what my parents believe, because I have researched and arrived at different conclusions. I found my own way.

Rabia: I love Islamic society when people follow true Islam. I don't rely on [secular] society's idea of Islam because most of the things they say differ from what the *Quran* says. I studied Islam in school and have read the Farsi translation of the *Quran*. I found that a lot of the things that the *mullahs* say are not mentioned in the *Quran*. I'm not a strict person, but I like to study the *Quran* and I have my own views and opinions. My dad used to teach the *Quran* to me when I was little.

Setara: I was born into a Muslim family, making me a geographic Muslim first. During the Taliban, I had this idea that I had to know what the so-called "real Islam" was that I saw in the government. So I started studying Islamic books, and I saw Islam to be something else. Now, I'm proud as a Muslim, but also very sad. Why don't I have the rights that Islam gives me?

Peggy: *What else do you have to say about Islam?*

Marzia: What I like about real Islam, not what we are practicing, is that it's a religion that cannot go too extreme; it's always moderate. I'm not a religious person, but I learned some things about *Shia* beliefs when I lived in Iran, even though I am Sunni. I can read the *Quran* in Arabic without any translation, but when I look at all the things that Islam or our Prophet says, it's always what you would do anyway if you're a smart person. Nothing in Islam seems extreme to me.

Zakiya N: Islam has many good things, but we Muslims don't implement them. Islam says one thing, but Afghans are doing something different. That's why many people in the world think that Islam is bad. They think that because Muslims [here] are like that, then Islam is, too. Islam is something quite different from the Muslims you see here. Islam is something that is useful for all human beings if it could be practiced the way it was supposed to be practiced.

Shakila: Another thing I like about Islam is that in the *Quran*, it tells us to be kind. I don't see this practiced much in Afghanistan, but Islam tells us that it's very important. We shouldn't be aggressive, but peaceful. When family members are peaceful, they can understand each other better.

Dr. Yacoobi: Sometimes it happens that a father wants to marry his daughter to somebody and he receives a lot of money from that person. In reality, he is selling his daughter. In our human rights program, we teach girls that they can say "no" if they don't agree to that marriage by using a quote from the *Quran*. We teach them that a woman can say, "No, my daughter is too young." Through those quotes, we are teaching women how to stand up and defend themselves, and it is working.

Peggy: *I'm also interested in your thoughts about the headscarf. You say that you believe in the deeper tenets of Islam, but not so much in the superficial ones. What are your beliefs about the choice to wear or not to wear the head covering?*

Shakila: There are some values in Islam that I question. For example, I can't find any reason why Muslim women should wear the headscarf. I've heard many different answers. I've heard that it will make them more secure, but I don't understand how. I've heard that a scarf keeps women from arousing men and makes them less provocative. My question is, why doesn't Islam ask the man to control himself? Why should I do something to protect him from his own feelings? I think men should be responsible for themselves in this regard. Why would seeing my hair arouse a man? For me, *hijab* is about wearing modest clothes, but I don't think it has anything to do with [concealing my] hair.

Dr. Yacoobi: It's a mistake when you look at Muslim women and think they are weak because they wear *hijab*. These women are very strong, intelligent, and resourceful. Wearing *hijab* does not mean that someone controls them.

Women in the Kabul bazaar.

Zainab

I met and Zainab at a literacy center aided by **Church World Service** (CWS). Even though there were only women there, she wore her *burqa* with the front veil raised, framing her face.

Zainab grew up in a Hazara village near Bamyan. At 18 she became engaged, and married two years later. Her husband died in a landmine explosion which also injured their oldest son. She now lives in Kabul and cleans houses to support her family. Besides learning to read, she earns money sewing quilts in a program run by the literacy center.

I liked living in the village, but it's impossible for widows to earn a living there. In Kabul I can work and live freely. In my village, people talked about me because I lived alone with my children without a man.

Peggy: *Tell me about life with your husband.*

Zainab: My husband was a good man, but he had a lot of debts. Finally, one of his creditors insisted on being paid, but we didn't have any money. So I sold my wedding gold to pay the debt.

Peggy: Gold or other items a woman is given as wedding gifts belong to her personally, to support her in case her husband dies or divorces her. Her husband can't legally take it from her. After Zainab gave her wedding gold to pay her husband's creditor, she was left with nothing when he died.

Zainab: I gave up my gold freely. I loved my husband and the creditor might have killed him or taken my daughter away, so I told my husband that it was better for them to take my gold.

Peggy: *When you were young, did you look forward to wearing a* burqa *like your mother?*

This question caused an angry debate between Zainab and my translator, Shakilla S., who didn't like what Zainab said and tried to elicit a more "politically correct" reply. To Shakilla's credit, she told me that this was Zainab's actual response:

Zainab: Yes, I liked the *burqa* when I was young and I like to wear it now. Actually, I don't like it, but I'm used to it. I feel ashamed if I don't wear it. It is *hijab*. I like it because it is good in Islam, it covers my body and people can't see me.

3/Women's Rights

Women's activism has and will continue to play a huge role in securing the rights of Afghan women. Like their counterparts around the world, Afghan women who successfully fight oppression emerge as bold, empowered leaders. While the murders of women who stand up, speak out, or just go to work or school may silence and paralyze some, these killings make other women more determined.

The Afghan constitution states, "The citizens of Afghanistan have equal rights and duties before the law." However, without a commitment to this ideal in Parliament and the ministries, the words are empty. It is up to Afghan women and the men who support them to make sure that these words are actually implemented.

Although the US government touted saving Afghan women as one reason for intervening in Afghanistan, it is now apparent that without substantial support from women around the world, and especially those in Afghanistan, the rights and gains of Afghan women will be jettisoned as the US searches for a face-saving exit from a realm of increasing religious fundamentalism.

Soraya Sobhrang
Commissioner for Women's Rights,
Afghan Independent Human Rights Commission

Just before I left Afghanistan in 2010, I was invited to accompany my friend Elizabeth Roberts and her husband Elias to this interview. Soraya's office overflowed with stacks of books and papers. She was inundated with work but was calm, soft spoken, and gracious, seemingly unaffected by the chaos around her.

Soraya was born in the western desert province of Herat and graduated from the medical university there as a gynecologist. When the Soviets came, educated people who didn't support them were considered enemies, so she and most of her colleagues fled to Iran. There, she practiced gynecology in a huge government hospital and worked with botched self-immolation cases. When she heard about the need for doctors in a hospital for refugees in Pakistan, she went there. But that, too, became dangerous as fighting spread, so she moved to Germany where she stayed until the fall of the Taliban.

If somebody kills you for your ideas and you work for human rights or for your country, it is common. But women's rights activists are dying in bed of natural causes. It's better if they die fighting. And so we must be hopeful and work and not be afraid.

Soraya was one of the first to repatriate when Karzai became president and invited Afghans to return. She served as Deputy Minister of Women's Affairs for three years and then was appointed to the Independent Human Rights Commission.

Masiha
Defense Lawyer

When I asked Masiha's employer, **Medica Mondiale** (MM), to connect me with an attorney, I received what may have been a form letter explaining that interviewing trauma survivors, even using a caring, sensitive approach, may re-traumatize them. MM's question, "Is the interview really necessary?" strengthened my belief that, for my book, it was not, so I didn't ask Masiha to introduce me to any of her clients. The organization's concern for trauma survivors' well-being deepened my respect for MM. I interviewed Masiha in the group's conference room.

Even as a child, Masiha was very interested in studying law and political science. She graduated from Kabul Law School, having studied secular law, *Sharia*[1] law, and political science during her four years there. After graduation, she took courses for defense lawyers given by the Afghan Women Lawyers Council (AWLC).[2] Her goal was to work in the Ministry of Foreign Affairs. When that didn't work out, she became a defense lawyer. She's been defending women since 2004.

Defending women is very important work, especially in Afghanistan. When I started my work here, there were no female defense lawyers. Now there are 54 of us.

Laila

Engineer, City of Kabul, Urban Planning Department

I visited Laila in her office in the distant outskirts of Kabul. The cavernous main room had a few dusty tables and chairs, some empty, others piled with untouched, rolled up city maps and unbound collections of reports written in Russian. On one wall hung a big plastic-covered map of the planned community, Macrorayon,

I'm very interested in helping women in remote areas. Those women are excluded from every kind of life. I could organize health care or sanitation projects. In some places, women are not even aware of sanitation.

where Soviet families had lived during the 1980s and Afghans live now. This spacious room surrounded a small inner sanctum, sealed off against the winter cold. This provided a cramped working space for five employees, who didn't seem to have much to do. In its prime, the office had been filled with 30 busy workers.

Laila's boss and two other women sat in on our interview. I've included some of their comments.

Laila was born in Baghlan Province, but completed high school in Kunduz. Throughout most of the Soviet war, she studied in Tashkent, Uzbekistan, where she learned Russian and worked on her Master's and PhD degrees. She obtained a job in the government housing construction department upon her return to Afghanistan, but this job doesn't utilize many of her skills, and she only earns $81 a month. She is happily married and has one son and two daughters.

Shakila

Former Assistant Program Director, 10,000 Women

In 2007, Shakila taught my husband, Bill, the Dari language while he was in Kabul. I first met her when she came to Texas in 2009. She'd been to a conference in New York City, and Bill and I flew her down to enjoy a visit and see another part of the US. It was fun to show her Austin and to see our town from her point of view.

Earlier that year, Shakila helped organize and participated in a women's demonstration against certain repugnant articles of the Shia Personal Status Law (aka Shia Law, Marital Rape Law) that had been signed by President **Hamid Karzai** in April.[3]

Shakila was the one who convinced me to return to Afghanistan in 2010. When I arrived, she introduced me to translators and many people of interest. I am deeply indebted to her.

Being part of this movement has made me feel more responsible for Afghanistan and its future. I didn't see any misery during the protest, just hope and life. It was inspiring!

Shakila was born in 1980 in a small village in Bamyan Province. Six years later, as Soviet forces attacked the area, her family evacuated to Arak, an Iranian provincial capital. Iran encouraged universal education at that time, and Shakila completed high school and a two-year nurse's training program. Her family returned to Afghanistan in 2004, moving to Kabul for its work and educational opportunities. Shakila worked as a nurse at Bamyan Hospital and later as a translator for **International Midwife Assistance** (IMA). She rejoined her family in Kabul when that job ended and began working as an Assistant Program Manager for the 10,000 Women Business Training Program at the American University of Afghanistan. In the fall of 2011, she began her studies in business in the US.

Zainab R
Director, Community Development Council

When I told Shakila I was going to Bamyan, she suggested I interview Zainab R. We met up at the bazaar in Bamyan City and took one of the few taxis to Azdar Village, a new community built to house returning refugees. Zainab's house was built of traditional mud bricks even though it was relatively new. Inside, light from

These mullahs *always provide challenges and problems for me. They are very much against changing the minds of people. But we older women have one goal and that is to fight with this kind of thinking. We have to change the mind of the people.*

the large windows illuminated the nicely plastered, painted, and carpeted living room. She was tired after her long day, and I found out afterwards that she was having some lung issues. Two days later, when I was scheduled to photograph her, she was in the hospital with pneumonia. In spite of her poor health, I could see the activist fire burning within her.

Zainab was born in Yakolang Province in the central highlands of Afghanistan, but grew up in Bamyan. Her mother died when she was nine years old. Shortly afterward some Kuchi people, nomads of Pashtun ethnicity, raided her Hazara village and forced the villagers out. Zainab and her family went to Iran, where she earned an Associate's degree in midwifery. Her father died when she was 15. Zainab has six brothers, a husband, four sons, and nine daughters.

The family returned to Bamyan after the Taliban were driven out. She now works in the hospital there and became head of the Community Development Council (CDC).

Fatima

Director of Women's Affairs, Bamyan

I met Fatima, her husband, and two lovely daughters over dinner at Belgheis' and Ali's home where I was staying, in the outskirts of Bamyan City. Quiet but not shy, energetic but calm, Fatima talked passionately about the work she's done to help women.

Fatima was born in the Bamyan area, but fled to Iran as a child to escape the violence. In Iran, she completed her education and teacher training. She worked in educational **Non-governmental organizations** (NGO)s and taught in a girl's school. She and her husband were among the first to return to Bamyan once the Taliban were overthrown. In 2002, the governor invited her to become the Director of Women's Affairs. She ran for Parliament in 2010 but lost.

We established a Women's Development Network and in 2009, we made a shelter for women who have problems with their families. We worked with 40 organizations in the Bamyan area to help women in various ways.

Humaira

I met Humaira late in the afternoon in her tiny office at Medica Mondiale. She'd just had a very full week and a long day, but was gracious enough to spend a short amount of time with me. Her desk was overflowing with books and papers and she was showing the effects of stress and exhaustion. Because of our limited time and her fatigue, I didn't ask her anything personal. She preferred not to be photographed.

Shinkai Karokhail

Founding member/director Afghan Women's Education Center
Member of Parliament

When I first met her in 2003, Shinkai was already a striking presence, a strong, grounded, motherly figure with a commanding aura. These qualities had solidified when I met her again in 2010. Unlike most Afghan women I met, Shinkai didn't mind being photographed without a careful application of makeup.

[Our demonstration against the Shia Personal Status Law] showed solidarity among women. Women have the same problems, they have the same pain and suffering, so it doesn't matter whether they are Sunni, Shia, or Hindu.

2003

Shinkai graduated from medical school at Kabul University but had to leave almost immediately due to the mounting violence of the Soviet war. Unable to get hired by a hospital in Pakistan since jobs were reserved for Pakistanis, she and some friends founded the **Afghan Women's Education Center** (AWEC), offering language and computer courses to women and motherly support to orphans and street kids. In 2011, AWEC finished building a school for some of Kabul's 60,000 street children.

2010

| Soroya | Masiba | Laila | Shakila | Zainab R |

Peggy: *Shinkai, what have been the biggest issues you've dealt with in Parliament?*

Shinkai Kaokhail: We worked against certain articles in the Shia Personal Status Law inside the Parliament for 15 months before we had a demonstration in April, 2009.

Peggy: *My Hazara friend, Shakila, commented that you were very active in fighting the Shia Law even though you are a Pashtun and a Sunni.*

Shinkai: Yes, because this is a human rights issue. I also saw that this Shia law would become the foundation of family law for Sunnis as well, because so far we don't have a separate family law. We use part of the civil law most of the time.[4] If this were to get approved, in the worst case scenario, we could never get anything for women. That's why we had to stop it and not let it become law.

At first, I was alone and not even the *Shia* in Parliament would support me. Shia extremists actually warned the moderates not to touch this law. They tried to blackmail the moderates by saying, "This is the first time we are getting our own law, so we should all approve it." Eventually I got the moderates' support. I told them, "I don't think religious issues should be used against the rights of women."

Peggy: Any law that applies specifically to one religious group would be anathema and illegal in the US. However, it makes sense in the case of family law (not criminal or civil law) in the cultures of South Asia and the Middle East. In Jordan, for example, there are separate family laws for Christians and Muslims. This is welcomed; neither group wants to be bound by the requirements of the other. In Afghanistan, there are differences between Shia and Sunni traditions surrounding marriage, divorce, and child custody. For that reason, Shia women I talked with were happy to have their own law instead of being bound by Sunni-dominated traditional and *Sharia* law; they just didn't like some of the articles this specific legislation contained.

Shinkai: The Shia Law was passed by the Parliament and then approved by President Karzai in February 2009. It only affected Shia Muslims, about six million

Fatima *Shinkai, 2010*

people. In some ways, it was supposed to be an improvement for Shia women because previously, customary law, or the law of the locality of any disputes, decided family issues. Decisions were made by male village elders or, in the cities, by the *mullahs*. The Shia Law brought the standardization of law, if not of actual practice.

Peggy: The bill was rammed through the upper house of Parliament without debate and sent to President Karzai, who quickly granted approval. Elections were fast approaching, and he wanted to win Shia votes. When Shinkai and her delegation visited Karzai to ask him to change his decision, it became obvious that he had no idea what the law contained. He agreed to revisit it due to Afghan and international pressure.

Shakila: When Parliament passed the law, we were not surprised because there were a lot of religious and conservative Members of Parliament (MPs). What we didn't expect was that Karzai would sign it. That really shocked me and opened my eyes about Karzai.

Shinkai: We believe that this Shia law was developed in Iran, because after a lot of searching, we could not find the people who drew it up. Locally, the powerful and hard-line Shia leader **Ayatollah Asif Mohseni**, who runs the Khatamun Nabiyeen Mosque,[5] also known as the Blue Mosque, supported it. The mosque's complex contains a large high school and university that are financially supported by Iran. Mr. Mohseni supported the law and he warned us that no one could touch it or amend it. In the end, he was willing and ready to accept 50 changes.

Peggy: *Wait, that never appeared in the Western press! We heard that there were two or three changes and that the "marital rape" part was taken out. There were really 50 changes?*

Shinkai: Yes, 50 changes. Five-zero. A lot of rubbish was dropped. For example, it was written that women should not wear makeup, which is no one's business! Whether or not I wear lipstick should not have to be approved by my husband. Such stupid things were dropped, including a schedule for having sex. They also wrote about child marriage without pegging a specific minimum age for marriage. Maternal child custody would have changed from the customary five years of age for boys and seven for girls[6] to two years of age for both, so women were really shocked.

Soroya   Masiba   Laila   Shakila   Zainab R

Peggy: *So in the case of divorce or the father's death, a two-year-old child would go to live with the father and/or his family, and before that age they would remain with the mother?*

Shinkai: Yes. Also, children could marry, and once they became adults they could cancel the marriage.

Peggy: That would make it very hard for the divorced woman to ever remarry, and would bring shame to her entire family, whether cancellation was instigated by the husband or wife.

Shinkai: There were a lot of stupid things like those, but I felt that these two issues, child custody and marriage cancellation, could garner good support.

Sunni and Hindu women, not only Shia, participated in the demonstration. There weren't many women. It would have been much bigger, but Mohseni used his own media and TV to promote his family law.

At the mosque, security guards and police circled the area and didn't let people enter. That's also why the numbers were not big. There were around 150 or 200 women, but I can tell you that if even one woman could stand in front of such a big religious place, where inside there were lots of people ready to throw stones, use bad words, and to try to frighten them, that is a big revolution in the history of Afghanistan! That was the first time women stood against a law that was based on a religious issue. It was… unreal. Even I could not dream that up.

Shakila: [Mohseni] presented his show promoting the law in the provincial mosques. He paid to have a generator so people could listen to his speech. Then he told the Parliament that all Shia women supported the law. He brought letters with thumbprints and signatures of provincial women to prove it. The only way for us to show our opposition was to hold the demonstration and stand up against the law. I understood that if we didn't participate, then everyone would think that Afghan women agreed with the law. People would say, "What's the problem with the foreigners? You can see that Afghan women want this law." We didn't have any other way to object. I'm very happy because our protest showed that there were

Fatima Shinkai, 2010

women in Afghanistan who are Afghan; not Christian, but Muslim, who didn't want that law.

Our protest was on April 15, 2009, at 10:00 a.m. The police stationed themselves between us and the men exiting the mosque. Counter-demonstrators told us that we were slaves of Christianity and said things like, "Long live Islam! Down with opposition to Islam!" Some people even threw stones.

Peggy: *Shakila, what effect did organizing and participating in that demonstration have on you personally?*

Shakila: I learned more about Afghanistan. It was very interesting because I saw people from other ethnicities organizing with us. Parliamentarians from other ethnic groups helped us greatly. It gave me hope that we could really accomplish something by working together. It really didn't matter what ethnicity we were, a new experience for me. Before, I had never paid attention to political issues. I found out that there were many women who thought as I did, and that we could become more powerful through forming organizations and working together.

Recipe for a Protest
By Shakila

In April 2009, a group of about 250 women gathered in front of the Blue Mosque in Kabul to oppose the Shia Law that violated women's rights. I was among them. It was a protest unprecedented in recent Afghan history and as a result, some articles of law were eliminated and some changed. But we were not prepared to encounter furious, stone-throwing men and shouting women. Thinking about this later, I've realized a very important part of our demonstration was that we began to learn how to organize. This is crucial because well-organized protests encourage Afghan women to take more responsibility in changing their situation and the laws that violate their rights.

To organize, first of all, an individual should form a group. Then, the group should explain clearly what it wants to achieve. Next, the group should divide responsibilities. The four main subgroups needed are: management, finance, marketing, and public communication. I was in the public communications group and went to the high schools to print off and distribute the protest announcement. The high school that we went to the day before the protest was attacked later in the day because of anger over our planned protest, and two people were injured.

Being ready for the unforeseen is very important. For example, on the day of our Shia Law protest, when we were gathering in front of the mosque, we heard that some women could not join us because a group of men blocked their way. When we heard this, we could not believe it and did not know how to help the women reach us. Still, we tried to stay calm and move forward.

Suddenly, a group of angry men moved out of the mosque toward us. They were shouting bad words, waving their hands, and throwing stones at us. Policemen and policewomen were the only line between them and us. Some women wanted to hold their ground to show that they were not afraid. Others asked us to retreat a bit. We did not know what to do.

A group of fierce women came out of another gate of the mosque and moved just behind us. They were yelling at us, condemning us, and coming to punish us, I felt. Now I could see that the women in our group were becoming really worried.

"Can police stop them if something happens?"

"Who knows?"

"Where should we go now?"

We were surrounded by an angry mob, and the policewomen made a circle around us. I was afraid of an explosion or of being attacked. We did not anticipate this and we were not ready for it. The policewomen helped us move from in front of the mosque to a less crowded part of the main street and from there, with their protection, we moved toward the Parliament Building. They tried to keep us as far from the mob as possible.

From this experience, I learned that a group always should be ready for a bad situation, and if something happens, the most important thing is to stay calm, be careful, and follow police instructions. This experience was hard but at the same time great for me because I learned many things about the women's movement that I did not know before. The protest was good, but if we had paid attention to some small but important points, it could have been much better.

This experience made me stronger and more active. Before, I always thought that if there were a law in this country, I couldn't do anything to change it. This was the first time I thought about taking action for something outside of my personal life. It was really a great experience and it boosted my confidence. Most importantly, I learned that I shouldn't be afraid to make mistakes. They are part of life and I should just do what I believe I should do to help improve women's lives.

The protest we did was really just a gathering. Yet I saw that if we were more organized, we could do anything. If we had a spokesperson at that time, we could show a stronger face and speak out because people would want to hear us. There are many risks for someone to speak publicly and to the media. They would become very vulnerable and someone might hurt them or their family. We weren't ready for that, so we simply gathered, but we held a significant gathering because we stood up to this unjust law. Another result was that we decided to start a discussion group to explore how we could nourish each other, inform ourselves about other activities going on, and organize ourselves better. [7]

The Khatamun Nabiyeen Mosque, also known as the Blue Mosque. The street side of this mosque was the site of the protest against articles of the Shia Personal Status Law.

Soroya   Masiba   Laila   Shakila   Zainab R

Peggy: Domestic violence is a big issue in Afghanistan, with one study[8] finding that 52% of the women interviewed reported experiencing physical violence. Five percent of those had received death threats from their husbands, and 39.3% said that their husbands had hit them within the last year. However, husbands are not the sole abusers in families; mothers-in-law were identified as the main abusers by almost a quarter of the women surveyed. Additionally, 59% of women were in forced marriages as opposed to arranged marriages.

Laila, why did you ask me to interview you?

Laila: I wanted to talk about the problem of domestic violence. I want to say that just because someone is educated doesn't mean that they don't experience violence. Even educated women have a lot of problems. Also, we cannot say that men are the only cause of violence against women. Women also do it. One example concerns mothers-in-law. Many of them abuse their daughters-in-law.

Peggy: *You mean they beat their daughters-in-law?*

Laila: Yes, but besides beating, there are other kinds of violence. For example, she won't let her daughter-in-law go outside, continue her education, or visit her parents. If she doesn't have a child, she faces more problems. Financial issues also make these relatives commit violence against the wife or daughters. Women also face political, financial, and man-caused violence.

Laila's Boss: We have a lot of problems and the most prevalent one is financial. If there are financial problems, there is violence against women. What is the motivation for the violence? My family consists of eight people and I only earn $94 per month. Because of our financial difficulties, I am violent to my wife. What should I do? I have to use that money for food, for rent, for everything.

Fatima   *Shinkai, 2010*

Peggy: This man had no shame over beating his wife. He sees himself as a victim of his situation and not in control of his actions. Even after questioning, he couldn't see that he might take responsibility for his violence or communicate his frustration in a more benign way. He had become accustomed to the government supporting him throughout his career under the Soviet system, when workers were given a small salary and also received uniforms and certain foods like flour, rice, and oil. Now, he's working for the government again, but he's not reaping the same benefits.

Addressed to two other women sitting with us:
Of all the women you know, how many experience violence in their homes?

Woman 1: About 50% of the women I know endure physical violence brought on by financial stress and unemployment.

Woman 2: I don't know anyone who suffers from physical violence. I don't know anyone here, nor where I come from in Herat Province, who has experienced violence from relatives.

Peggy: The same study noted above went on to say: "Only 18% of women knew other women who had been beaten by their husbands, suggesting that most women were isolated in their experiences of violence." Also, "Almost a quarter of women were dissatisfied with domestic relationships between men and women in Afghan society."

Over 75% of married women claimed to be satisfied, or at least not dissatisfied, with their relationship with the men in their families.

On the other hand, the report also says, "Domestic violence is highly normalized in Afghan society… many women noted satisfactory marital relationships while simultaneously reporting experiences of violence in the home."

Soraya: A lot of the women who experience familial and societal violence come to the Human Rights Commission to complain. They also go the Women's Ministry (Ministry of Women's Affairs, MOWA). Before, these abused women thought violence was their husband's right. "He is giving me food, a place to stay, and clothes, so he has the right to beat me." Now, it is very difficult for her husband when she says, "Why are you beating me? I'm going to the Minister

Soroya   Masiha   Laila   Shakila   Zainab R

and the Human Rights Commission." Many women come; last year alone, 3000 women come to our offices around the country.

When they come, we give them guidance. For example, one woman came with her family and said, "My husband didn't tell me that he's already married to another woman and I want a divorce." In that kind of case, we mediate. We asked this woman what she needed and we offered it to her. Sometimes they don't want a divorce because they don't have a job and they have a family they would have to support. The women say, "This situation is not acceptable to my family, but I love my children and so I just want you to talk to my husband because this is unjust." So, we talk with her family and her husband. This takes a long time; however, we are successful in many cases.

Peggy: *If the woman gets divorced, does she lose her children?*

Soraya: Yes, and this comes from Islam. Boys can stay with the mother until seven years of age, and girls until nine. After that, their father will come and get the children. This is very painful for everyone, especially the children. This is a very big motivation for women not to choose divorce, because they love their children. In other cases, a woman wants to stay with her family, but the husband doesn't want her. Sometimes at the end of mediation, we have to show him that if he doesn't behave well, he will have to go to court. They have to be a little afraid of the law, although we don't pose any ultimatums.

Peggy: *You can take them to court?*

Soraya: Yes, especially if they are criminals.

Peggy: *Are there shelters for women who are beaten and just can't take it anymore?*

Masiha: Yes. We have some shelters here, but many families aren't aware of them or they think they are shameful places, like prison.

Peggy: *How does one find out about them?*

Fatima   *Shinkai, 2010*

Masiha: Some women who have run away go directly go to MOWA and people there will direct them to the shelters. Most of them, however, go to a police station and then are referred to MOWA. There's only one shelter where women can go without a referral from MOWA, run by **Women for Afghan Women** (WAW). In that case, they go to the WAW office and are taken to the shelter's secret location.

Peggy: WAW does a lot of work helping women (and men) who have had their human rights abused. In Kabul, they have a family guidance center with a "battalion of social workers, case workers, and lawyers who help each client get justice or attain the solution they desire for their problems."[9] Their secret shelter is a place where a woman can go if she is in danger or has nowhere else to go.

Peggy: *What services are available for women suffering abuse here in Bamyan?*

Zainab R: The level of literacy in Bamyan, especially for women, is very low. Because of this, very few people are connected or know how to get help. For example, a woman isn't able to go to the Human Rights Commission or NGOs if the husband is against it. Also, it is very dishonorable if they go to the Human Rights Commission and say, "My husband attacks me." Instead, they just put up with the situation. This generation accepts the situation. We have to wait for the next one.

We made a center of empowerment for women.[10] This center offers literacy classes and courses that explain the laws to women. Since there isn't electricity during the day, we even adopted solar energy.

Peggy: *Is there any place women can go, or anything they can do, to get help if they are in danger from a violent husband?*

Fatima: We established a shelter for women who have problems with their families here in Bamyan with the help of the **Shuhada Organization**. These women are brought into the shelter where they try to solve the problems with their families and then go back to a better situation. I worked very hard to establish this shelter. It's my proudest achievement as Director of Women's Affairs in Bamyan.

Peggy: One interesting difference between domestic volence shelters in Afghanistan and the ones in America is that in the US, counseling is aimed at

helping women get out of their violent situations and into a life separate from and independent of their abusers. In Afghanistan, where shelters are few and not respected nor understood by the population at large, the goal is to mediate between the women, their husbands, and their in-laws. They work to help women go back to a better life with the same family. This may seem crazy at first blush, but in certain cases is surprisingly effective. Because of segregation between males and females, husband and wife often have little understanding of each other or the other gender. Violence is seen as a normal way to deal with women and children, but through education, other ways can be learned.

Zainab: This country is very traditional, and changing the minds of these people will not happen overnight. We have to go step-by-step and make our people understand every woman's and every girl's right to education. Then, girls can help support their families, which will lessen the financial pressure on the family, and thereby lessen violence.

I also try to help women who suffer from domestic violence. Some women only have small problems that I can resolve myself, but others have bigger problems and I send them to the Human Rights Commission.

Does mediation generally have a favorable result?

Humaira: It depends. Most of the time it works well. Often, the level of literacy is low and the expectations of husbands and wives are different. They don't know how to communicate with each other, so of course they have a tense relationship.

Post-childbirth is also a stressful time for both parents, and men may not understand the physical and psychological effects that childbirth has on their wives. Sometimes, traditional practices affect the relationships in a negative way. By making them aware of the effects of these practices, we can help them behave in a better way. Mediation can help them understand each other better, and improve their relationship. But sometimes, a case just ends badly.

For example, on January 25, 2010, we had a case where a 22-year-old girl from Paghman Province was suffering from a forced marriage. She had been in love with a boy and after she had been married awhile, she escaped and ran away

Fatima   Shinkai, 2010

with him. As long as the couple hasn't had premarital sex, which is illegal, running away is not a crime, but is often treated as one. The couple got the support of a defense lawyer and the girl was put in a detention center. We held a mediation and one of her uncles signed a paper saying that he would guarantee her safety. By eight o'clock that very evening, that same uncle had killed her. So I cannot say that all the work we do is perfect or that it always helps the woman. Often it works, but sometimes, because of honor killings, stigmatization, and the taboos about women going to prison or the police, we can't really help.[11]

I believe that capacity building is a good place to begin social change. Medica Mondiale started with grassroots activities that help people understand Islam and its real meaning. Whenever I give talks, I always say that we want women's rights, but not according to the European approach. We want women's rights that reflect our Islamic values. We want equal participation of women and men because women make up half of the country. We need to be safe. This is not against the law.

We also train *mullahs* because they are very influential in society. These *mullahs* come to our workshops, but they really don't come with the desire to learn anything; they just come to eat something or to get free transportation. After we talk with them about the medical and psychological consequences of violence, they begin to understand. My colleagues with a *Sharia* law background talk with them about legal issues, and then they accept it. Now, one of the *mullahs* who was trained by MM is promoting the use of condoms!

We need to change the thinking of women as well as men. A woman came to us crying about how her husband beat her, and then went on to say that it was his right because she over-salted his food. Sometimes women say, "He beat me because I came home late when I should have come home before dark." Once she understands her fundamental rights, she can see that Islam doesn't deny them. Sometimes a woman has a horrible gynecological problem and doesn't know that it's okay to refuse to have sex.

In 2007, we provided training for 500 police officers in seven districts throughout Kabul. We trained them on women's protection issues, standard treatment of prisoners, trauma, the health and psychological effects of violence, and its consequences on the well-being of women. We showed them how to identify cases of violence. They learned how to interact with women without judgment and without intensifying their symptoms.

We've seen a huge improvement in the cases referred to us, especially regarding women in prison. One police training course can have an immediate effect, but it soon dissipates as officers revert to their customary behaviors. Permanent attitudinal and practical changes are impossible with only one training session, because these things exist in our culture and are a part of our society. We need to do a lot of follow-up training to ensure that alterations stick.

Peggy: *When the police arrest a woman, how is the case processed?*

Masiha: When a woman is arrested, the police take her to the detention center. Part of my job is to go there regularly to find women who need our help. When we find a case, we follow it from the detention center through the Supreme Court or to the highest court before our client is released. For example, if we find a woman who has been raped, we try to send that woman to the doctor for an examination so we can have some documentation to prove her case in front of the judges.

Peggy: *So, you gather evidence for the case and go before the judges, is that right?*

Masiha: No. When a case comes to the detention center, the investigating prosecutor comes to gather information. Then he sends the case to the follow-up prosecutor. The prosecutor writes the charges against the client. The case continues to primary court, where the judges will make a decision regarding the client. The case then returns to the prosecutor to see if he or she accepts the verdict. If not, the case goes to the secondary court, and if there is still no agreement, it goes to the Supreme Court.

There are three judges. One is the president of the court. Sometimes the lawyers are present, but many times not. We follow our cases by ourselves; we try to find out the day and time our client will be tried, so we can participate in the trial. We have to do this on our own because the judges don't notify us. According to law, they should inform the lawyers five days before the court session, but generally they don't do it. Sometimes we can't find out in time and the woman faces the judges alone.

Suraya

Suraya was working for the **International Rescue Committee** (IRC) as an integration specialist at the age of 23, when I met her. She invited me to spend the night in her family's home in a quiet, middle-class Kabul neighborhood. The horseshoe-shaped, mud-brick house was plastered and nicely painted on the inside, with a beautiful large carpet covering the floor. Along the walls lay *toshaks* that served as both couches and beds. When the electricity came on at about six in the evening, the family turned on the TV. In 2003, there were mostly local news shows.

An hour or so after my arrival, Suraya's mother and sister brought out an oil-cloth "table" and platters of lovely food. After dinner, we settled in and watched a Bollywood DVD before we slept.

Suraya began school at age five during the Soviet occupation. Soon, Kabul became too dangerous, so her family packed a few things, locked up their house, and slipped away to Pakistan

Studying gives you the strength of standing with men, of going with men, not behind them.

where they spent the next 14 years. There Suraya finished high school and took extra courses that led to her employment with the IRC. When the family returned to Kabul in 2002, they unlocked their house to find everything: the carpets, refrigerator, TV, and other belongings just as they had left them.

Peggy: *What was your life like before you left Kabul?*

Suraya: Society was not so conservative then. When I left in 1988, girls were wearing short skirts and socks. For example, when my mother was young, she wore skirts above her knees. **Amanullah Khan** brought these things. His wife returned from their European tour wearing a short skirt and Amanullah said everybody should wear them and take off their *burqas*. That was in 1910. From that time until the government of the *Mujahidin*, the people here were very modern. My mother's wedding dress was knee length.

When the *mujahidin* came in 1992, it all changed. We had to cover ourselves, even while we lived in Pakistan. Fundamentalists poured acid on some women with exposed faces. When the Islamia [fundamentalist leaders] came back to Afghanistan, they lost a little control over Pakistan, and then we were fine there just wearing scarves.

Peggy: Throughout the Soviet war, Islamic fundamentalists controlled the lives of Afghans in many refugee camps, and to some degree in the Afghan sections of Peshawar and other Pakistani border cities. When the Soviets left Afghanistan, Afghan fundamentalists in Pakistan dominated the refugees. The breakdown of the Afghan *Mujahidin* government drew these extremists back to Afghanistan to fight each other, and their influence in Pakistan lessened.

You are Pashtun and yet your household seems to be run by your mother. Is this common?

Suraya: Not all Pashtuns are strict. My mother has seven older brothers, and when she was born, they were so happy to have a girl, they killed six sheep for the party. Pashtun people like daughters very much, and my grandfather gave my mother the same rights as her brothers. He insisted that my mother be educated, and agreed with her intent to be a nurse over the objections of his brothers. He declared that she be allowed to finish her degree as a condition for marriage. In my own case, some of my uncles were telling my mother how stupid she was, wasting her money on daughters. "They will get married and go to their husband's house and then what is the benefit of it?" they would say. But my mother told them that her daughters have more rights than her sons. I share this opinion.

Peggy: Suraya's family benefited immensely from this stance. Suraya's father, who had worked as a veterinarian for the government, became disabled and lost his job. Her mother worked as a nurse by day and sewed jackets until late at night. This work provided the family with food and educational classes. Suraya is now a major contributor to the family income.

Also interesting was that Suraya's mother, Raisa, manages the family. Suraya asked permission of her mother rather than her father before taking courses or applying for jobs. It was her mother who stood up to Suraya's uncles over the matter of educating her daughters.

4/RAWA

Not all activists for women's rights operate openly and publicly in Afghanistan. **Meena**, an Afghan student activist, founded the **Revolutionary Association of Women in Afghanistan** (RAWA) in 1977. Even though the communists supported women's rights in many ways, they also violated basic human rights. RAWA opposed the communists. When it became too dangerous to remain in Afghanistan, the organization moved its headquarters to Pakistan. There, Meena launched their magazine, *Payam-e-Zan* (Women's Message). The publication became a major recruiting tool. Before her assassination by fundamentalists in 1987, Meena established schools for refugee children, hospitals, and handicraft centers. When the Taliban took over, RAWA established a network of secret schools throughout Afghanistan.

In 2003, the Taliban had reportedly been defeated and Afghanistan was inundated with international efforts toward education and women's rights. I thought that perhaps Afsana, below, whom I met then, was a bit paranoid in continuing to work underground. History has shown her to be prescient. In the intervening years, more and more fundamentalist leaders have gained powerful positions and been incorporated into the government. Karzai approved policies conducive to welcoming the Taliban into the government. He signed the Shia Personal Status Law and approved Parliament's legislative assault against domestic violence shelters. Only after sufficient pressure both from Afghan civil society and international donors, Karzai revisited the **Shia Law** and reversed the majority of its most odious aspects. In the end, he also supported the shelters.

I first met RAWA activists in 2003 in Pakistan. I visited various RAWA projects around Peshawar. The Malalai Hospital was sparkling clean but very basic; a small, well-organized institution staffed with compassionate, dedicated professionals. RAWA's girls' school was also basic, and full of eager students. Orderly children who sang and performed somersaults for me filled a cramped 25-bed orphanage. My last stop was an apartment where a group of RAWA members lived. I had read Ann Brodsky's *With All Our Strength*[1] on the long plane ride over. It gave me a good understanding of the intense dedication that RAWA women possess. Now I saw first-hand their frugal lifestyle.

During one conversation I asked, "Why do you keep the word '*Revolutionary*' in your name? It must keep many people and organizations from funding you." Afsana answered that promoting women's rights in Afghanistan today *is* a revolutionary act and that people who understand that support them.

RAWA aspires to help "establish a government based on democratic and secular values in Afghanistan."

A RAWA school in Pakistan. (2003)

Afsana

Afsana met me at the Airserv crew house where I stayed in 2003. She arrived in a taxi driven by a RAWA sympathizer and was accompanied by a male RAWA supporter. She told me that I wouldn't be allowed to photograph her, but when our interview was over, she agreed to be photographed in a non-recognizable way.

Afsana and her three brothers were educated. Her father had been an officer in the communist government. Even though her mother was illiterate, she participated in dinnertime political discussions about women's and human rights and democracy. During the internecine struggles within the communist government prior to the Soviet invasion, Afsana's brother and other political activists were arrested. Her brother hasn't been seen since. Shortly afterward, Afsana and her family went to Pakistan where she joined RAWA.

When we accept the way of struggle against the fundamentalists, we accept that we can die in this way. I am never afraid of death. Other members of RAWA are like this. So when we see the fundamentalists, we go against them.

Maral

I met Maral in 2010. She was in her early 30's and had a no-nonsense air about her. She and a male supporter arrived at the SOLA guesthouse where I was staying and we found a quiet space in the living room. Her escort stayed with us throughout the interview. Maral didn't mind being photographed, but I only took

a few shots when the interview was complete. She posed herself after re-wrapping her scarf.

Maral was three years old when the Soviets invaded and her family left Kabul for a RAWA refugee camp in Pakistan. Her mother was already a RAWA member. At the camp, her mother began teaching and involving herself with various social service projects. When Maral was old enough, she attended the RAWA school in Peshawar. Because a RAWA member had reared her, she was allowed to join at age 16 rather than the usual 18.

Education is the only way to change the minds of people in a good way, but it takes a long time.

Peggy: *How have things changed for RAWA since 2003?*

Maral: We have more social and political activities than we had before in Kabul. We educate women because we believe society will develop if they are educated. Still, we need the help of men and women together to build our country. Boys have more opportunities for education and work, so we focus on education programs for women and girls. Now we have literacy classes, handicraft courses, and income-generating projects. We give micro-credit loans. We also have political awareness classes. It's very important that women know their rights or else they will always submit to pressure in their home and society. We have support from some Members of Parliament who support our ideas and we help with their campaigns. They are not RAWA members, but we support them.

There is just one school left for Afghans in Pakistan since the refugee camps have closed: our Herat High School in Islamabad. We also support an orphanage for girls and boys in Kabul, but it's not under RAWA's name. We helped to start it, and now we're the only ones supporting it.

Peggy: *How do you locate the children who live there?*

Maral: We conduct surveys in very poor areas of Kabul and other provinces to find the neediest children to bring to the orphanage. On our website, we post photos of the kids and ask for supporters. Each child has a sponsor. The more donors we have, the more children we can care for.

Peggy: *Why is RAWA still underground? All of your activities are legal and in fact encouraged by the government.*

Afsana: Yes, the kinds of activities we do are now being encouraged, but RAWA is a very political organization and we are always against the fundamentalists. If the fundamentalists come back into power and we are not secret, they will know who we are and they might kill us. Our founder, Meena, was assassinated.

Peggy: *Tell us about some of your activities.*

Maral: We demonstrated to protest the Shia Marital Rape Law.

Peggy: Since Maral often talks with Westerners, she used the term for the Shia Law that most foreigners have heard.

I have a friend who helped organize that demonstration. I asked her what she knew about RAWA's participation and she told me that she didn't know anything.

Maral: That's because we didn't use our name, we just advocated our policy there.

Peggy: *How does RAWA find prospective members?*

Afsana: Sometimes women read our newsletter, *Payam-e Zan*, like our message, and contact us. They work with us for a year, and we investigate them and their family to make sure they aren't fundamentalists. We observe them to see what they are like and what they do well. When we are satisfied, we invite them to join RAWA. It takes a year to become a member.

Maral: We get new members through our literacy classes and educational centers. Through members, we gain access to their relatives and neighbors. After we get to know them, we invite the most trusted ones to become RAWA members.

Peggy: *So someone who comes to your literacy class may not be a prospective RAWA member or supporter at first, they just come to learn to read?*

Maral: Yes. In the beginning, they don't know about RAWA, but after some education and slowly getting to know them, we can see whether we can trust them and invite them to join.

Peggy: *How does one become a RAWA member?*

Afsana: You must be 18. I heard about RAWA when I was 16. That was 1980, when the government was arresting a lot of students, many of whom were fleeing to Pakistan. My family was in great danger because they were very political. By the time we went to the refugee camp I was 19, so I contacted RAWA and joined.

Peggy: *What is your life like as a RAWA member?*

Afsana: We do not have personal lives; we do not have a family. We belong to RAWA and our lives are political. We have meetings every five or six days. There are different sections in RAWA and those groups sit together and discuss issues that come up. The senior member resolves any disputes that arise.

Every RAWA member has her own situation. Some live with their families, some live with their husbands, while a few live in RAWA hostels as I do. Sometimes when I have been given a job I don't like, I don't do it, but then another RAWA member will come and do that work for me. When this happens, I feel bad. Why should she do this work that was given to me? When we have given our lives to RAWA for the struggle, why should it be acceptable for me not to do what I'm given to do?

Peggy: *Do your parents know about and support your membership in RAWA?*

Afsana: Yes, my family knows and they encourage my membership because they know it is a good organization.

Peggy: *When you are angry, how do you deal with it?*

Afsana: Personally, I am very angry. Whenever I see injustice or bad treatment of women, I become angry. If I see something unfair within our group, I become angry. Yet within RAWA, we should not be angry so we have meetings to discuss everything. We learn to control ourselves that way.

Peggy: *What do you do to calm yourself in the face of fear?*

Afsana: First, I am never afraid of anything. When some women are alone in their homes, they become fearful that someone may come and abuse them, but I am never afraid of this. When I joined RAWA, I knew it was dangerous. Our leader, Meena, gave her life for woman's rights. When she gave her blood, we knew that women were vulnerable and our enemies could attack us. Knowing this gives us more strength and helps us work hard. Our cause gives us courage.

Peggy: *How were the RAWA refugee camps different from other camps?*

Maral: Our camp had different types of people, but RAWA had organized it and most were RAWA members. We told our supporters that if they left Afghanistan, they should come to our camp. We provided them with free education, a free clinic, simple homes, security, and an orphanage. We did this on our own with no help from the UN.

Peggy: *I thought the UN and other international aid organizations had started all of the refugee camps.*

Maral: Yes, they set up camps, but the UN just provided tents, some food, and blankets for their camps. We built houses, with walls around the camp for security.

Peggy: *I've heard that some of those other camps were horrific; that gang members controlled them.*

Maral: Yes, **Sayaf** ran one camp and **Hekmatyar** ran another. The fundamentalists took control of certain camps so they would have a place to hide their leaders. Conditions were awful.

Peggy: *How do you find students for secret schools?*

Afsana: There are no literacy courses in the villages around Kabul so we contact our members in those areas and ask if there is any interest. Those members arrange the classes. Other RAWA members go there to teach them.

Peggy: *What do you think is the best way to change the minds of those who have fundamentalist ideas about the treatment of women?*

Maral: Education is the only way to change their minds. Besides making women aware of their rights, men's minds should also be changed. People have been deprived of education and access to their rights for 30 years. Before the wars, women had education, we had our rights, we had everything during and before **Najibullah**. We even had foreign students who came to study here at our universities.

The wars caused people to change and to welcome the fundamentalists. America helped to bring these fundamentalists by supporting them to drive out the Russians. American support for Pakistan helped create the Taliban. The wars have pitted the ethnic groups against each other. Our ethnic issues were minor before the wars. Education is the only thing to change the minds of men and women, and it takes time.

Peggy: *Are schools the only way you educate?*

Maral: We educate through schools, literacy classes, gatherings, meetings in the mosques, and through the media. Unfortunately, Afghan media is not very good. Mostly Indian soap operas are on; there really are no good public information programs. A good media is the best way to change the minds of people.

Peggy: *Have you ever thought about having your own television station or radio channel?*

Maral: We can't have our own program because of security, but it's a good way to educate many women and men. We could do it in the future by supporting some organization to produce a program with our messages.

Peggy: *What is your main work for RAWA now?*

Maral: I work as a speaker. A month ago, I returned from six months in Australia and before that I spent four months in America. It's a good way to spread awareness about Afghanistan and to get more people to support RAWA and our activities.[2]

Peggy: *How has support for RAWA held up?*

Maral: After 9-11, we got a lot of attention and support. After America attacked Iraq, support decreased and we had to close some schools.

Peggy: *How is it now?*

Maral: During the Taliban, we were the only organization who had a webpage that showed the Taliban's crimes. We posted a film of a woman being executed. After that, we had many more supporters. It's steadier now and we have supporters from different organizations like SAWA[3] in Australia, a group in Italy and other places. We still have financial problems and we've had to close many of our activities, but we're hanging in there. We still need more support to restart programs we've had to close and for new activities.

Peggy (in 2003): *If you could have lunch with US President George W. Bush, what would you say to him?*

Afsana: I would tell him, "You have two politics. On one side, you are against terrorism. On the other, you bring terrorism into power in Afghanistan. The fundamentalists are now in the government."

Peggy (in 2010): *If you could have lunch with President Barack Obama, what advice would you give him?*

Maral: I would tell him that he's failing his mission because he's following Bush and his policies. I would say, "You said you would change things but you didn't. If you really want to support the Afghan people, you must pull all of the troops out of Afghanistan. We don't want more war in Afghanistan. We just need security and freedom for our people."

Peggy: *What do you think would happen if Obama pulled all of the American troops out of Afghanistan? Do you think that the war would end?*

Maral: If the troops leave Afghanistan, people say a civil war will start. We say that there already is a civil war. We have American troops bombing innocent civilians on one side, we have Taliban whose influence is increasing, and we have the Northern Alliance and other warlords. People are fighting on three sides. If one of them leaves, we will be left with two enemies. If the Americans leave Afghanistan, then Afghans will think about how to rebuild their country. We need more intellectuals and more democratic, open-minded people in order to unite Afghanistan. We need years and years to make this happen, but the point is that it should come from Afghans. No other country can give it to us as a gift. We have to sacrifice and struggle.

Peggy: *How can Western women support RAWA and the women of Afghanistan?*

Afsana: The job of Western women is to convey this message to their government and ours: "Don't bring fundamentalists into power in Afghanistan. Do things for the betterment of society, not just for your own benefit or your own political ends." Western women can publicize the activities of RAWA in newsletters and on television. Let us Afghans run our own government and choose our own leaders. Don't come to us and say, "This is your new government."

Maral: International people around the world should put pressure on their governments to stop bad policies. If they really want to support Afghan people, they should come independently of the American government. They should help rebuild our infrastructure. We never need war and bombs. The US is spending more than $1,000,000 a day in Afghanistan. Can you imagine what a difference it would make if this money were going to educate Afghan people?

Street photographer. These once-ubiquitous box cameras
contain their own darkrooms. By 2010, they had mostly
been replaced by digital studios.

5/Welayat Prison

My first visit to Welayat Prison in central Kabul was as a tag-along with an aid group bringing light-weight fabric to the prisoners so they could make some new clothes for summer. A long line of scribes waited across the street from the prison entrance to help customers fill out official forms. Each scribe sat behind a small table shaded by an umbrella. In 2003, when I interviewed the prisoners, another line of photographers sat ready to make the passport-type photos required for certain forms. They offered pictures-while-you-wait, processed in darkroom-in-a-box cameras.[1] By 2010, a digital photo studio had taken up residence down the street, displacing most of the box camera photographers.

Entering the flimsy-looking prison gate in 2003, I saw vehicles being "wanded"[2] to check for explosives. We pedestrians were shunted through small guard rooms, women to the right side of the gate and men to the left. First our bags were searched, and our cell phones and my camera were activated to show that they weren't disguised bombs. A female guard patted us down before we were allowed to proceed. Our entourage meandered among the prison buildings until we came to a rough-cut stone structure with high windows, circa 1934, housing the female prisoners. A prominent white checkmark scrawled on the iron-clad wooden door assured us that the building had been checked for landmines. An elderly man waited patiently on a bench outside.

Behind a six-inch hole in the door sat the matron who granted admittance. She reached through the hole to fit a key into the lock outside, and the door creaked open. We followed her down a dark corridor barely lit by a single bulb hanging from a cord. Rough walls flanked uneven stone floors, and a dank, musty smell conjured up thoughts of medieval dungeons.

Then the matron paused and opened a door into a bright, recently renovated room where four beds rested on a room-sized plastic mat. A casement window let in brilliant sunshine and a view of a woman in the courtyard hanging laundry. Three women were sitting on the beds. Seven or eight more filed in behind us and arranged themselves on the floor, backs against the wall. A few small children quietly crawled onto their mothers' laps. The aid group women explained their purpose and passed out fabric as I, after motioning my request for permission, snapped a few pictures.

Usually, if a woman goes to prison, the children stay with relatives. But in modern Kabul, many residents became separated from their families and extended families when they returned from exile, so there are many children who have no place to go except into prison with their mothers.

In 2009, **Women for Afghan Women** (WAW)[3] created a residence so that children of female inmates may now live outside the prison and receive counseling and education. Within the women's prison, WAW teaches inmates vocational skills and offers counseling as well.

Prisoners' children lead precarious lives. If their father and mother are estranged and the children live with the father, they are at the mercy of other wives in the household or grandparents and aunts who have negative feelings toward the imprisoned, "immoral" mother. Those feelings are often directed towards the children. If their father should die, the children may become little more than servants catering to his family. Ultimately this depends on individual relationships and the specific family situations.

One of the aid workers I accompanied told me about bringing and personally delivering a requested box of tea to one of the inmates. Upon the worker's next visit a few weeks later, the same woman asked for tea again, claiming she'd never received the first box. I asked if the inmate was trying to scam the worker, but the aid worker said that many prisoners suffer from post-traumatic stress disorder (PTSD) and other psychological issues stemming from abuse and their war experiences. She went on to say that this particular woman also has memory issues.

With this caveat, the stories in this chapter are true as they were told to me, but that doesn't mean they are necessarily the "Truth." For example, I found an interview with Hador conducted in 2004 in Ann Jones' book, *Kabul in Winter.*[4] There were significant variations in the details of Hador's story. It could be that she remembered things inconsistently as time passed, or that our translators interpreted her story differently or, for whatever reason, she told us different things.

After my first experience at the prison, I was eager to go back. I used my Airserv connections to gain access, but ultimately the photos I'd taken gained me admittance because I'd promised to deliver prints to the women *in person.*

On my subsequent visit, I saw four other rooms of different shapes and sizes, all freshly painted and furnished with beds rather than traditional *toshaks*. A fifth room, the largest, was vacant and had yet to be refurbished. Its dingy walls crackled with peeling paint. The dirty, rough, uneven floor and ill-fitting windows showed me how dispiriting the place had been before the renovations began.

Prisoners who wanted to tell their stories were brought into our room one-by-one. The matron came in to watch for a while and asked if I would photograph her as well. I told her that I would be happy to do so once I was finished with the inmates, so she left to attend to other duties.

When I had interviewed about half of the women, the warden came in, matron in tow. The warden asked me about my project and then said it was all fine except that I couldn't take any pictures. I hid my disappointment and agreed. She left, and I told the matron how sorry I was that I couldn't take her picture since it was now forbidden. "Oh," she said, "Don't worry. Just keep the camera hidden if the warden comes back." And so I continued with my photography and interview sessions.

Note: In this chapter, I recount one woman's story at a time, followed with comments by Masiha, the women's defense lawyer I met in 2010; Najia, my translator; and myself.

Entrance to the women's prison. The man on the bench
runs marketing errands for the women inside.

Zakiya

As Zakiya walked into her interview, her four-year-old son and eight-year-old daughter trailed behind her.

Zakiya: My husband and I were renting a small room and a garage but we needed some money, so we sublet the garage to another man. One day the landlord came and told my husband that he needed to use the garage, so my husband told the renter that he had to move out. The renter got very angry and had a fistfight with my husband and beat him. My husband can't walk because something is wrong with his back and his feet don't work. Four months later, that man barged into our house at two in the morning. My husband was sleeping in his chair. That man grabbed my husband by the throat and began beating him; saying that he would rape me right there. He was shouting all kinds of crazy things. But our room was very small and my husband was able to grab an axe that was lying nearby and hit the man over the head. He died instantly.

I ran out of the house screaming and then the police came. They arrested both my husband and me. At first I was given 12 years but in the secondary court, they reduced it to ten. Because my husband was handicapped, he only got six years. Since we have no family here in Kabul, our oldest two children are in an orphanage and the younger two are here in prison with me. When my husband gets released, my older children will go to live with him, but their life will be very difficult because my husband can't work. Perhaps the boy can sell some things in the bazaar to earn a little money.

Peggy: I asked my translator why they would also arrest Zakiya because, according to her story, she was completely innocent.

Najia: No one knows what really happened. Perhaps her husband held the man down while she hit and killed him. Perhaps she had committed adultery with the man, perhaps the dead man's family paid money to the police to keep them in prison. The judges could have thought any of these things.

Z

Because of the delicate nature of Z's story, I have not included her picture.

Z: A *talib* came and forced my father to give me to him to marry, but I didn't want that. The *talib* raped me, so now I can't leave him because no one else will want to marry me. I told my father that I changed my mind and wanted to get married to him, but my father got angry, refused, and had me put in jail.

Peggy: *How long will you stay here?*

Z: It's up to my father. If he agrees to let me get married, I will get out. If he says no, I will stay here.

Peggy: *Are you saying that you'd rather stay in prison than go back to live with your parents?*

Z: Maybe my father will have a fight with my fiancé and then we can see who will be the winner. If my fiancé wins, then I'll get married.

Peggy: I had never heard a story like this before; that a father would put his daughter in jail and bring shame upon the whole family. It also seemed that the father had initially agreed to the marriage, whether he'd wanted to or not, and it would have been shameful for him to break it off. Surely it couldn't be broken off without repercussions, possibly dangerous ones. As I was puzzling this out, Najia, my translator, was talking with some other women and she later told me this very different story:

Najia: Z had been in a sexual relationship with a taxi driver. Someone informed the police and one day they were both caught and arrested. Z's family wants her to marry the taxi driver but the driver doesn't want to or can't marry her. They are both in prison until it can be resolved. The situation looks very bleak for her. Even though her family might like the couple to marry, his family most certainly would never agree to bring this "dishonored" woman into their household. Even if they did, because of her shame, his entire family would likely abuse her. If the taxi driver's family has money, it's possible that they can buy him out of prison and the situation will be resolved for him. However, it will haunt Z forever. When she is finally released, unless she can be accepted into a shelter, her only refuge would be her own family, where the chances of an "honor killing" would be very high.

Peggy: While this second story makes sense, we can't know for certain that the other prisoners who told it weren't making it up for their own reasons. I also found it interesting that Z volunteered to tell me her story at all.

I'm curious, does this make sense to you? What might be the outcome of a case like this?

Masiha: According to our law, if a girl or boy runs away, the case would go to the family court. If they get married and live together, everything is finished. Running away is not a crime as long as the couple didn't have sex before they got married. If they did, it's a problem, because adultery is a crime and by law they should be punished.

Peggy: *How can anybody tell if they had sex or not if the couple doesn't say so?*

Masiha: There's a doctor who checks and he would know if the girl has committed adultery or not. But it's more difficult to prove for a non-virgin woman. Often when we get these cases in the police station or the detention center, we talk with both parties and try to get the families to accept the marriage without any punishment. Sometimes we have success, but sometimes we don't.

Peggy: *In this particular girl's case, if the family doesn't agree and if it's proven that she did commit adultery, how long would she likely have to stay in prison?*

Masiha: For women who are married and have a husband who might complain, punishment will be more severe. For an unmarried girl, the punishment is not too much. It can go from six or eight months to a year-and-a-half.

Peggy: *Once she gets released, what are the odds that her family will kill her to regain their honor?*

Masiha: It's a big challenge to know whether or not this will happen. [Now in 2010,] we have a mediation center in Welayat and we try to help families accept the daughter. In order to reintegrate the woman or girl, we have to talk with their families. If the family won't accept her, we try to refer her to a shelter.

Peggy: *Before you were sent here, did you know anyone who had been to prison?*

Z: No. I didn't even know that there was a prison for women. I never understood anything about prison.

Peggy: *What do the prisoners here do to comfort each other or help each other when* *they're sad or troubled?*

Z: We give each other advice.

Peggy: *Have you made any friends here that you will want to stay in contact with when you get out of prison?*

Z: No.

Peggy: *Do women here teach each other things or learn things from each other?*[5]

Z: Yes, sometimes we teach each other. One of us knows sewing and she has taught us.

Peggy: *What advice do you have for young girls, perhaps your future daughters?*

Z: I will advise her to be a good girl and get educated. But education is not the most important thing. She must also be a good girl. One girl came here who worked as a translator for a foreigner and she also has the same problem I have.

Peggy: *How much education have you had and how old are you?*

Z: I'm 18 and have completed eleventh grade.

Hador

Hador: I've been a widow for the past 11 years. I had a normal life living with my mother, brothers, and son, who was born just after my husband died. About a year-and-a-half ago, my cousin came from Pakistan and lived in our house as a guest. After a few months, he raped me and I asked him, "Why did you do that to me? Now you should marry me," but he said, "No, I don't want to." He continued to rape me, so one night when he was sleeping I poured benzene on him and set him on fire. He died. My whole family went to prison but my mother and brothers have been released.

Peggy: *How long will you have to stay in prison?*

Hador: The primary court told me I should be here for 15 years, but when we appealed, it was reduced to ten; then when I paid some money, it was reduced to six. A few months ago I went to another meeting and they reduced my sentence to three years. I've already been here 11 months. When my son comes to visit, he doesn't want to leave and he cries. It's very hard for me. My mother is taking care of him until I get out. He's 11 years old and in fourth grade. I get to see him once a week.

Peggy: *How can a woman's sentence get reduced?*

Masiha: Sometimes they can pay the judges. As you know, corruption is a big problem in the judicial system. But for some crimes, like kidnapping and national security cases, they won't reduce the sentence. In some other cases, President Karzai can recommend a legal reduction of the punishment. Still, it's necessary that the woman completes at least half of her sentence in order to be eligible for release.

Peggy: *What happens in a case where the woman has been very badly beaten by her husband and then she kills him?*

Masiha: In that situation, the woman goes into detention and is punished because she killed her husband.

Peggy: *It doesn't matter that he almost killed her?*

Masiha: No.

Peggy: *How much prison time is she likely to serve?*

Masiha: The punishment will probably be between 14 and 18 years, but sometimes it's only five. I had one murder case where the woman was punished for ten years, but she had killed her husband with the support of her brother and cousin. The three of them killed that man. She was punished for ten years but she's happy because she doesn't have her husband anymore.

Peggy: *And were the other people who helped her punished, too?*

Masiha: Yes. Her brother and cousin got 16 years from the primary court and 18 in the secondary court. My client's sentence did not get increased, because I showed the judges that her husband was very cruel to her. Those judges really listened to me and supported my client and me, but they didn't help her cousin and brother-in-law because those men didn't have lawyers. I kept telling them that I couldn't help them but could give them a referral but they refused and wished to defend themselves.

Peggy: *What can prisoners do to comfort each other?*

Hador: When new prisoners come, we talk to them to ease their nerves and try to help them with their problems by offering ideas and advice. We talk to them so they won't feel sad.

Peggy: *How do you do that?*

Hador: We hug each other and cry together.

Peggy: *Do you also teach each other things?*

Hador: If they want to.

Peggy: *Is it something you normally do?*

Hador: There is a woman who makes beaded balls [decorative balls with beads pinned onto a core] and she taught the women in her room how to do it. She also tried to teach it to others, but they weren't interested. Also, the people who work with us here are very kind and they help us a lot.

Peggy: The matron had stepped in for Hador's interview, but left after hearing those words. When she was gone, Hador told my translator that what she'd said about the staff helping them wasn't true. In fact, she said, the matron brokered the women as prostitutes. The clients were generally guards from the men's buildings. If the women had enough money they could pay for themselves and avoid being prostituted. Also, they could keep a bit of the money to purchase food and other necessities that may not be provided to them by relatives.

I was able to talk briefly with the matron later, who said that her (very low) salary kept her family from starving. She is a widow with three children and also supports her widowed sister and her children. I didn't discuss her role as "madame" of the prison, so as not to jeopardize the inmates, but if it's true, she's just playing a part in the system. If she were to refuse, she would be replaced with someone more cooperative, and be unable to support those who depend on her.

I heard from several sources that women's prisons are often used as brothels, so I believe this story about the matron is likely true. Still, it might also be possible that the prisoners have a grudge against her, or that Hador told me this to get the matron in trouble. There are many layers to unravel to get at any truth, and in prisons there are even more.

Mehro

Mehro: My name is Mehro and I didn't do any crime. Somebody shot a commander and injured him. They thought my son did it so they came to our house. When they didn't find my son there, they took me, my younger brother, and my daughter. They say that I have to sit here for seven years or until I tell them where my son is. My son didn't shoot him, but the commander says that he did. I have been in this prison for two years. Before that, I was in a private security center basement that belonged to the commander. There I was given electric shocks, raped, and beaten. This was a place for men, but they kept us there for one year. After a while, my older brother found out where we were and went to the government. My younger brother was freed and I was released from there and sent to this prison. I have no idea what happened to my daughter, she just disappeared. It's likely, though, that she was sold to a brothel either here or in Pakistan. That commander is a big man in Kabul and no one can touch him.

Peggy: I can't imagine that Mehro knows the whereabouts of her son at this point. It's been two years and he is certainly in hiding or has left the country. But even if she does have an idea where he might be, what a dilemma for a mother! She can rot in prison or inform on her child, which would certainly lead to his death, or more likely his torture and death. When she finally goes free, I'm sure the commander's henchmen will be watching to see if her son comes to visit.

Can you talk about the conditions in prison generally? I know there are Welayat prison and Pul-e Charki, the notorious prison of the Soviet era. Are there other prisons for women in Kabul?

Masiha: There are no women at Pul-e Charki now, only men. The women are at another prison called Badam Bagh. They have a new building where the rooms are separated and the prisoners are divided into categories. Dangerous ones or instigators are put on the third floor. There are also children in Badam Bagh.

Peggy: *When I visited Welayat in 2003, the prison had been rehabilitated and the walls painted. There were four to six women in every room, and they could move freely about the entire building. They washed their clothes at the well in the courtyard. A man [the old man who I'd seen sitting in front of the prison] would come inside to take market orders that the prisoners paid for themselves. They did their own cooking. Is that still the situation, or is it different now?*

Masiha: The situation has changed in the detention center because they built a new building for the detainees, but it's not completed yet. Because of this, they're at another site where the situation is very bad; they can't even leave their rooms and if they could, it wouldn't be safe. Each room is very crowded.

In Badam Bagh, the women can cook for themselves and participate in various hobbies. WAW has made a center where their children can learn to read and write. It's hard for their kids to go to regular schools because other kids will ask them where they live, and when it becomes known that their mother is in prison, will tease them and say bad things to them. It's like an orphanage except that they get to visit their mother once or twice a week.

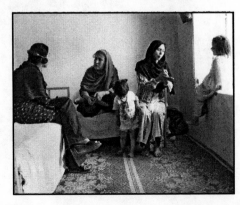

Rehabilitated prison room. The children live with their mother in the prison.

Eager students at the Aisha Durani School. (2003)

Lacking classrooms, classes are sometimes held in tents. (2003)

6/Educators & Education

Kabul University (established in 1932) offered free tuition and had nine colleges by 1967. Eight hundred primary schools and 300 secondary schools existed in Kabul and regional cities in the mid-1980s. Realizing that the future of their nation lies in the education of their youth, Afghans have established 45 universities and institutions of higher education around the country since the Taliban left in 2001.

Daoud's communist government of the 1970s promoted education for all, though most schools were in urban areas. Authorities would come to villages and "draft" girls and boys to attend their schools, fueling anti-communist feelings and the development of anti-communist educational materials. Exiled Afghan officials wrote reading and math texts featuring violent imagery and promoting *jihad*. Fifteen million books glorifying the rebel fighters and encouraging children to take up arms were published. In the 1990s, these books still occasionally surfaced in schools because various groups, including the Taliban, stole the content and reprinted it.[1]

Students in Kabul received a fairly decent education under communist rule. Schools remained open during the civil war years (1992-96), but many teachers and students stayed home for long periods when fighting was especially intense. As a result, the **All Afghan Women's Union** (AAWU)[2] began encouraging the teachers to give instruction to neighborhood children from their homes. During the Taliban era, all the girls' and many of the boys' schools closed. The boys' schools were discontinued due to lack of teachers, since all female teachers had been sent home. Educated women often taught students secretly in their homes, sometimes on an individual basis, other times with different networks. The Revolutionary Association of Women of Afghanistan (RAWA) was best known for creating underground schools, but there were many other groups and individuals who secretly taught. Once the Karzai government arrived, public schools reopened and students were tested and placed in the proper grade levels.

Now, education is a booming business, evidenced by Kabul's vast number of private universities and schools. Signs everywhere promote courses in computer skills, English, and especially test score improvement. Anyone who can afford it tries to send their children to a private school; siblings work to pay each other's tuition so the whole family can benefit.

Although the government provides free schooling, teaching methods are often archaic and the school day lasts only three or four hours. The price of school supplies and uniforms puts such "free" education out of reach for many poor people. Numerous children attend school for a few hours early in the morning, work during the day, and do their homework late at night.

In 2003, Kabuli schools were still being rehabilitated. Many students were taught in tents. One teacher might have younger students in the morning and older ones in the afternoon. Less fortunate schools had three shifts a day. Teachers relied heavily on rote memorization and physical punishment for those not learning quickly enough. Thankfully, this is changing. The government recognizes the need for newer methods and has contracted with the **Afghan Institute of Learning** (AIL) to train some teachers, but doesn't have enough funding to conduct modern training throughout the country.

Education is also expanding outside of Kabul. Julia Boltz created an NGO, **Ayni Education International**, that has built and equipped 18 new schools and refurbished and supplied 20 more in the early part of 2000. Since 2002, Ayni has served a total of 25,000 children in the Balkh area of northwest Afghanistan. Ayni only enters communities where they've been invited and local citizens will work with them. Communities provide land and labor for building schools and teachers' salaries, while Ayni provides building materials, guidance, and teacher training. With communities paying teachers' salaries, schools will be able to survive even should sponsoring organizations leave.

AIL builds women's centers and schools using a similar model. In addition to schools, their centers provide simple health clinics and workshops on topics outside the normal school curriculum, like human rights and nutrition.

Canadian Women for Afghan Women (CW4AW) and **Catholic Relief Services** (CRS) create schools using a different community-based model, suitable and affordable for tiny villages in remote areas. Village leaders identify potential teachers and send them to their provincial capital for education and training. The new teachers return home to teach in existing public buildings such as mosques, or in the teachers' homes.

Rural and remote-area education are some of the best ways to eliminate abusive traditions such as *baad*. Educating girls will raise family living standards and educating boys will one day help shape the now-male-dominated *shuras* and *jergas* that will decide issues for both men and women in their villages, provinces, and country. This long-term endeavor, may be the best guarantee for enduring changes.

Girls studying at Omid School (School of Hope) in Kabul, 2003.

Krayba

I met Krayba in in 2003 at the vocational section of a school run by **CWS** where women received training in tailoring and literacy. She had an air of worry and sadness about her but smiled easily.

Krayba married shortly after finishing high school in Kabul. She and her family lived there throughout the civil war, but moved after a rocket landed on their house, killing her brother and brother-in-law. As they were moving, taxi-load by taxi-load, neighbors entered through the rubble and stole their household goods. Her husband, a mechanic, disappeared during the civil war. She teaches tailoring and takes her sewing machine home each night so she can supplement her income with private tailoring clients.

All of us are human and we must learn how to live and how to help each other. Never fight, never kill. It is bad for everyone. My first priority is to guide women to find the power to work with and help each other.

Hamida

Hamida lived in a simple mud-brick house in Azdar, a village 10 miles from Bamyan. Before 2004, Azdar was an empty valley, but by 2010 was populated by about 50 households of returned refugees. Their mud-brick homes look primitive from the outside, but inside are plastered and painted. Room-sized carpets covered Hamida's floors.

Hamida was born in the Bamyan area but her family moved to Iran once the fighting became too intense. They returned to Afghanistan when she was 13. The only high school was in Bamyan, so she and some friends walked 20 miles round-trip every day to attend classes. She married at the age of 15, but only on her parents' condition that she be allowed to complete her schooling. While she was still in high school, she taught other women in the village to read. Now she manages the village women's center.

I teach illiterate women and I am so proud that now my students can read and write. This is my favorite accomplishment. As the manager of the women's center, I work hard to remove illiteracy from this valley.

Hanifa

King Amanullah commissioned the construction of the Aisha-e Durani Girls' School in the 1930s. An impressive, Greek-style building, by 2003 it appeared dilapidated. Construction materials and machinery lay scattered throughout the schoolyard on one side and a row of temporary classroom-tents stood along the other. As I entered the school, I was surprised to find classes in session. The dark hallway floors were covered with construction debris, with narrow paths leading through it to the classrooms. I met with Hanifa in a teachers' meeting room, probably the most beautiful room in the building. A giant bay window dominated the front wall and a few dusty tables and chairs were scattered around.

Hanifa has "always lived in Kabul and always will." She stayed throughout the entire war period and completed high school and teacher training under the communist regime. She taught boys until the *mujahidin* commanders assigned all female teachers to girls' schools. During the Taliban years, she and her sister secretly taught 200 students in their home. When the Karzai government was installed, she became Director of the Aisha-e Durani Girls' School.

One day towards the end of Najib's [Najibullah] presidency [at the end of the Soviet war], bombs were falling on our school and one fell right through the ceiling. I was teaching a class, but we didn't stop our studying. We stayed calm and didn't lose our courage.

Sahera Sharif

Sahera is campaign savvy and always knew what poses to strike for my camera. I enjoyed her use of proverbs. When talking about Ireland's problems, she said, "It's easy to deal with your problems when your neighbors are fish." Mentioning interference by Afghanistan's neighbors in its internal affairs, she quipped, "When the waters are muddy, it's easy to catch fish." We met in 2010.

Sahera started school in 1970 in the shade of a large tree in a mosque courtyard. Her classmates were a few other girls and her teacher was a *mullah*. Her family moved from Khost City to Kabul after she completed second grade. When she reached sixth grade, her father, who had always been against her education, said she'd had enough. When crying and begging didn't work, she locked herself in a room, refusing all food and drink for two days. Finally her father agreed she could continue. When her parents moved back to Khost a decade later, she stayed in Kabul with her brothers, to look after them and to continue her studies.

While I was researching women in remote villages, I found five women who had bachelor's degrees but were carrying firewood and milking cows.

She married and had three children while earning Bachelor's and Master's degrees in education from Kabul University. The Taliban regime wouldn't let her continue her research, so she and her husband escaped to Pakistan where they both taught in refugee camps. When she returned to Afghanistan during Karzai's first administration, she became Director of Women's Affairs of Khost Province. She found and trained female election workers. When women were sought to run for Parliament, she was encouraged to run, did so, and won. She was re-elected in 2010.

Dr. Sakena Yacoobi

I met Dr. Yacoobi in 2010 at the **Institute for Economic Empowerment of Women** (IEEW) conference in Dallas, Texas. Driven and passionate, direct and plain-spoken, I had the feeling that this woman would stand up to anything. She's indefatigable at the age of 61.

If you want to do something, do it from your heart, and keep your objective in mind, then you will reach your goal. Compared to my goal, my life doesn't mean that much. Not then [during Taliban] or now.

Sakena was born in Herat. Her father was illiterate, so she acted as his secretary from a young age. At 16, she received a scholarship to study in the US, eventually earning a Master's degree in public health. In 2007, the University of the Pacific awarded her an honorary Doctorate of Laws. She gave up a professorship at Michigan's D'Etre University in 1990 to work in an Afghan refugee camp in Pakistan. In 1995, she started **Afghan Institute of Learning** (AIL). During the Taliban era, she returned to Afghanistan and set up 80 secret schools, providing education for 3000 girls. Dr. Yacoobi has won numerous awards, including being one of 1000 women to jointly receive the 2005 Nobel Peace Prize.

Najia

Najia was my translator during my 2003 trip to Afghanistan. After we interviewed her former teacher Hanifa, Najia told me the story of her own education.

The youngest of five sisters, Najia was four when their father died. Her family stayed in Kabul throughout the wars. She studied nursing in Jalalabad and after a year, during the Taliban era, began work at the Jalalabad hospital. She helped birth over 700 babies, counseled pharmacy customers, and later educated villagers in sanitation and basic health.

She then worked for the **US Agency for International Development** (USAID) teaching accountability and transparency to government ministers, until she quit due to death threats. Her training with **10,000 Women** has enabled her to start her own food processing and sales company.

My mother begged me not to continue with school, but I had to go and learn.

Peggy: *What was it like going to school during the civil war?*

Najia: I remember most strongly my time at the Aisha-e Durani Girls' School where Hanifa was a teacher. We had quizzes every day. One day, rockets were falling nearby and one hit the school. We were afraid and wanted to run outside and go home, but our teachers kept us inside. The rockets fired from 8 am to 12 pm, stopped for an hour, and then resumed. Many students were killed. Two of our classmates left to go home, but while they were waiting for the bus, a rocket landed nearby and they died.

Krayba   Hamida   Hanifa   Sabera   Dr. Sakena Yacoobi

Shelling continued that way for five years. For a year and a half, we didn't go to school at all because of fighting among the warlords. Rockets crashed throughout Kabul, but the area near the school was hit hardest. No school for a year and a half. When we returned, we took an exam to see what grade we would be in. Although the teachers helped us pass, we didn't understand anything. We got promoted and I went into tenth grade, but school kept stopping and starting because of the fighting. I studied at home a lot.

When we entered twelfth grade, the fighting had stopped. The Taliban appeared two months before the end of that year, but they withdrew to another area and sent rockets into Kandahar. By the year's end, they had captured a place close to Kabul and the rockets came every day again.

I was with my classmates when we got the results from our final exams and I saw that I was third in the class! At that moment, planes bombed Kabul. It was chaos! All the students cried and screamed. We were very sad because we wanted to celebrate and because we knew we wouldn't see our friends again for a long time. We went to the bazaar, had ice cream at a restaurant, and then went home.

We had finally graduated and sat at home waiting for the University exam, but it was canceled.

Hamida: I began my schooling in Iran. The school was good, but I always felt like an outsider. Some Iranians told us we should go back to our own country, but we couldn't because the Taliban were there. My family was always afraid the Iranians might attack my brothers. When the Taliban left, we returned, but it was difficult because the social environment was closed, especially here in Azdar Village. With my parents' support, I continued my education and now, after six years, I am free and not afraid.

Peggy: What Hamida means when she talks about the social environment is that while living in Iran, she had the freedom to participate in society and mix with males, but when she returned to rural Bamyan, her social access was limited. Not all Afghans in Iran experienced this much freedom. Whether in Iran or Pakistan, Afghan refugee camp leaders and conservative families sometimes kept girls from participating in opportunities that society allowed.

Najia, 2003

So your father and mother encouraged you to go to school?

Hamida: Yes. My parents are illiterate, so they want their children to be educated. I got married when I was in seventh grade and now I have two children. My parents wouldn't let me marry my husband unless his family would allow me to finish my education. My parents took care of my baby while I studied.

Peggy: *Do all of your family and your husband's family live in this village?*

Hamida: Yes, we all live here.

Peggy: *Did your husband live in Iran also?*

Hamida: Yes. That's one reason his family agreed to let me finish my education.

Peggy: *In this village, how many emigrated and how many stayed in Afghanistan?*

Hamida: Around half of the people in this village had lived in Iran. The rest came here from other places nearby. Six years ago, this valley was vacant. Most of the refugees who returned to Afghanistan didn't have any land to build on, so the government distributed this land among the poor people.

Peggy: *In this village, how many children go to school? Do some families keep their daughters home?*

Hamida: Every family in this village sends their children to school.

Peggy: One reason rural girls sometimes aren't allowed education is that the nearest school may be in a neighboring village. Fathers may wish to educate their daughters, but don't think it safe for them to walk to a far-away school. Azdar Village has its own primary school, so safety isn't an issue.

Dr. Yacoobi: When I was working in the refugee camp, I saw all of these people who were traumatized and really suffering. They didn't trust each other so no one would talk with anyone else. After hearing countless stories of murder, rape, and violation they had endured at the hands of the Soviets and their Afghan collaborators, I saw that these people were trying to protect themselves by keeping silent. Many women and children were alone because their men had been killed

Krayba   Hamida   Hanifa   Sahera   Dr. Sakena Yacoobi

or were off fighting. They had come to these supposedly protected camps inside Pakistan, but the Pakistani police would come in the middle of the night and go tent-to-tent doing whatever they wanted. Nobody could stop them.

I decided that the best thing we could do was to start some educational programs. In the beginning, the elders of the camps refused, but somehow, with God's help, they began to agree. So in one year, we went from 300 students to 15,000, all girls. They were so delighted to be able to learn! We started classes from the first through sixth grades, then to the tenth, and then the twelfth. Since they didn't have anything to do after graduation, we started a university for them, Goharshad University. We started it in one small house, in three rooms.

In 1995, I started AIL. At first, AIL's job was to train teachers in modern teaching methods. Building schools is the easy part, but finding good teachers is much harder. So AIL began training our own teachers at Goharshad.

Peggy: *Tell me about your program and the women's centers.*

Dr. Yacoobi: When I started the women's programs, I thought it would be good for women to meet and talk together. From that, we added a literacy program, a mobile clinic, and an income generation program. The income generation program includes sewing, embroidery, and weaving. We teach women about their rights, and we also teach computer skills in some centers. A lot of people have copied my programs, but their success has depended on how well they managed them.

Peggy: *How do you get communities interested in your centers?*

Dr. Yacoobi: First let me tell you that before the Russians came, 70% of the population was illiterate. The Russians forced their education system and ideology on the people. That is one reason why people were against education.

Once communities saw results from our centers in other villages, they could see that we were teaching everything inside of Islam and Afghan culture. We have been establishing centers in Afghanistan since the Taliban left, and before that in the refugee camps, so they have come to trust us. As a result, many come to us asking to make a center for their community. Before we have a chance to tell them

Najia, 2003

what we offer, they tell us what they want, because they have seen our centers in other areas, and we design our programs accordingly. Then we ask what they can provide. Some offer a roof, others a guard, still others offer money for teachers' salaries. Sometimes, they offer little things like soap, but such contributions are equally important because they give people a share in the program. That way, they come to trust us. Even the men can see how education has changed the lives of their people and tell me that they want their wives and children to be able to read and write. This is how we know we're having a positive impact.

In our schools, we teach the government's school curriculum so they can transfer to the government schools. We also teach subjects like peace education, law and order, ethics, sharing, sustainability, human rights, justice, family spacing, and environmental health. We teach critical thinking and how to communicate and ask questions. These are the topics that will help us get rid of those barbaric people [Taliban and warlords] and build a peaceful environment for Afghanistan.

Peggy: *Tell me about some of the workshops you offer.*

Dr. Yacoobi: We offer seminars in life skills, health, and nutrition. In one village we asked women what course they wanted, and you know what? They chose our course on women's rights. In the evenings after class, the women would go home and tell their husbands, "It says in the *Quran* that girls *and* boys should be educated. It says that men and women are supposed to respect one another and treat each other kindly." We teach the girls that they can tell their fathers "no" to an arranged marriage because the *Quran* gives them that right. We teach the mothers that they can say "no" to marrying their daughters too young. By the end of the course, the women reported that it greatly changed their lives. Their children respected them more and their husbands treated them better.

Peggy: *How was it to teach in the refugee camps?*

Sahera: We worked for a German NGO but we weren't paid enough. Even though my husband and I both worked, our rent and school fees were so high that I had to take a second job.

Peggy: *What was it like teaching under the Taliban?*

Krayba   Hamida   Hanifa   Sahera   Dr. Sakena Yacoobi

Hanifa: My sister and I taught over 200 students in our home. It was dangerous because if they caught us, we would be beaten, even more than our students. So we had the students come and go at different times. They would always carry a *Quran* with them in case they were stopped so they could say that they were going to the mosque to study. Teaching was very good for us. I was not married, and I'm still not, so it was important for us to be able to contribute a little bit to the family income. It alleviated boredom and it was something small we could do to resist the Taliban.

Dr. Yacoobi: During Taliban, we were asked to start some underground schools inside Afghanistan. We went back and forth providing supplies and teachers' salaries and training. From the beginning we could see the change in women's lives. They were healthier and more assertive, and they saw that teachers could help support their households financially. The women were even having fewer children. All these things were the result of education.

What was it like working in Khost Province after the Taliban left?

Sahera: My husband lectured at a university temporarily located in Pakistan, but when Karzai came, it moved back to Khost. We followed. There weren't any female professors then, but I volunteered to teach psychology because I wanted to show everyone that women could also study and teach at the university level. At first, the male students were embarrassed to be asked questions by a woman, especially one without a *burqa,* but after a while they accepted it. I also taught them other important points so that when they would go home they would help their sisters and mothers. Once, one of them told me that after I talked to them about women, he went home and made salad for his wife.

My husband also helped bring the Department of Women's Affairs to Khost and he helped me become the Director. All the time I lived and worked in Khost Province I never wore a *burqa.* I was strange and different from the other women in that province. Everyone stared at me and some people told me that I would be killed, but still I didn't wear it.

When I came to Khost, there was one school for girls and it only went to

Najia, 2003

the third grade. There weren't enough students, but also there weren't enough good teachers. So I began to go house to house out in the province to encourage parents to allow their girls to come to school. Slowly, it had an effect. When I started, only one of the teachers had graduated from twelfth grade and was an official teacher. By the time I left, the school had six grades and all of the teachers were certified.

I also noticed that there were a lot of educated women in Khost Province. During the Taliban, they all had to stay home, but even after the Taliban, the men wouldn't allow their women to go out. One day a woman came to our office and told us that her husband was a teacher. She said that she herself had finished school in Kabul but couldn't take her exam because her husband wouldn't allow her to go outside. She said, "I spend all my time collecting firewood from the mountains and carrying water from a very far place." My husband and I invited her husband to our house. After a lot of talking, her husband agreed that she could be a teacher. We found a position for her husband and they moved from that remote area. Several years later, that same woman spent two months in Japan training to be a teacher.

Peggy: This and other stories I heard told of men who changed their minds about allowing their women freedom to work. It requires a lot of time in one-on-one discussions, but as more minds are changed, the social context of the area changes, making future transformations easier. The woman who became a teacher also became a role model for her daughters, students, and other women in the area. The downside is that her husband left a teaching post in a rural area where his skills were no doubt badly needed.

Sahera: We set up literacy classes for older girls and women. We found other educated women who lived in remote areas who weren't allowed to work outside their homes, so we had them teach students inside their homes.

We also made radio programs for families. I recorded them in my house and gave them to the radio station. Doctors told me that some village women were sick because they were too dirty and didn't know how to keep clean. They would be ashamed if the doctor tried to talk to them about it, so I made those women aware of sanitation through radio broadcasts.

Peggy: *What are the most important issues in education?*

Dr. Yacoobi: Teacher training. When I was a student, we had to learn by rote memorization. Some of my classmates couldn't read or write even after three years.

Krayba   *Hamida*   *Hanifa*   *Sahera*   *Dr. Sakena Yacoobi*

When students learn from AIL teachers, they can learn to read and write in three months because we use student-centered techniques. We ask the students questions. We do role playing. Sometimes we work with students in groups. This is all modern. People come to us constantly requesting teacher training. So far we've trained 14,000 teachers, but many more need training. We have 48 centers and training our own teachers is our first priority. After that, we train government teachers.

Education done the right way teaches people how to think. If a woman has learned to read and write, it gives her some confidence. If she has learned critical thinking and learned to ask questions, then nobody can abuse her because she will be able to respond logically and appropriately.

It's also important to work with men, not just women and girls. Men become frustrated and take it out on their wives. If the man doesn't have a job, he can't support his family. It's traditional for men to be breadwinners, but many are sitting at home with nothing to do. As a result, women or the children work.

This creates a problem between generations. When a boy is finished with high school, he knows English and computer skills. He gets a job at a fine organization and brings money home. Then he tells his father how he will live his life and the father can't say anything because the son is the breadwinner.

Young girls also get jobs because of their English and computer skills. When they come home, they rule the house and the family must bear it no matter what. As a result, there are many problems inside families. War and poverty are to blame for tearing our society apart.

Peggy: Some successful women, like filmmaker Sahraa and my translator Najia, do not abuse their power in the household but foster mutual respect among their relatives. Kindness and respect build peace and strength in the family and make the process of change less painful.

What are some reasons for your success?

Dr. Yacoobi: Confidence. Acting as my father's secretary gave me confidence. I also learned a lot from my years of setting up schools, for example, "rush rush rush" doesn't work. Yes, there are many important things to be done, but it's

Najia, 2003

important to stop and listen to people. The Taliban did not find even one of our 80 secret schools because we had the support of the people. They trusted and protected us because we *listened* to them.

Peggy: *What do you see for the future of AIL?*

Dr. Yacoobi: My goal is to have AIL in all 32 provinces of Afghanistan. I hope that in ten years we will not be able to find a single illiterate person in the country. I want everybody to be able to read and write. That's my life's priority.

Peggy: *What is the best way to help Afghan women?*

Dr. Yacoobi: We need things, but it is very difficult and expensive for people to send them, especially to the places where they're needed. The best thing is just to send funding. That way you can help support the Afghan economy as well as the women. We also need to do more human rights and leadership training for women.

I also think that more money should go to education rather than the military. I really believe that if we put one-fourth of the money being spent on the foreign military into education, we will not have the problems we have today. We have so many people becoming suicide bombers, so many innocent people being killed, and women and children being kidnapped and sold. All of these problems come from a lack of education and skills. If people are able to provide food for their families and have access to health care, then they will not do these bad things. I really believe that education has a direct link with the economy, poverty, war, and success.

Peggy: *What would you say to the US President?*

Hanifa: Please stop the invasion of our neighbor, Iraq. We've had enough war in Afghanistan. We don't need another country's money. We can make a lot of carpets. We can produce things bit-by-bit if we have peace.

Peggy: *Do you want the American troops to leave Afghanistan right now?*

Hanifa: If the American forces leave now [2003], then within a few days, Pakistan will attack. It's necessary for the International Security Auxiliary Forces (ISAF)[3] to be here now. America did not invade us, they just came to get rid of the Taliban, and when they finish they will leave. That is not invasion.

Krayba   Hamida   Hanifa   Sahera   Dr. Sakena Yacoobi

Dr. Yacoobi: We have opposition groups everywhere creating problems, not just the Taliban. Troops can provide some security, but a lot of innocent people are being killed when the foreigners raid homes. The situation is so bad right now [2010] that it's impossible to start peace negotiations and engage in a two-way conversation. I think that right now we need troops to maintain security, but our own, not American ones.

If the United States really wants to help stabilize our country, it should work on planning and developing infrastructure; it should provide jobs for Afghans. Countries need some sort of national security, but most foreign troops are not primarily focused on protecting women and children. Their focus is on beating the enemy, which is very different, and ordinary citizens become collateral damage in the process.

Peggy: But infrastructure development, while important, will backfire unless it's implemented very carefully in ways that don't add to corruption or feed into tribal or personal rivalries. Policymakers would do well to consult closely with humanitarian workers with long-term experience in the area of the country they're considering "improving."[4]

Dr. Yacoobi: Many people tell me that Afghanistan should have democracy. But I ask you, how can a nation have democracy when people don't know how to read and write? How can you implement a democracy if people don't know their rights? We have a constitution, but it needs to be implemented. We cannot just *talk* about democracy. We have to *prepare* people for democracy.

In the cities where we and other NGOs are working, the lives of women are better because women are taking more initiative. The more money spent for women, the better outcome you will have. You see billions of dollars going into Afghanistan. It's given to an elite group who spend a lot of it on themselves. Organizations that are not connected to this elite, those that are working at the grassroots, don't get money.

Right now, the people of Afghanistan are really against foreigners. They are really hurt because they have been promised money over and over again and it never came, or it went to people who did very little to help common people.

Najia, 2003

Peggy: *What has the greatest potential to change Afghan society?*

Hanifa: Take the guns away from the militia commanders, make a strong Afghan military force, and don't let people with selfish motives make the leaders do things they're not supposed to do. Give leaders the power of their position.

Peggy: *Are you in this situation of feeling pressure from special interests?*

Hanifa: Yes, sometimes. As a school board member, I am threatened when I reprimand certain students who have powerful families. The *Mujahidin* government changed the psychology of the people. No one followed the law, they just did what they wanted. We still have psychological problems from this.

Peggy: *What plans do you have for the future?*

Hamida: I worked as a teacher in this village when I was in high school. Now I'm the manager of the Women's Center. I want to continue this.

Peggy: *What do you enjoy most about that job?*

Hamida: I manage and supervise different activities like weaving carpets, washing clothes, and baking cakes, but mostly I like baking cakes. We train women how to bake them and we are planning to sell them in hotels and to foreign NGOs. We supply the ingredients, the women make the cakes, and we will sell half of their cakes and let them keep the rest.

Peggy: *How can Afghanistan recover from its traumas?*

Krayba: Experience from the past gives us tools for the future. Our country must come together to solve our problems. Guiding my students is very important to me. All of the women in this center have similar situations to deal with and it is good to help each other. If this center can develop and there can be more like it throughout Afghanistan, then we can become more aware of human rights. This can help change Afghanistan and bring hope for all of us. It's not easy to do things alone, but if we learn from each other and work together, we can make big changes. This will help make our society peaceful.

Peggy: *What challenges are you dealing with in your life right now?*

Krayba   *Hamida*   *Hanifa*   *Sahera*   *Dr. Sakena Yacoobi*

Krayba: I finished school at the end of the Soviet occupation. I was very young when I got married, but we were happy.

My husband was a mechanic, and one day someone brought a car to his shop to be repaired. After they had repaired it, my husband took it on a test drive to the bazaar so he could purchase something. I don't know what happened, but someone abducted him. He and the car disappeared and I still don't know what happened to him. I searched everywhere for two years but haven't found him. Six months later, I found the car by its license plate, but I couldn't do anything because that car now belonged to a commander. Because of that, no one would help me find my husband. The car that my husband test-drove was a taxi. Perhaps the people who captured him thought he was someone else because he was driving it.

Now I must pay the former owner of the car. After I finish teaching, I sew clothes until 11 pm when the electricity goes off, so I can pay this man. One day he came to my house and no one was home except for my daughter who answered the door. He asked to marry her instead of taking the money. I will never give her to that horrible man! I earn A9500[5] per month at the school. [$190] I only keep A500 [$10], and give him A9000. In two more months I will finish paying him.

Peggy: *What gets you through all of this?*

Krayba: I keep thinking of how I can make the situation better for my children. Our children must have hope. I urge everyone to avoid war because humans aren't meant to kill each other. All of us are human and must learn how to live together and how to help each other. Never fight, never kill. It is bad for Muslims and all people. My advice for women is to find the power to work and help others.

Hamida: My family always gives me hope and motivates me to fight with my problems. When I feel sad, I talk with my family and they tell me not to be disappointed. Now I know that everything I want to do is possible with my family's protection and support.

Krayba: Teaching tailoring to widows gives me the opportunity for food and life. I want to teach this skill to all women, and they can use it to help others. In one area of Kabul alone there are 1250 widows.[6]

Najia, 2003

Peggy: In 2003, there were 40,000 widows registered with the government in Kabul. The latest estimates for the entire country range from several hundred thousand to two million.

Krayba: If all of us help and coordinate with each other, we will lessen our poverty and our country will develop. I share my story with my students to show them that if I didn't have these skills, I couldn't live my life. All women must have skills and be able to work to earn money for themselves.

Peggy: *What would you like to say to women in the West?*

Hanifa: We could use help with our education system, especially for teachers. We need to teach teachers modern methods, because the methods they use now are very poor.

Hamida: First, I really appreciate the Americans for helping people in Afghanistan. I would like to say we want women to have jobs. We want to graduate women. We want to work like men and have the same opportunities. However, women lack access to income and jobs. Women potentially have the necessary skills, like weaving carpets and making other things, but we don't have an opportunity to sell them in the international markets. We want this.

Peggy: *What would you like women in other countries to do to help Afghanistan?*

Dr. Yacoobi: Don't underestimate the people of Afghanistan. We are a people who have never been conquered and we never will be conquered.

Also, don't pity us Afghan women. We don't need your pity. Afghan people are very proud. We have all the things we need to make Afghanistan a good country. Maybe we need some help with training and security, but Afghans can create a good country for themselves.

With security, women could do so much for Afghanistan. We are intelligent and powerful. Don't leave us alone; support us and help us to build our support. I see a very bright future for the people of Afghanistan, especially the new generation because they have the strength and strong desire to be independent and self-sufficient. They have the potential and the energy to overcome their difficulties. That would be my dream come true.

School in Band-e Amir National Park.

Horigal

Besides becoming teachers, I wanted to know how education really helped illiterate Afghan women. Horigal, whom I met at one of two literacy centers I visited, had a compelling reason for literacy education: land mine awareness.[1]

Although Horigal was only 45 when I photographed her, she looked over 60 as a result of malnutrition, tragedy, and a generally hard life. She had been studying at a literacy center aided by **CWS** for two months when we met.

Horigal was born in a village in Ghazni Province and came to Kabul during the Taliban era. During their jouney to the city, a rocket killed her husband and three of her four sons. She continued on to Kabul where her cousin was living. Now her daughters earn money by washing clothes and begging for food. Her surviving son goes to school in the morning and spends his afternoons washing cars for a shopkeeper or selling plastic bags in the bazaar.

Every day, I bring the information from this center to my children.

Peggy: *What was your life like growing up?*

Horigal: From the start, my life was very hard because my father didn't earn much by selling hair and make-up products, so we could only afford to eat bread. He brought home dry bread, which we soaked in water to make it edible. Dry bread and tea was a very good lunch for me.

Three months ago, some people came to survey widows to see if we would qualify for their program. They told me about this center where I could learn to read and sew. That was a very good day for me.

Peggy: *How has literacy training helped you?*

Horigal: I can count from one to 200 and write my name, but the most important thing I've learned has been about the mines. Before, I didn't know their dangers, and I sent my children to collect metal scraps to recycle. Now I know that the metal pieces could have been landmines! Thank God nothing happened to my children.

7/Women in Business

Business training can be an effective tool to improve women's and children's lives. If women's businesses succeed, female entrepreneurs are likely to employ more women, extending the benefit. Contributing to household income increases women's status and stature within the family and society. Women's income helps reduce domestic violence, easing economic pressure, while at the same time equipping women with more power to stand up for themselves.

Training programs such as **Peace through Business** (PTB) in Kabul and in Kigali, Rwanda, empower women entrepreneurs. PTB's model uses three phases. The first offers basic business training in each woman's home country, culminating in a business plan. The second phase includes a week of high-level leadership training and mentoring in the US. Women complete the third phase by helping educate others in their home countries.

Another training program is Goldman Sachs' **10,000 Women**, designed by faculty at the Thunderbird School of Global Management and held at the American University satellite school in Kabul. Over the course of ten months, women learn the basics of marketing, finance, and operations management. Instruction is in Dari. One of my interviewees, Shakila, was the assistant director of this initiative and another, Najia, graduated from it.

Habbiba took courses and later became a trainer at the **Afghan Women's Business Council** (AWBC), a United Nations Development Fund for Women (UNIFEM) program. In the summer of 2003, AWBC emerged as a "partnership between women entrepreneurs and leading Afghan NGOs in enterprise development."[1]

The beauty of AWBC is that instruction is in Dari, Pashtu, and English. This makes training accessible to a wide range of women, including the uneducated who, with a little training and support, can become adept entrepreneurs.

Farzana

Farzana appeared both delicate and strong. Her husband had driven her and their two-year-old daughter from Kandahar to Kabul to attend weekly training with PTB. The risks of this trip are substantial, including land mines, abduction, attacks, and car accidents.

Farzana has faced and surmounted many challenges throughout her life, beginning when her family evacuated to Iran when she was ten. She completed her education with a degree in mass communication from the University of Tehran. When the Taliban was defeated, she and her family returned to Kandahar. She has established a training center for women there.

Kandahar has intelligent, smart women. They just need to improve their education. There are many strong businesswomen here in the South who don't have access to any training programs but if they did, they would attend.

Rahela

Rahela was a barely contained bundle of energy: quiet, soft-spoken, but very strong.

Rahela was born in Kabul in 1970. She attended medical school and worked as a doctor until the civil war made that too dangerous. She and her family went to Mazar-e Sharif, a provincial capital in the north, where she taught in the medical college. Later she taught at Bamyan University, where she helped establish a primary health care clinic as well as literacy and computer courses for women. When Taliban fighters came to Bamyan, she and her family went to Pakistan, but returned once Karzai came into power. Rahela also earned a Master's degree in public health from the University of Antwerp. Her 2010 bid for Parliament was unsuccessful. She now owns and runs Afghan Women Empowerment Organization (AWPO). In the fall of 2012, Rahela began studying for her Master's in Public Policy at Georgetown University in Washington, DC.

Sometimes I was thinking that a woman who is working in social activities is going into the fire and she has to eat the fire. I have faced a lot of problems but the main problem is that men have the power and they don't like women to work.

Kubra Z

Kubra had a very warm and generous personality.

Kubra grew up in Herat, earned a pharmacy degree in Kabul, and upon returning to Herat, worked with the AWBC where she established the Business Association of Herat Women.

Men or women should confront their challenges. Women have big challenges in Afghanistan. We shouldn't worry about them, we should fight with them. I am proud of the Afghan businesswomen who have only started recently but have become very successful, even within two years.

Habbiba

I interviewed Habbiba in her jam factory office. She gave me a tour, showing me her simple equipment, some of it awaiting repair. A collection of about 50 jars of different jams and flavored waters sat on the floor in one corner of a room. I didn't see any set-up for processing fruit, but perhaps that was done simply with a few big kettles and propane burners during the harvest season.

Her office was dusty and bare. An empty desk, a tall black file cabinet, and a few chairs filled the space. She told me that she doesn't have a computer, and perhaps she doesn't need one to sell locally.

Habibba was raised and married in Kabul. After she completed her degree at Kabul University, she worked in Najibullah's government until she had to flee the *mujahidin* takeover. Soon after arriving in the refugee camp, she began buying things in the Peshawar market to sell to her neighbors. Six months later, she had saved enough to move her family into a house. She kept that business and also worked as a teacher for the 12 years they lived in Pakistan. She taught at a public school when they returned to Afghanistan in 2003. Her

My father always told me, "Whenever you face a problem instead of sitting still, you have to act to get yourself out of that problem." He was very supportive of me when I was young and always encouraged me. He was an educated person.

interest in business drew her to AWBC, at first to take courses, and then to work as a trainer, mostly in Uruzgan Province. She and other members of a co-op run a jam-making business in Kabul. Through her work with AWBC, Habbiba has trained over 2000 women in basic business since 2003.

Najia

2003

2010

My income really helped me solve my family problems. Otherwise no one would have listened to me.

Najia, my translator during my 2003 trip to Afghanistan, seemed sweet and not very imposing, but underneath she possessed an ironclad internal fortitude. It was a pleasure to work with her because she was clear-headed, practical, adventurous, and a terrific translator. One moment remains especially clear in my mind. We were to meet a friend of Najia's at Kabul University. Her friend was late and we didn't know if she'd show up, so Najia offered to approach random women on campus and ask them for interviews. Even though this wasn't customary, it wasn't offensive. She introduced herself to a few women, but they all declined to be interviewed. Shortly afterward, her friend arrived.

When I saw Najia in 2010, some of her light youthfulness had been replaced by a more overt strength and determination, a solidity of focus and purpose that hadn't been as apparent before.

Najia worked for **USAID** teaching accountability and transparency to government ministers. She quit after receiving death threats. Her training with 10,000 Women enabled her to start her own crisps[2] factory.

Touba

Touba made me wish I lived in Afghanistan. Her self-confidence, intensity, and commitment to making a difference all made me want to be among her friends. Unfortunately, I met her near the end of my trip, and she was leaving later that day to vacation in Dubai.

Touba's father worked in King Zahir Shah's government until the king was overthrown in 1974. The family left the country when Touba was five and went to Canada. After she earned an MBA, she returned to Kabul on her own and created a consulting business which helps girls get jobs in appropriate companies. She also trains them in how to conduct themselves, work, and get along in a business environment.

Here in Afghanistan, I feel that if I make a difference in one person's life, they can go back and support their family and kids. If I can do that in one person's life, I can do that in many more. That's even greater.

Muzhgan

Confident and well prepared, Muzhgan sent me her Powerpoint CV prior to our meeting to save time during the interview. Her resume was very impressive.

Muzhgan grew up in Herat and moved to Pakistan when she was 12. In 2003,

she opened a coffee shop in the Women's Garden and three years later established the first women's shopping mall, tenanted with 33 women-owned shops. She simultaneously created Wafiq, a production company employing around 120 women who make handicrafts and jewelry from home. For the past three years, she has run a business consulting company with her husband. She's only 25 years-old, has a Master's degree, and studied with PTB.

Business and life are the same. To have a good life, you must be a good manager and planner. You need to coordinate. It is the same in business. You must be a good leader for the employees and the customers; and in life, for your children.

Peggy: *What prompted you to start your own business?*

Muzhgan: It was my dream to be a business owner. Since childhood, I was always trying to be the leader of the other children and later became the leader in my office. I never wanted to work under someone else. I prefer to work by myself and for myself. That's why business was the only thing I could do.

Peggy: *Did your family encourage you and your dream?*

Muzhgan: Yes, of course. My family always told me, "If you want to do business, then you must not wait. You can start now, anytime you want." So I started my first business in 2003 when I was 18.

Touba: I have a strong sense of responsibility, a sense that I have to do this, that I am connected to Afghanistan, even though I was raised in Canada.

Peggy: *And certainly there is so much you can contribute…*

Touba: Yes. This is one of the biggest reasons I'm here. In Canada, I had a great career, but at the end of the day I didn't feel that I was contributing very much to society as a whole. Here in Afghanistan, I can see the effect of my mentoring on girls in the workplace. I can be a role model for them.

Rahela: When I was teaching at the medical college in Mazar-e Sharif, I saw people's homes that were destroyed during the war. People kept asking for help, so some friends and I started a women's commission. Through the commission, we began activities like primary schools for girls and income-generating projects for women. While teaching at Bamyan University, we started public health education, made efforts to improve the local health system, and offered literacy and computer courses for women. Yet, I kept noticing that women had remarkably low educational and economic status, and I wanted to do something to create jobs for them. So I started the AWEO.

Najia: I wanted to be a businesswoman and had an idea for a business, but little knowledge about how to start. I studied business administration at Kabul University, then got another chance with the 10,000 Women program at American University, so I went there to learn. That program helped me a lot. Now I know how to make a business plan and market my product.

However, I still want to start an NGO. Its name will be "Women's Power." Unfortunately, in the past, I was too busy and my partners were not good nor strong enough. We applied for many grants, but the donors said they didn't give money to small NGOs. Now USAID is coming to support local NGOs… finally! They give very little funding, but if an NGO is successful, then it can get more money.

Peggy: USAID's Afghan Women's Empowerment program[3] is a very smart initiative. In early 2010 they put out a request for proposals to local women who wanted to start projects to help other women. They were inundated with applications! In the end, they supported 44 projects. Personally, I believe it would be beneficial to find a way to support almost all of the projects. Training and

Farzana Rabela Kubra Z Habbiba Najia, 2010

classes could help women whose proposals weren't up to par improve their plans. Mentors could help them become successful.

The desire to become self-sufficient is strong in Afghanistan, especially since jobs for women are scarce. Training Afghans, especially women, how to employ themselves and others would go a long way towards solving this country-wide problem. Unfortunately, with the scheduled withdrawal of American forces, USAID's Afghan budget has been severely cut.

Kabul University didn't teach you marketing or how to write a business plan?

Najia: I didn't take many courses from them. 10,000 Women provided the first course where I studied business administration. It was very practical, while the Kabul University program was very abstract. With 10,000 Women, I made a business and marketing plan. I did a market survey and everything. Then I searched for start-up funds and my business was launched.

Peggy: *What inspired you to create a business?*

Kubra Z: I became a member of AWBC in 2003 and then decided to start a business association of Herati women. I had my first business experience in an AWBC workshop with UN Habitat and there I learned how to start my own business. After some time, I got the idea to start a small association to encourage Herati women who already have their own businesses to expand.

Habbiba: I had a position in the government and a really nice life here in Afghanistan. But when the *mujahidin* took over, it became very dangerous for anyone who had worked for the communists, so we had to leave. We left Afghanistan suddenly and could take hardly anything with us. In Pakistan, our only alternative was to move into a tent in a refugee camp.

I had always been interested in business, but it became a matter of survival there. I had to do something to make our life better so we could get out of our tent. I asked the people in the camp what they needed. They wanted things like

Touba   *Muzhgan*

candles, soap, and sugar, so I went to the bazaar and brought those things back to the tents to sell. There were some Afghans who had brought their cows and chickens and would make butter and cheese that they sold in the market. When I first started this business I made 100 Pakistani rupees, and later 1000. Within six months, I was able to move my family out of our tent to live in a house in Peshawar.

Through this experience I slowly, slowly got to know more about business and what makes it successful.

Peggy: *What personal things made you see that you needed to change your situation? What gave you the impetus to take action when so many people just waited for help?*

Habbiba: My father was so supportive of me when I was young and he always encouraged me. He was an educated person. Also, I wasn't used to the uncomfortable and dangerous life in the camp.

Peggy: *And was your mother educated also?*

Habbiba: My mother was not educated, but she went to the mosque to learn different things.

Farzana: My education center is an NGO. My mother teaches in a government school. She showed me how to help educate people. My mother was my inspiration.

Peggy: *Kubra, what is the nature of your Association?*

Kubra Z: Since I established the Herati Business Women's Association in 2006, I have given workshops to help women introduce their products to both the international and domestic markets. I help them make handicraft products based on modern styles.

Peggy: *What particular products do you work with?*

Kubra Z: Carpets and various handicrafts. I established a marketing center in Herat called Herat Women Handicrafts. After I came back from the Peace through Business trip in 2007, I expanded the center and signed an agreement with several international hotels to open small handicraft shops in their lobbies.

Farzana   Rahela   Kubra Z   Habbiba   Najia, 2010

Rahela: Right now we at AWEO have a program that trains women in aquaculture, animal husbandry, and literacy in rural areas. We also teach them housekeeping and quilt-making.

Najia: In my crisps factory, we make baked crisps from corn and potatoes to provide a healthier option. You can buy imported crisps coated with Pakistani or Indian masala [spices], but Afghan people are not used to this, so I make them with Afghan spices. Many young people don't want to eat fried food because they're afraid of getting fat, so we bake our crisps. Maybe there will be a market also in other countries.

Peggy: *What is it like to be in business in Afghanistan?*

Touba: Well, I get propositioned a lot, but it's done indirectly. Mostly it's government employees. They say, "We will work with you on this project, but you know, what about me? You know I'm doing so much for you, what can you do for me?" I know where they're trying to go with this, so I just send them a small gift so that they know that I appreciate their help and that we're working together.

Peggy: *And that works?*

Touba: With some it does, with others, definitely not. It's challenging.

Peggy: *But it's something you can deal with and remain firm?*

Touba: I can deal with it because I've been groomed in the professional world. However, it's more difficult for the new generation entering the workforce. Some of the people I'm training don't know how to deal with it. They are really sad and disappointed when they are faced with these kinds of issues. They don't know what to do and they usually just fall victim.

Peggy: *Oh no, they just give in?*

Touba   Muzhgan

Touba: They think it's the thing to do, they think it's normal, they think they have to.

Peggy: *Habbiba, how did you go about training your 2000 women?*

Habbiba: Since I trained both educated and illiterate women, I would give visual presentations so they could see and understand what business is and how to start and run one. I usually just spoke with the educated women and offered them a workshop, whereas I spent more time teaching and supporting the uneducated ones.

Peggy: *Was this with the AWBC?*

Habbiba: Yes. They would introduce me to the courses and I would go out and teach them.

Peggy: *How long did these courses last?*

Habbiba: They lasted 25 days for uneducated women and 15 for the educated. The women learn how to do tailoring and embroidery. Sometimes they bring their products to the AWBC to show and sell them. We teach them how to produce and sell their products so they can have enough money to support their families. We just want to create more jobs because there is less violence if the women can earn some money.

Peggy: *Are you saying that women get beaten less if they are working?*

Habbiba: Yes. Life is much easier when women work. They can take care of their kids' needs, including education. This leads to less violence. I've seen it in practice in Uruzgan [Province] where I held a workshop. When I followed up, some women told me that they generated some income for their household. Their unemployed husbands had a lot of stress, but when their wives brought home money, they were happier and less prone to hitting them. These ladies also take literacy classes to learn to read and write. This improves the quality of their lives and contributes to earning income.

Peggy: *Why are you so focused on Uruzgan Province? Are you from there?*

Habbiba: I do training sessions for the Afghan Women's Business Training

Farzana   *Rahela*   *Kubra Z*   *Habbiba*   *Najia, 2010*

Association (AWBTA) that currently focuses on Uruzgan. Sessions last nine months.

After one year of working with AWBTA, I realized that if we want to teach women how to do business, it would be beneficial for trainers to have a business to demonstrate the process and hire women to work with us. So ten of us members invested $1000 each and started a business to make these products. I'm the director of our enterprise.

Peggy: *How do you deal with challenges in your business?*

Rahela: A lot of people help me. When I was in Mazar-e Sharif trying to go to Bamyan, I got support from MSF [**Médecins Sans Frontières**; a.k.a. Doctors Without Borders] for medicine and other things. I have had a double challenge, not only because I am a woman, but also because I am Hazara. I have faced a lot of injustice in our society, in school, in the university, in the workplace, just everywhere.

Peggy: *How do you deal with this prejudice?*

Rahela: I just have the passion and I go forward. All the time, I think about how to fight with all my problems, but sometimes I get tired. All of my life, I have fought my way forward through unfairness.

Peggy: *So the fighting made you stronger, right?*

Rahela: My biggest help was knowing that my father, my brothers, my husband, and my mother all supported me. Now I have four children and my husband still encourages me in my social activism. This made me successful, but I still face many challenges from society.

Najia: Everyone has difficulty finding funding when starting a business. I've faced troubles, too. I have some money, but it's not enough. I try to avoid credit debt so I've borrowed some money from friends and I've also been saving. I've had

Touba   *Muzhgan*

to be creative. I was looking for crisp-making machines on the internet, but they were too expensive. So I looked at the pictures and took them to a shop that could make a similar machine for me inexpensively.

Peggy: *How will you sell your crisps?*

Najia: My plan is to have our company's stands set up outside shops. When people walk by, they will see them. It's good advertising for us. We will start out by selling in only one district of Kabul at some of the 2000 medium-sized shops there. Once sales are high enough, we will target Kandahar, Herat, and Mazar. In my plan, we will have targeted all of Afghanistan after five years.

Peggy: *You said you hired your husband to work with you as a marketer? How is that working out? That's a challenge no matter where you live.*

Najia: In Afghanistan especially, it's not easy for a woman to do business or go and talk with people outside her home. I know how to do the marketing, but the people who run shops often have little education and don't think that a woman should have a business or a factory. They will think that I'm not a good woman and they will not buy my product. That's why I have my husband market for me. I cannot trust anyone else. Of course I'm doing the bookkeeping and accounting, but I need a man to take care of distributing and marketing.

Peggy: Progressive individuals face censure from their friends and relatives. Batool told me that her husband would help around the house except when guests came. Najia's husband faced social pressures as well and began to resent not being the boss. In November, 2011, she wrote to me:

"It is impractical for a husband to work for his wife in Afghanistan. It was working in the beginning but not anymore. He does not listen to what I say and now tells me that it was he who built up the factory, that I didn't have any role. He is not helping me anymore and I am looking for a lady partner. However, we still need a man to do the marketing."

By Spring, 2012, Najia had hired her brother-in-law to market for her and in June her chips appeared in all of the small and large shops throughout two districts of Kabul.

Muzhgan: I have faced many problems finding project funding. When we submit our proposals, the Afghan staff doesn't let us meet the international heads

Farzana Rahela Kubra Z Habbiba Najia, 2010

of the projects. Once, I knew I had the best project but the Afghan staff did not add it to the pile for further review. So I found the contact number for the head of the project, met with him, and showed him my proposal. I told him that I'd like to know why I was not the winner of the project funding. I told him that if my proposal had technical problems, I wanted to know. In the end, I have gotten many projects by forcing my way in, by facing the many problems.

Peggy: *So, you have persistence and then follow-up.*

Muzhgan: Yes. Because of all of the wars, everybody's doing something for their relatives or friends. That's why it's not possible for us to get a project just with our qualifications or skills; we have to know someone. Meeting the project manager, however, helps us get in.

Farzana: In Kandahar, the big challenge is security for women. When I go to the office, I must wear a *burqa*. It's very… I'm not comfortable. It's long and heavy, but I'm forced to wear it for security. There are no women [in Kandahar] who go out without a *burqa*.

The other challenge is Kandahar's closed culture. They have very old ideas about women, like they have no rights to education. Women are supposed to just stay at home, take care of their babies, and obey their husbands. Nothing else.

Peggy: *Is your husband from Kandahar? If he is, he must think differently.*

Farzana: Yes, but he was educated outside of Afghanistan; that greatly influenced him. He's one of the very few educated men in Kandahar.

Most people there don't like my activity. They think my education center is not suitable under Islam. But my centers exist to help women improve their lives with education. This is actually *encouraged* in Islam.

Touba: We are Pashtuns, and our ancestry goes back to Kandahar. That's highly respected. It's very tribal here. I never knew about that before I came, because in Canada there was no discrimination. Here, the first thing they ask me is, "What

Touba   Muzhgan

is your tribe? Who is your father?" When I first came to Afghanistan, I went to different meetings where people never asked my name or qualifications. They didn't know why I was there. Yet they would ask, "Who is your father? Who is your grandfather?" I had to go back to Canada to find out who my grandfather was, and he turned out to have been a very prominent man in Afghanistan. Now when I mention his name, they say, "O.K., we know who you are." Usually that helps because things here are mostly based on relationships.

Peggy: *What has your employment meant to you and your family?*

Najia (in 2010): My husband respects me, especially after I told him that I am not a woman who will blindly follow what he or my family says. I will listen to them and then I will decide. I know and understand my rights under Islam and Afghan law.

My husband's family knows that I am working at a high level with the government. If I were uneducated, nobody would listen to me. Unfortunately, there are many uneducated women here who have to put up with nobody listening to them, and they're not strong enough to talk about their problems.

Peggy: *You are so resolute. What gave you your courage, what made you so strong?*

Najia: I think I learned a lot from my situation and from society. I grew up without men. My father died when I was four. Because I have no brothers, my mother made me go to the bazaar to buy what we needed. I was the youngest child, and if my teenage sisters went out of the house, people would think they were not good. I always had to stand up for myself, so I learned to be very strong.

Peggy: *Do you have any advice for your (future) daughters?*

Rahela: One of my daughters and my son are in school and I'm trying to provide them with equal opportunities. My daughter is very strong even though she's only in the third grade. Sometimes I ask her to do something at home and she tells me, "I will, but my brother should do it, too." And her brother agrees.

Muzhgan: If my daughter wanted to become a businesswoman, I would advise her to fully understand business, the Afghan market, and computers. It would also be important for her to get financial as well as human support. Then she could be successful.

Farzana   Rahela   Kubra Z   Habbiba   Najia, 2010

Habbiba: I tell all children, including my daughter, to get a good education so they can work and help the family.

Peggy: *What are some important things you've learned in your business training?*

Muzhgan: One of the most important things is how to treat employees. I've learned that it's very important to be friendly with them. It's important to have a democratic environment in the business and get advice from everyone you employ.

Peggy: *What can businesswomen in the West do to help you?*

Farzana: When I was in New Jersey last year, my mentor asked me the same question. I told them, "You should come to Afghanistan one time, then you will really understand everything about the life of women. You will see what we face more clearly. Hearing something from the media and newspapers is not enough to know Afghan women."

Also, the Peace Through Business program should be extended into southern Afghanistan. There are many strong businesswomen there who don't have knowledge of nor access to the program, but if they did they would certainly participate. I have the capacity to come to Kabul but many other women don't. I have this opportunity because my husband and family support me. It's very difficult for Kandahari women to come every week for two months because the road is very dangerous. It's also very expensive to come, so if the program can expand to the south, it will help those women a lot.

Peggy: *Is there a place in Kandahar where women could gather and have this course?*

Farzana: Yes, and the women will come.

Muzhgan: Organizations who want to help Afghan businesswomen should have good follow-up programs. They should have a systematic way to follow the women's businesses and help them deal with future challenges.

Rahela: Some women, especially the educated ones who have more complex

Touba   Muzhgan

business ideas, need some technical support. When I studied at the University, I learned a lot about how to start and run a business and realized that technical support was as important as funding.

Peggy: By "technical support," Rahela means that they need role models, mentors, and information on the mechanics of running a business.

Kubra Z: Foreign women could help a lot by sharing their experiences with Afghan women and helping them write business plans. It's also good if they come to Afghanistan and invite Afghans to go to the US to show them their businesses.

Habbiba: My request is that foreigners help us spread business knowledge among girls so that we can help them have successful businesses. The economy in Afghanistan is bad, so their support is very important.

Najia: I hope that a high-ranking American government official hears this because I want to say that they should help women of Afghanistan earn their own income. This will reduce a lot of familial and general violence. It doesn't matter how much they make, but women should believe that they can do *something* [of value]. Some women have told me that they are uneducated and don't know what to do. "We can't go out of the house, so how can we earn income?" There are a lot of ways they can earn money.

Peggy: *Like what?*

Najia: Well, I know some women who live in Shamali [an area just north of Kabul] where there is a lot of fresh, wholesome food. They can make jam or pickles because they already have all of the raw materials; they can use fruit from their own trees, vegetables from their own gardens, and make things in their houses to sell. And this is only one example. In some villages women can grow trees from seeds and sell them after one year. They can take care of other people's children in their home. Most donors want to start sewing projects, which are also good, but more time-consuming.

Peggy: *What is the market for sewn things? Is there a lot of demand?*

Najia: No, there's not, because many things are imported from China or Iran and they are very cheap. But if they make jam in their houses, it won't have chemicals in it like the jams from Pakistan. If they get some support to buy a cow, they can make cheese from the milk that they can also sell. A lot of things come from Pakistan and the products are marked "for export only." Why? It's because the raw materials are not good. It's because there are no standards on what chemicals or materials they use. If we make these things in our own country, it will provide income for women and the products will be better.

Peggy: In August, 2012, I received an update from Najia telling me that her husband had been kidnapped. She negotiated with the kidnappers to lower their ransom down to $200,000 from their initial demand of $300,000. She sold her crisp-making business, and some properties they held, and gathered money from relatives. The kidnappers released her husband, telling him that if the family didn't leave Afghanistan immediately, their sons would be kidnapped. Now they are in India awaiting word on their refugee status. Due to previous death threats she'd received during the time she worked with foreigners, Najia believes that this kidnapping was a way for the Taliban or others of their ilk to get back at her for her efforts on behalf of USAID to end corruption in the Finance Ministry's procurement department.

Women learning tailoring.

Siebewal

I met Siebewal at a **CWS** literacy center. She smiled during our interview and looked remarkably well adjusted despite everything she'd been through.

Siebewal: I lost my husband during the civil war. When he went to the bazaar one day, somebody killed him. Two months later, my two babies died when a rocket exploded on my house. As I was moving some of my things to my brother's house in a safer area of the city, my neighbors came and stole my remaining belongings. I was only in that house for four months when another rocket fell and killed my mother, brothers, and sisters. I escaped with my three remaining children.

All of this made me crazy, but it was easier after I started to work washing clothes for neighbors. I couldn't earn enough money to live on because sometimes no one would hire me, so I sent my children out to work. I sent one child to work in a butcher shop and others out to wash cars wherever traffic stops. Unfortunately, a rocket landed on the butcher shop and killed the owner. My boy was also injured and has not recovered. Now, the only way I have to make money is with this quilt-making project [at the literacy center]. My son needs medicine. I've forgotten my own mental problems because I'm so concerned about him.

Peggy: *What have you learned from all of these horrible experiences?*

Siebewal: They were a good experience for me also. Now we try to help each other. Not fighting, not bringing black days for others... We must have cooperation.

The Community Midwife Training Program's school in Bamyan.

8/Women's Health Workers

Save the Children made headlines in 2011, rating Afghanistan as the worst place to be a mother. The 2009 national average there of 1600 maternal deaths per 100,000 live births gives only a partial picture.

In Kabul, where qualified medical practitioners and adequate facilities exist for those who can afford and/or access them, the maternal death rate is one-quarter of the national average. It is in remote rural areas where rates are horrifically high. In Badakshan Province, the northeastern mountainous area where researchers had to ride donkeys up and down narrow, rocky paths to reach many villages, the maternal death rate in 2002 was 6507 per 100,000 live births, the highest number ever recorded.[1] Sadly, 80% of those deaths might have been prevented had a skilled birth attendant been present.

Afghanistan's National Association of Midwives says that Afghanistan needs up to 8000 midwives to curb its high maternal death ratios. During the 1950s, '60s, and '70s, midwives were trained, licensed and regulated. The Afghan Family Guidance Association was founded in 1968 and trained midwives until 1992. They resumed training in 2002 after the Taliban left.

There are currently 3000 midwives throughout the country. Three to four hundred are trained at 31 midwifery schools every year. At this rate, it will take 14 years to get the other needed 5000.

Headway is being made. Thirty-two of Afghanistan's 34 provinces have midwifery schools. Women selected from their communities commit to returning there to practice upon graduation. Communities with midwives have higher rates of vaccination and birth control use. The number of health care facilities throughout Afghanistan rose from 500 in 2002 to 1700 in 2009.[2]

My friend Jennifer Braun, a co-founder and former executive director of **International Midwife Assistance**'s (IMA) project in Afghanistan[3] wanted to make use of the long lineage of traditional birth assistants (TBAs) who have provided maternal care to rural and urban women throughout the centuries. Jennifer's idea was to help the TBAs update their skills in light of modern sanitation and understanding. But over the course of several years, she could find none in Bamyan. She learned that many of them relocated during the Soviet fighting and the rest of these knowledgeable, literate, and often uppity women were murdered during the Taliban era.

To fill the need, women with little knowledge of herbs and techniques began working as birth asssistants. Most new birth assistants were illiterate village mothers and grandmothers relying on superstitions, hearsay, and experience within their own families.

Saleha

Saleha invited Shakila and me to visit her family in Herat during Now Ruz, the Afghan New Year. She and Shakila became friends while working together at the midwife school in Bamyan. Saleha, her two-year-old daughter, her husband, and her husband's elderly mother live together in a modern five-room apartment in the Hazara section of Herat. Saleha is a devout Muslim. Since she's of the younger generation, instead of wearing a *chador*, she put on a beautiful zippered

and hooded *abaa* when she went out. Saleha was quiet and shy, but had a good sense of humor. She told me that her best qualities as a midwife were to listen carefully to her patients, admit if she didn't know something, and then research and network to find answers. If I were a pregnant mother, I would confidently put myself into Saleha's hands after seeing her conscientious manner and knowing she has backup from doctors and the Herat Hospital should anything go wrong.

When Saleha was two, her family fled the Soviet war in Herat and moved to the university town of Mashhad, Iran, where she met and married her husband. Although she had a strong interest in painting and literature, Saleha chose midwifery as her university major so she could better help

My father always wanted me to be successful and help the people of this country. But it wasn't until after he died that I realized how much he supported me.

I want to tell my daughter not to let society's limiting ideas stop her.

her people. When she graduated, she and her husband returned to Herat, but she could only find a job at the Bamyan hospital, so she went there alone to work. In 2006, she returned to Herat to reunite with her husband and set up her own midwifery clinic.

Shakila

It was fun to travel to Bamyan, where Shakila had formerly worked, and see for myself the things she described. She was instrumental in making my Bamyan visit a success, rescuing me from my grubby hotel by finding a friend, Belgheis, to host me, as well as connecting me with other old friends. We also traveled together to Herat to visit her midwife friend, Saleha.

Yes, [being a midwife] was very good; at times it was very hard. I'd never experienced women's labor and delivery before, but I had to help them because the male nurses couldn't do that. It was a matter of learning.

Soraya Sobhrang
Commissioner for Women's Rights

There's a lot of self-immolation in Herat and nearby provinces. Most women who try to kill themselves in this way have lived in Iran. Self-immolation was very rare in Afghanistan before the wars. If a woman wanted to kill herself, she'd take pills or slit her wrists

Najia

Najia, my translator, introduced me in 2003 to two of her sisters: Ramzia, a doctor, and another who is a pharmacist. Later, when we were reflecting on our conversation with them, she told me about her own training and experiences in the medical field.

[My challenges] taught me that I cannot be like other women, shy and unconfident. If something is very difficult I tell myself that I can do this. I can do it; and so I do. I decide first, and then say I can do it. I pray and then make a strong decision.

Ramzia

Najia brought me to Macrorayon to meet her oldest sister, Ramzia. Her apartment building was pockmarked with bullet holes from the civil war. The stairwells were dingy, but her apartment was clean and bright. She had furnished it with overstuffed couches and chairs rather than the traditional *toshaks*. Ramzia had an authoritative presence and a warm sense of humor.

There were two best times in my life, the first was when I entered medical school and the second was when I finished.

Ramzia is the oldest of five sisters. Their father died when she was 13. In spite of his strictness (*he was a very dark man*), he encouraged his daughters to get an education, at the time under the Soviet system. Because they had no paternal uncles, she and her sisters were allowed to choose their own husbands. She married a fellow doctor, had her first child in 1991, and a few years later graduated from medical school. The Taliban allowed her to practice only because she could work with her husband. She was sent, along with Najia, to a remote village in Nuristan Province for the duration of their rule. Now she supervises a government midwifery program in Kabul.

Kobra

I met Kobra at the Bamyan Midwifery Training Center. When I entered the compound, I saw one of the Buddha grottoes in the distance beyond the school. Classes were out of session and the clean, spacious halls were empty except for handmade posters illustrating how to care for certain medical conditions.

Kobra's office was comfortable and well lit, and Kobra herself was at ease being interviewed. Kobra, Shakila, and Saleha had all worked together in the Community Midwife Training Program (CMTP) in Bamyan.

Kobra was born in Iran and her family returned to Bamyan when she finished high school. She joined the first class of the CMTP in 2004 and graduated 18 months later. She became a teacher after six months of working in the Bamyan hospital, and now she's the course coordinator.

Bamyan has the second highest rate of maternal mortality in Afghanistan.

Peggy: *Kobra, tell me about the program you offer at the midwifery training center.*

Kobra: Our program aims to create midwives for remote areas. When we first started in 2004, only a few people applied, but now we have a waiting list.

Peggy: *What qualifications must your students have?*

Saleha Shakila Soroya Najia, 2003 Ramzia

Kobra: They must be at least 18 years old, have completed ninth grade or higher, and have a recommendation letter from a related NGO or from a *shura* in their community. They must promise to work in their own area for five years.

Peggy: *Where do they come from?*

Kobra: They come from all over Bamyan Province. We try to select several students from the same village. When they finish their training, they will go back to work in a clinic in their village. It's good for them to be able to support and consult with each other. Since I've been here, only one girl has dropped out. She had health problems.

Unfortunately, we can only accept 25 women for each 18-month course. The students study normal labor and delivery, postpartum issues, and immunizations in the first section. Then they study complications of pregnancy and sick newborns. We also teach family planning and reproductive health.

Peggy: *How well is family planning accepted?*

Kobra: In the beginning, very few people wanted it. Now we have a lot who come for IUDs and for depo-provera, maybe 1500 or more. They accept the use of condoms also.

Saleha: At my clinic in Herat, I deliver a lot of babies, but most of my patients come for family planning.

Peggy: *How much practical training do the students get?*

Kobra: [Our training center] is close to the Bamyan hospital and student midwives work night duty there.

Saleha: When I studied midwifery in Iran, we spent three years in classes and then we went through practice. But in Bamyan we would study in the morning and go to the hospital to practice every afternoon. We saw so many kinds of cases.

Kobra

It was very practical and much faster. And we didn't only see one patient, but five or ten every day.

When I worked for the Bamyan hospital, often there weren't enough doctors, so I had to take care of the whole ward by myself. But doing that gave me the confidence that I could handle it. Because the midwifery school was there, we could hire a few of their new graduates, which gave them experience and filled our need for more help. Sometimes it happened that there were just two people working in the ward. Maybe this was not good for the patients, but it was good for us, because it gave us a lot of experience. The students also got a lot of practice and they learned to help like nurses because they had to support us.

Ramzia: At Kabul University Medical School I didn't get any practical experience. When the [civil] war started it became even harder. [When I graduated] I didn't know anything and had to work really hard to learn what to do.

Peggy: *How can the hospital or midwife center help their graduates when they're back in their villages?*

Kobra: We give on-site supervision to all graduates twice within the first six months and once a year after that for five years. We send someone out to their villages to see how they work and to talk with them about any questions they have. We also offer refresher courses to our graduates here at the center, where they can meet other practicing midwives. Part of their duty as midwives is to send feedback on how many people they help, what they need, and what more they need to learn.

Peggy: *Does one midwife typically serve only her village or many villages?*

Kobra: The school selects several students from the same village. When they are trained, they will work at the basic health clinic in or near their village.

Peggy: Near Band-e Amir, the midwife in Jaroo Kashan Village worked at a clinic that served five villages in and near the national park.

Shakila: A few graduates from the midwifery center went to work for Bamyan Hospital, but most of them went back to their villages where everybody already knew and trusted them. Sometimes though, after living in Bamyan, they didn't want to go back.

Saleha   Shakila   Soraya   Najia, 2003   Ramzia

Peggy: *About how many women come to deliver their babies at the Bamyan hospital each week?*

Kobra: At most, we perform 100 deliveries a week. For pre-natal and post-partum care, it's about 500.

Peggy: Hemorrhage is the most common cause of maternal death in Bamyan and most of Afghanistan, but in Badakshan most childbirth fatalities are caused by obstructed labor. Malnutrition, especially lack of viTamim D and calcium, is a major factor leading to a contracted pelvis and obstructed labor. High rates of opium use among women in Badakshan lead to childbirth problems as well.

What kinds of complications do you see most commonly?

Kobra: We see eclampsia and preeclampsia,[4] hemorrhage, and shock mostly. Women in Afghanistan and especially here in Bamyan don't come to the hospital unless they have a complication. Many of them live very far away and it's difficult for them to get to Bamyan. Another issue is poor nutrition.

Ramzia: There are many problems. A lot of women don't want babies, but their husbands make them have children. Because they've had so many children, the deliveries are dangerous. Sometimes they are malnourished. They don't have enough iron. Maybe they can find a midwife in their area or they just get an experienced person. A lot of women die. Only our midwives can help them. We give them viTamims and iron and sometimes help them deliver their babies.

Peggy: When I met Ramzia in 2003, there were only 200 or so trained midwives in Afghanistan and most of them worked for the government.

How do your midwives operate? Do you have a clinic?

Ramzia: The midwives have one room in the government health clinic. Women come to the clinic for their initial visit, but after that, midwives go to the women's homes. My job is to train and supervise the midwives.

Kobra

Peggy: *What traditional midwife practices have you seen?*

Najia: There are local midwives in villages, but they are uneducated. These women only have experience with their own kids. Sometimes they give oxytocin at the wrong time, even before the women are properly dilated. Many women have died from this. I saw more than 200 children who had tetanus because of unclean knives. Also they put henna on the cord if it doesn't come off soon enough. It's not sanitary because the water they mix it with is not clean. Sometimes they use cow dung.

Peggy: In Afghanistan anyone can walk into a pharmacy and buy any available drug just by asking for it. Oxytocin is sometimes given to induce labor, and after birth to contract the uterus and stop the woman from hemorrhaging. It must be injected to be effective, so the issue of clean needles arises. Also, the dosage must be very accurate or fatal complications can result. Its use does not fall within traditional practice by definition.

Henna (*Lawsonia inermis*), an herb traditionally used to dye skin and hair, has also been used in many cultures in the belief that it protects newborns from "malevolent spirits" in conTamimated water sources. However, it must be mixed with clean water, and can raise the risk of hyperbilirubinemia, or breast milk jaundice, and should not be used on newborns.[5]

Shakila: Sometimes there are people who have TBA skills but there are times when their remedies don't work. In fact, sometimes they just create more problems because the TBAs don't have any idea about physiology. Maybe in some ways they were helpful, but with eclampsia cases, nothing they did would work.

Peggy: *Najia told me that one of the old customs was to put cow dung on the umbilical cord after cutting it. Did you ever see that?*

Shakila: In some places people do that, but in Bamyan they don't. There may be different customs for different villages. Different TBAs have different skills, too. Once I heard about using parts of animals to stop the bleeding and to deal with infection. They learned later that they shouldn't do that, so now they use string and tie the baby's cord off.

Peggy: *I know that sometimes no matter what you do, you lose the mother and baby. How do you deal with that sadness?*

| Saleha | Shakila | Soraya | Najia, 2003 | Ramzia |

Kobra: We try as hard as we can to save the mother first and then the baby, but if they don't survive, we believe that it is God's will. It's all up to God.

Peggy: *Shakila, after seeing all these complicated deliveries, does that make you afraid to have children?*

Shakila: No, because I know how important it is to have good nutrition and good exercise. The ones who have difficulties are the ones who were weak or who do not have enough food. But for the strong, healthy women it was so easy. But I understand now what they mean when women would tell me that if they don't have any babies it's one problem, and if they do, then it's another!

Peggy: *Saleha, How old were your youngest patients when you worked in Bamyan?*

Saleha: Our youngest maternity patients are 17 or 18 years old. Many girls in Bamyan get married at 12 or 13, but they don't get pregnant until they are older. But maybe it's different in different areas. In Iran, girls would get pregnant at 10 or 12. Maybe it has to do with nutrition.

Peggy: *And the oldest women?*

Saleha: Around 40, but not older.

Peggy: *Kobra, what would you like for the midwifery school if you had the money you'd need?*

Kobra: We would hire a teacher to teach new mothers how to take care of their babies well. If we had a lot of money, we'd like to build our own building. If the landlord wants to take this building back he can, and there are no other suitable buildings in Bamyan.

Kohra

Peggy: *I have heard Herat referred to as "the self-immolation capital of the world." Why do you think the rate is higher there than elsewhere?*

Soraya: Self-immolation is not only high in Herat, but in Farah, Nimruz, and Kandahar provinces. [Except for Kandahar, these provinces border Iran.] Many women in these provinces went to Iran during the wars. There they got educated and were able to experience having their rights and freedom. Their minds were changed from the traditional way of thinking.

Then they came back to Herat and the other neighboring provinces. This area has a very fundamentalist society. There is a lot of violence against women. For many of them, it's the first time they've ever had to wear the *burqa*. It's very difficult to wear. So there is always a conflict between the society and the hope residing in the women's minds.

Peggy: It is heartbreaking that these women who grew up in Iran, who have developed their minds, experienced freedom, become aware of their rights and their personal potential, should be forced to live in a restrictive, abusive, and isolated environment. I would think that it would be easier to bear if that were all one knew...

On the other hand, nothing will ever change unless women first get awareness of their rights and an idea that their lives and society could be different. It's important for women to have the tools and the inner resources to help move themselves forward. The idea that they can make changes, even small ones, can give women the hope they need to help them overcome their depression and anger; it can give them the vision and impetus to teach their sons and daughters something different. If those who are allowed out of their houses can ally themselves with like-minded women in their village, they can encourage each other and help each other persevere. Those who had an active and educated life in Iran or elsewhere are in a position to fundamentally change Afghan society over the long run.

Soraya: During my six years working in the Iranian hospital in the early 1980s, I was assigned to the burn cases. One day an Afghan woman came in who had done self-immolation. This woman had poured benzene and oil on herself. This was a new thing among Afghans.

There is a lot of difference between life in Iran and in Afghanistan. In Iran, women are very educated and active in the civil society. Women could walk

| Saleha | Shakila | Soraya | Najia, 2003 | Ramzia |

alone in the streets because of Iran's good security. There are a lot of women's organizations working for gender equality, and Afghan women also value this.

Peggy: This is true for middle-class women who lived in the cities. Those who spent their Iran years in refugee camps may not have experienced this education and freedom nor mixed with Iranians as much.

Soraya: The relationship between husbands and wives is more egalitarian in Iran, as well. Men may not order their wives to do this or that. So when women who've experienced this come to Afghanistan to live in a village with their in-laws, they will have to get up early in the morning to cook and make tea and do all the housework. In Iran, many men will help in the kitchen and the husband and wife work together to keep the house.

But in the Afghan village, there is a mother-in-law and father-in-law and a big family. They are living like they did in the 16th or 17th century. The women who had lived in Iran were used to having everything: computers, internet, and television. Sometimes when they are watching television in their village, a show comes on and they think, "This TV character is also a woman, so why do I have to be treated like a servant?"

Shakila: Sometimes catching oneself on fire is accidental because some women don't know how to use an oven, or they must cook over an open fire. But in many cases women burn themselves on purpose. They're under a lot of pressure from their in-laws and they cannot deal with it. Sometimes in the hospital a woman will ask the nurses to do something to kill her.

Peggy: I've also read stories of men who bring in their burned wives and ask the medical staff to finish them off. Certainly, if the women were badly treated and depressed before, it would only be worse after they recover.

Kobra

Peggy: I've been trying to puzzle out the psychology behind self-immolation. Not only, *What in a woman's life would cause her to want to kill herself,* but also, *Why would they choose to do it in such a painful way?* Women under care at Herat Hospital's burn unit often weren't forthcoming about their reasons. Out of a combination of shame and fear, many women lie about how they were burned, denying that it was a suicide attempt.[6] Researchers have come up with a variety of explanations for self-immolation's increase.

Women may think that self-immolation will be a quick, sure death. "Young women especially set themselves on fire thinking that if they burn themselves then 'everyone will be kind to me.'"[7] They see it as a dramatic act, a way of crying out their emotional agony when no other way is available. Since suicide brings shame on the family, it's also a way for a woman to get back at her tormentors, especially if they have shamed her with sexual abuse or accusations against her honor. Doing any harm to one's body is forbidden in Islam, so suicide or attempted suicide is a profound statement.

One type of situation, as described by Shakila and Soraya, is the educated woman who goes from an urban environment, often in Iran, to living with her in-laws in a rural village. The woman can't deal with this change for a variety of reasons. These can include in-laws' prejudice toward the woman, who is seen as having had an easy life in exile, or the woman's prejudice towards the illiterate in-laws whom she sees as stubbornly backward. The in-laws then respond with more abuse.

Women in some forced marriages also may suffer such unbearable abuse at the hands of their husbands and/or in-laws that they can't or won't take it anymore.[8] Malcolm Garcia says, "For Afghan women, self-immolation has become a way to externalize private injustice, to push hidden pain into the public square. They are expressing a demand for human rights in a culture that does not allow them to articulate that wish."[9]

Dr. Aref Jalali[10] of Herat General Hospital's burn unit credits sexual abuse within the family as a common factor. Other times, the cause is repeated emotional and physical abuse. "Fear of their husbands is another cause." Dr. Jalali adds, "Forced marriages lead to problems and often the cause is young women forced to marry old men. They are sold, or swapped for sheep or even opium. Sometimes girls are engaged as babies to baby boys – this is common outside the cities." Most of the women Dr. Jalali sees are between 15 and 25 years old and up to 85 percent of them are impoverished, illiterate, and "unable to deal with problems within their families." In the first six months of 2010, the hospital had seen 69 cases, about the same number that was seen in all of 2009.[11]

Saleha   Shakila   Soraya   Najia, 2003   Ramzia

The real rate of self-immolation is much higher, though, because many never make it to the hospital. Faizullah Kakar, advisor to President Karzai on health affairs says, "over 2400 women kill themselves by self-immolation per year."[12] He continues, "Based on my research, depression is the main reason for self-immolation. Sexual violence, violence in in-laws' homes and many other social problems have also been regarded as the cause for suicide among women in Afghanistan."

"Selling" a daughter because one needs the money is horrific, but for a father in dire poverty, it can seem like a rational and culturally-approved temporary solution. Many times, for example, a creditor demands money to pay for the seeds from a failed crop or an eradicated opium crop. The family may be near starvation. Sometimes the bride-seller is a widow who needs to raise money to nourish her other children. More and more often, money is needed to feed an addiction to opium or heroin, since no recovery programs are generally available.

Ghulam Sakhi Kargar Noor Ogholi, a Public Health Ministry spokesman says, "The idea for Self-Immolation Day was to involve schools and mosques in a public information campaign. We must start in the schools, we must use the media and the *mullahs* at the mosques to get the message across. We need to set up centers that focus on young women, helping them learn how to deal with and solve their problems. So we set aside October 10 as Self-Immolation Day."[13]

This is a beginning, but rather than teaching women how to "deal with their problems," efforts should focus on eliminating root causes. There are already laws prohibiting marriage under the age of 16, but they will never be enforced unless there is buy-in from the local communities. Deborah Smith, in an article on forced marriages,[14] acknowledges that in many communities she studied, people were aware of problems associated with high bride prices, large age discrepancies between the husband and wife, and exchange marriages.[15] However, parents weren't necessarily free to act on this awareness unless the whole community accepted the idea of change. This awareness is an important precursor for change.

In December, 2010, the governor of Khost Province met with the Nadir Shah Kot[16] village elders and religious leaders to discuss the negative consequences of *baad*. This tradition gives a daughter from a perpetrator's family to his victim's family in recompense for a crime. After discussion, the elders and religious leaders

Kobra

all agreed to stop that practice, and also to eliminate high bride-prices in the areas they control. Since then, seven other neighboring villages have followed suit.

Educating girls increases the possibility of females contributing to the household's income honorably, lessening the poverty that sometimes leads to using wives as prostitutes.

Educating boys in gender respect would enable males to see females as human beings rather than objects or possessions, and therefore address some of the fundamental issues leading women to suicide.

Dr. Jalali has set up a research foundation called *Nejat*, meaning "rescue" in Dari, at Herat General Hospital's burn unit. He hopes that the foundation can uncover enough information to be able to help put a stop to what he calls the "horrifying increasing trend" of self-immolation in Afghanistan.

The Women's National Basketball Team practice at the Olympic gym.

9/Sports and Fitness

Imagine my surprise! Six teenaged girls in bright red uniforms were performing Taekwondo forms onstage at one of several International Women's Day events in Kabul. When it came time to demonstrate their kicks, Mosakan, their bearded instructor, walked up to hold the target paddles. I loved seeing women practicing a sport, and even more so one most often performed by men. Doing so onstage gave an excellent example for others.

When the Taekwondo players left the stage, I made a beeline after them. In their dressing room one girl, semi-fluent in English, invited me to visit their dojo. I was directed to what looked like an ordinary middle-class house compound. It was the home of the instructor, Mosakan. He and his family lived above the dojo, located in a half-underground basement. The tiny room, maybe 10 feet (3 m) wide and 30 feet (9 m) long, had rough, whitewashed walls covered with sports posters. When I arrived, eight class members were jogging around the edge of the cramped space. Soon they began working on punches, advancing along the length of the room. The girls' faces were focused and determined.

Large signs sporting scantily-clad, muscle-bound Aryan men flexing their muscles commonly advertised gyms in 2003 Kabul. In 2004, when Ismail Khan, Herat's fundamentalist governor, left his post, women's gyms began sprouting in that city. By 2010, there were maybe a dozen or so gyms in Kabul owned by and run for women, but no signs at all advertised their locations.

Kabul's Olympic stadium is infamous as the location of public executions during the Taliban era. Now it is again used for soccer matches. Buildings surrounding the stadium house training facilities for a variety of sports, among them women's Olympic teams including judo, boxing, kick-boxing, volleyball, hockey, badminton, Taekwondo, handball, soccer, and basketball. Afghans who fell in love with cricket during their Pakistan exile have formed a women's cricket team.

Najiba

Najiba was born in Kabul but spent the civil war and Taliban years in Bamyan where the fighting was less intense. In Bamyan then, there were no schools for girls except for a few run by NGOs. She was lucky to attend one of those. Their teachers were refugees who had returned from Iran. Najiba studied until seventh grade but had dropped out to help support her family. She and her family returned to Kabul in 2004 when she was 12. When we talked, she was back in school.

I really look forward to going to competitions in other countries. Maybe one day I can be a famous person and make my mother proud.

Hanifa TKD

Hanifa and her family lived in Ghazni and she studied at home during the wars and the Taliban era. They moved to Kabul in 2003 when she was 13 and in seventh grade. In 2010 she finished high school and is now preparing to go to a university.

Taekwondo forces me to work out physically. It helps keep my mind open and keeps me healthy. I believe that exercise is important to keep my health. When I found out that our teacher was encouraging women I wanted to come.

Freshta TKD

Freshta and her family lived in Iran for nine years. When the Taliban left, they came back to Kabul. She was 14 years old and in high school when we met.

The best day of my life was the day I joined this Taekwondo club.

Maihan

Maihan is a petite dynamo. Self-assured beyond her years, her rapid-fire speech shows her intelligence and high energy. We talked in the Olympic gymnasium right after basketball practice. When we finished and she went into the locker room, I could see the jovial camaraderie and respect between her and the other girls on the team.

Maihan's family went to Pakistan toward the end of the Taliban regime when she was six. They returned only a few months later when Karzai came into power. Her thirst for education led her to continually take courses in English and computers outside of school. She began playing basketball in 2006 and is now captain of the National Girls' Basketball Team. Since graduating from high school, she has worked on a medical radio program and volunteered with the **Afghan Women's Network** (AWN).

Teamwork is the best thing that I've learned because teamwork develops unity, and unity can be in every part of our life. It's the most important thing.

Kobra M

I first met Kobra in the fitness center at the Women's Garden. This eight-acre woman-only oasis, developed in the 1940s and 1950s under King Zahir Shah, was closed by the Taliban and used as a dump. It looked rather shabby and barren in March, 2010, but about 30 women were enjoying its sanctuary as their kids played on the swings and slides. Small groups of women congregated, some with picnic snacks, others walking and talking.

The garden closed again soon after my visit and reopened seven months later with 5000 freshly-planted rose bushes. In a few years 3500 new trees will screen women from the view of onlookers in near-by high rise apartments.

This haven also includes women-owned shops, a kindergarten, restaurant, mosque, computer lab, job training center, and basketball court. Kobra opened the Garden's fitness center in 2005. After a brief tour of the facility, she and I made an agreement to meet later at her gym.

Exercise and sports has helped me avoid going to the doctor for my back problems and gives me hope that I can continue my vigorous life. Because of sports and exercise, I stay far away from illness.

Tucked away in a quiet, tree-lined neighborhood, one would never guess that a school and gym lay beyond the unpretentious blue metal gate. Kobra guided me past her office and around the crowded courtyard to a large room that had been converted into a gym. She showed me a row of exercise machines lining the walls as a teacher led six students in aerobics.

| Najiba | Hanifa TKD | Freshta TKD | Maihan | Kobra M |

Both of Kobra's parents were educated. She loved sports as a child and played whenever she got the chance. She earned a university degree in history and philosophy. While still in college she had the idea to open gyms for women, but her dream was put on hold when the Taliban came. She and her family moved to Pakistan until Karzai took office. Back in Kabul, she opened her first gym in 2005. Currently she has ten gyms in Kabul and one each in Herat and Mazar-e Sharif. She also helps train Afghanistan's women's Olympic volleyball and gymnastics teams.

How did your parents feel about your playing sports?

Kobra: My parents were both educated and encouraged me to exercise and keep strong. When I was young I used to play badminton, but when I grew older I didn't have much chance to exercise. I began to get sick a lot but once I started to exercise again on a regular basis, I stayed healthy. My husband is happy about this because I'm stronger and healthier and don't have to go to the doctor all the time. He supports me a lot.

Hanifa TKD: My friend and my brother don't like me to study Taekwondo, and sometimes I face some difficulties with them. But I have the encouragement of my mother and father and I really want to come.

Najiba: My family is happy that I study here but when I began asking around to find a Taekwondo club to join, people made fun of me. Now, it's more normal for girls go to the club as well as the boys. First I found a club that charged money, but I couldn't afford it. Then I found this one, which is free for girls.

Maihan: At first my parents were a little worried about it because of the environment. People in our society don't understand that a girl might want to play sports, so at first they were worried, but right now they're very proud of me. My younger sister is also the captain of her football [soccer] team.

Peggy: *Have you ever played outside of Afghanistan?*

Maihan: Peace Through Sports took me to Jordan for 15 days and I was a youth delegate to the UK for an exchange program a few years ago. In 2009, I went to Washington DC to participate in a basketball training program.

Peggy: *What is the most important part about sports for you?*

Maihan: Sports teaches teamwork. It also teaches you how to deal with sad things because sometimes you lose and you have to learn to be a good sport. Sometimes other things make me too sad to talk about them so I just play basketball. It is one game that you can play by yourself or with a team. Playing makes me focus so that I forget about my sadness or depression or anything else. It improves me both mentally and physically and it gives me more energy.

Peggy: *What has basketball taught you?*

Maihan: There are a lot of things I've learned from basketball. It's important to give love and respect for each other. The respect that we have for each other on the team and the teamwork is a really important part of life. I especially learned teamwork when we trained in the US. Teamwork brings unity and unity can be useful in every part of our life.

Peggy: One of the more discouraging things I saw in Afghanistan was disunity among women working for the same goals. An organizer of the Shia Personal Status Law demonstration told me that she'd invited one woman to participate who answered that if THAT (a third) woman was going to be a part of it, she wasn't interested. When I asked one woman (whom I deeply respect) for contact information for another, she told me not to interview that person, not to listen to her, because "she causes a lot of trouble."

After years of struggle for one's own existence, the survival of one's family, one's tribe, one's ethnic group, it's natural that people would think of their own needs first. However, that works to the detriment of individual women and also the greater society.

Peggy: *What has studying Taekwondo taught you?*

Najiba: Today is only my second class. Before this, I trained by myself at home. In these two classes, I've learned about the braveness of women.

Najiba | Hanifa TKD | Freshta TKD | Maihan | Kobra M

Freshta TKD: I love learning the Kendo and techniques. During the war years, girls did not have the freedom to play Taekwondo. Our teacher taught me and all the students that women are brave.

Peggy: *Kobra, how many students do you have in the academic part of your school and how many come to the gym?*

Kobra: We have 600 students who study academics and 45 who come to the gym. We teach English, holy *Quran*, mathematics, and sewing. The students pay a fee for every class, but for the gym they pay about A500 [$10] per month. I offer one fitness class per day and they can work on the machines anytime they like. But without the academic and sewing classes, I couldn't afford to keep the gym open.

Peggy: *What do you advise your students regarding fitness?*

Kobra: First I advise them to work under the Islamic framework. Secondly, I tell them to get an education but also not neglect sports and fitness. Part of the problem is that most women are working at home and eating oily or unhealthy foods. So I tell them not to eat those things, or if they are served at a specific holiday to limit how much they eat.

Peggy: *Hanifa, when you were living in Ghazni did you find a way to exercise?*

Hanifa TKD: No. During the Taliban we were stuck in the house and there was no one to teach us or lead a class. We couldn't exercise in our compounds because sometimes the Taliban could see into our yard.

Peggy: *I know those times were very difficult, but did you learn something from that?*

Hanifa TKD: The only thing I learned from it was the importance of women's education and women's freedom. It made me more determined to study and to help women.

Peggy: *When you have difficulties, how do you help yourself feel better?*

Freshta TKD: When I'm sad or discouraged I come to the class. If it isn't class time, I do other exercises.

Hanifa TKD: I look for other situations. I try hard not to give up, and I keep on trying. I tell myself that maybe I can't do this thing, but I can do that one.

Najiba: Those people who have power over me make me discouraged so I keep silent in front of them so they won't harm me. For those who can't harm me, I will struggle with them.

Peggy: *What has been the best part of your life so far?*

Maihan: Everyone has good and bad things in their life, but what I love is playing basketball and playing for the national team. I'm working hard to make my people proud of our country. Besides, I've found lots of good people here playing basketball and have made some very good friends.

Peggy: *What do you see for the future?*

Kobra: I have confidence that my gyms have a bright future because I started with just two women, and now we have 500 in all of my gyms. A lot of gyms are opening around the city. This means that more people are becoming aware of gyms for women.

Before, most men were against this gym and didn't allow their wives to come. Now, however, they're getting used to the idea, especially when they see the health benefits for their wives. And so they changed their minds. When women get together in one place, they can talk and they come up with new ideas, so there's a community that builds around the gym.

In general, women aren't very interested in exercise. But these days women are getting more encouragement, so now when they have back problems they come to build their bodies. Then they go outside and talk with other people. That encourages both of them. But still many women face problems with their families. When they come here and talk about problems with their families around their going to the gym, they see that they are not alone.

Maihan: For myself, I want to finish my studies in computer science or information technology. A Finnish NGO trained me to do photojournalism and I hope to make that my career. With that training and my experience with the

Najiba   Hanifa TKD   Freshta TKD   Maiban   Kobra M

radio station, I hope to find a good job to help my people and my family.

I think that the first thing Afghanistan needs is real unity. This means showing respect and not lying and cheating people anymore. This means talking and then bringing our speech into action.

Freshta TKD: I want to finish school and become a doctor. And besides studying I want to continue my classes in Taekwondo and work with that.

Hanifa TKD: The women in Ghazni Province still don't have the right to work or study, but we, the new generation, are trying our best to take our rights back and get our freedom. We are working for Afghanistan to provide all those necessities for women that they don't have now.

Peggy: *In what ways are you doing that now?*

Hanifa TKD: The first thing I'm doing to help Afghanistan is to get myself educated. The second is that I'm working with some organizations that help women. In my job I have to walk door-to-door looking for women who need help. That forces me to exercise.

Peggy: *How does Taekwondo fit into this?*

Hanifa TKD: Taekwondo helps me keep my mind open and keeps me healthy. Exercise is very important to keeping our health. The second thing is that our teacher is encouraging women. That's why I joined this club. I also want to carry Afghanistan's flag in other countries, in international competitions.

Peggy: *What gives you the most hope for the future of Afghanistan?*

Kobra: I think the most important thing right now is changing the view of sports in Afghanistan because every day athletes are winning gold medals and championships. I hope that we can do something good through sports at least.

Peggy: *What do you see for your own future?*

Hanifa TKD: This year, I finished school and took the TOEFL test. [Test of English as a Foreign Language]. I want to go to a foreign university but my score wasn't high enough. But I'm planning to take some courses and take the test again. I really want to study law. So I'm continuing my education, and meanwhile I help organizations do fundraising. My hope is to finish my law education so I can support women's freedom and talk about women's rights in the provinces.

Najiba: I want to finish my education and help solve my family's financial problems. God is great, and he will help me finish my education and come to the position where I should be. I'm looking forward to being able to compete in other countries and become a famous person and make my mother proud. *Insha'alla.*

Peggy: *What can women in the West do to support Afghan women playing sports?*

Maihan: As you can see, Afghanistan is not yet in the position that we should be regarding sports. We still have a lot of problems here, but most of them are social problems that girls face every day. All of the girls' families are worried about their daughters arriving safely here to the Olympic training area, so I think we need a transportation system that will bring us here and safely back home.

Another thing that I think would help a lot is to have more exchange programs for the athletes. That way they can learn drills and new techniques. They will also be able to understand lots of other things about other countries' cultures. This can also teach them about their own country. The new president of the national Olympic Committee is supporting all the teams very well so we will see what happens.

Peggy: *What would you like to say to women in the West?*

Maihan: I would just like to thank all those who are supporting Afghan teams. Afghan girls and women in all parts of the country participate in a lot of exchange programs and I want to give appreciation for their work and their future support.

Hanifa TKD: Women in foreign countries can help by supporting institutes to teach Afghan women vocations. These kinds of programs can financially help women.

Kobra: I really need support for my gyms. My dream is to make them bigger because sometimes it gets very crowded. It would be good to have new sports technology. On the north side of Kabul there are no gyms for women. My dream is to open a bigger place with different areas for football, volleyball, and an athletic center. I can't do this without the support of an organization. Most women can't afford higher fees.

Peggy: I was very impressed with Kobra and her determination. When she asked if I knew anyone who could help her, I recommended that she go to American University's 10,000 Women program for help with her business plan and possibly with funding sources. I heard that she went all the way across town to visit them that very afternoon.

I was surprised by the acceptance of male instructors for girls. Maihan's basketball coach and the Taekwondo coach were men. Kobra had a male math teacher in her gym-school. In every case, the particular man made a big difference. Men can earn the right to teach girls if they have a good reputation, treat them respectfully, and maintain propriety.

Other factors also come into play. For one, families who allow their girls to play sports tend to be more educated and have more liberal ideas than those who don't. For another, many of the dojo students and their parents had spent a decade or longer in urban areas of Pakistan or Iran, where there was often more gender mixing. In the dojo, both teacher and students were from the Hazara ethnic group, slightly more liberal and often more open to mixed gender activities than others. One may also note that the Hazara appear physically different from other Afghans. They are therefore more vulnerable to persecution and harassment for being Shia than the Pashtun or other Shia. Hazara girls' parents more readily encourage their study of martial arts.

Training in Mosakan's dojo

The Male Instructor: Mosakan

Afghan society is very segregated by gender. Women in conservative families are not allowed any contact with men outside their immediate family. In public elementary schools, children attend class with boys on one side of the classroom and girls on the other. But by the time girls reach puberty, they must be in all-girls' classes taught only by women. There are exceptions. One was Mosakan, who had been sought out by some girls' parents to teach their teenaged daughters Taekwondo. Another was the math teacher in Kobra's gym/school. Maihan's Olympic basketball coach was also a man.

Mosakan lives with his family above his dojo and his students reside in his neighborhood. People already knew and respected him because their boys studied Taekwondo under him. The fact that his students, both girls and boys, sometimes come home with cash prizes and that his classes for girls are free makes a difference as well. On the basketball team, the players came from different ethnic groups, but being Olympians

Last year, 11 girls [whom I'd trained] went to foreign countries and they came back with medals that they won for their country.

carried a lot of respectability and prestige. In Kobra's case, she and her school have a good reputation and the male teacher is from a respectable family. Kobra would ultimately be held responsible, however, if something bad were to happen.

What makes the bigger difference is that all of the students and players were female. Most would probably not be allowed to play on a mixed team, nor after puberty study in a mixed class. On the other hand, university classes and many private courses are mixed.

Mosakan was a quiet, gentle man who welcomed me into his dojo and encouraged the girls there to talk with me. When I asked him how people in the West could help him, with a mixture of pride and slight bitterness he said that he doesn't need outside help anymore. When he needed it, no one would help him, but now he has all that he needs.

Peggy: *Mosakan, how did you get involved in Taekwondo?*

Mosakan: I was 14 years old when I left Ghazni Province and went to Iran. It was at the beginning of the Soviet war. There I played football and started studying Taekwondo. But seeing the hard time my mother and sisters had, my only feeling was for women and how hard their lives are. So I dedicated myself to helping them. I wanted to make something for women that could take them out of the hardship of life. That's why I started these classes for girls.

When I first came to Kabul, I started teaching boys. One night while we were training, two girls came and said that they wanted classes as well. I told them that they had to talk with their families and the families should come and talk with me. The fathers came and asked me to teach their daughters. That's how it started.

The following year, Olympic training began in Kabul. I talked with the Olympic supervisor and they agreed to interview my girl students. Eventually, with the help of television and newspapers, I got 200 female students to come here for training. Most of these are now going out for competition internationally. I've trained 750 students and 200 of them are girls. They are from 12 to 18 years old.

Peggy: *What benefits do you see from women practicing Taekwondo?*

Mosakan: First, it helps them study better. Second, it helps them be in better condition so they won't get tired from housework. Third, it makes them stronger when they are pregnant. Fourth, it gives them the idea that they can defend themselves if they must. And fifth, it allows them to go outside of Afghanistan, so they can see how other people face their hardships. It gives them confidence.

The problem is that many of my students come from poor families and can't pay any fees. So I made the club free for girls. I earn enough money from the boys to support my family.

Peggy: *What advice do you give your students to help them?*

Mosakan: I teach my students how to face the difficulties of life, how to challenge others, challenge themselves, and I teach them how to face a situation that looks impossible. And second, I teach them that exercise can help them financially. President Karzai gave the three students who won medals in the free fight competition about A100,000 [$2000] each. He also promised them more facilities for more training.

Peggy: *Where do you see these women and your training facility in five years?*

Mosakan: I think that in five years all of my students will be great women in this country and their bravery will be a source of pride for our nation.

For my dojo, I don't need help from others. My students are strong enough to stand by themselves and be proud for the nation and proud of their class. The time when I needed help, no one came to help us. I had some problems in this area; some of my neighbors and the *mullahs* were not letting me teach the girls.

Peggy: *So how did you deal with that?*

Mosakan: I had a big argument with the neighbors and the *mullah*. Then I sent one of my students to bring the *mullah*'s daughter into the class. When she reported back to her father about the class, he stopped saying bad things and let her continue.

A woman surveys the scene much as Bibi must have watched for her brothers from her rooftop

10/The Elderly

Afghan lives revolve around the family. Traditionally, elders are respected and given an important role in family decision-making. They are taken care of within the families until they pass away. Not only would it be shameful to send an elderly relative off to a retirement or nursing home, but no such places exist. While the average life expectancy is now 48 years old according to the World Bank,[1] people regularly live into their 70s and 80s.

I heard three very distinct life stories from Bibijan, Bibi, and Sakina. *Bibi* means "wise" and *jan,* attached to the end of a person's name, means "dear." It is often used respectfully to mean "Grandma," but some young people are nicknamed Bibi as well. It's interesting that, try as I might, I never learned the given names of either of the two Bibis, but Sakina was only referred to by her given name. It might be because the Bibis were Pashtun and Sakina, Hazara. It might be because I was introduced to the Bibis by their family members and Sakina introduced herself. Age might make a difference as well. At the time I interviewed each of them, Bibi was the eldest at 85; Bibijan was 75; and Sakina, 60. Since then, Bibi and Bibijan have both died.

Bibijan

I saw Bibijan sitting on a cushion in the corner of a hallway when I came out of an interview with her niece. She seemed to be in a world of her own. I had my translator ask if we might talk with her and she agreed. Bibijan was a sad and bitter woman, raised by a harsh, conservative father who married her to a cruel, vindictive husband. She passed away in 2005 at the age of 77.

Bibijan's pain and hopelessness showed in every one of my photographs of her even though she had spent the past 25 years living in a home where she was treated kindly and cared for well.

When Bibijan was young, she lived with her mother and her mother's co-wife. Her mother was the first wife, and since the second wife didn't have any children, Bibijan had to do chores for both women. When she was born, her father promised her to another powerful man's young son, whom she married when she turned 13.

For me, my only good time was working with the cows. At that time, I was the most free.

Bibi

I met Bibi while she was living in her nephew's house. I had come to interview the nephew's wife but he wouldn't allow it. He permitted me to interview Bibi, however. When we finished, he requested that I also photograph his six-year-old daughter. I agreed, and he arranged her in seductive poses that he must have seen in fashion magazines.

Bibi was the oldest child of five brothers and two sisters in a very wealthy family in Charbagh, a village outside of Jalalabad. Her father owned the entire village as well as a sugar production factory that processed the sugar cane they grew.

Their wealth earned them numerous enemies, especially within their own family, as different factions of uncles and cousins tried to wrest land from Bibi's father. Bibi had a strong personality and controlled her household, even as a young woman while both of her parents were alive. Neither Bibi nor her sister ever married because they and their father wanted to avoid marriage into the family of an especially cruel uncle who was after their land.

I was very happy when my brothers, sisters, and I were together and my parents were alive. But the time when I was most happy was when my first brother got married.

Sakina

I met Sakina with six other refugees who came to my translator's home to be interviewed. She stood out from the younger women in that she looked me in the eye with engaging assertiveness and sparkle, despite her illiteracy and grinding poverty.

Sakina grew up in Wardak Province where her father was a sharecropper. Although he farmed, they often went hungry. Her father died when she was young, but her older brothers *were like a father* to her. At 16, she was married to her cousin and in spite of their poverty, she has had a good marriage with him.

The life of us poor people is just trying to find something to eat. We have to sit and pray for God to give us something. I tried to get some work cleaning houses, but most people say I'm too old.

Peggy: *What was your life like when you were young?*

Sakina: My father was a farmer on land owned by other people. Sometimes I helped my family in the fields. We grew onions, wheat, and potatoes.

Bibijan: When I was young, I lived with Mother and her co-wife. Father was a strong man and we kids were afraid of him. He beat us a lot.

He was a *khan* [a wealthy land owner and village leader], so he married me to a *malik* [an elected official who represents the village to the government]. When I lived at my father-in-law's house, he never let me go out to visit my mother or friends. When I went to work in the orchard or with the cows, I had to wear *duloq* [pants with a huge, high waist and tight ankles]. I wore the *duloq* over the light-weight embroidered trousers that I wore around the house. Over that I'd have to wear a big cotton burqa that went to the ground all the way around. I could hardly walk wearing all that. My job was to care for the cows, and there were a lot because my husband was rich.

Bibi: My cousins and uncle were always trying to steal our land. Our fields and the sugar cane factory were far away from our house. Once when my brothers were coming home, I was on the roof and saw my cousins waiting for them. I shouted out, which scared my cousins, and it saved my brothers because the cousins didn't want a witness. I went out to meet my brothers and walked them back home.

Peggy: Najia, my translator, told me that Bibi worked like two men.

So, what happened that you and your sister never married?

Bibi: My worst uncle was a very cruel man. If someone's cow wandered into his pasture, he would cut the tongue out of the cow's mouth. He was very jealous of my father, who had inherited their father's land. It is customary that if a man dies in the presence of his son, that son doesn't inherit anything from him. My uncle was present when their father died, so my father inherited most of the land. My uncle got some, but he wanted more. After that, he kept trying to kill my father, but he couldn't.

My cousins all wanted to marry me so they could get some of the inheritance from my brothers. But I loved my brothers and wanted them to have it. If I'd

Bibijan   *Bibi*   *Sakina*

married anyone outside the family, my uncle would have just killed him. So we decided that it would be better if my sister and I never married.

My mother was a simple woman. My father died when I was 26 or 27 and after that my uncle would come and beat my brothers while they were out working the land. They were only 14 and 16 at the time, so I would go into the fields to confront him. When I was there, my uncle would have to stop because I was a witness to him beating a child. Finally, he got sick for a year and died. After that it was better.

Peggy: *What are some of your happiest memories?*

Bibi: I only liked working with the cows. We milked the cows and made yogurt.

Bibijan: The only time I was ever happy was when I was working with the cows. After I married, I worked in my husband's orchards and fields. We grew apples, melons, and grapes. Working there allowed me to get out of the house but I was never allowed to go into the village. I liked working with the cows best. My father gave me a cow as a wedding present. It was my own cow, but my husband returned it to my father and told him that he didn't want it.

Sakina: When I was working in an Iranian family's house it was a good time. We lived with them and were able to save some money. We bought some carpets and other things for our room. The Iranian lady was nice to us.

Peggy: *What were some of your hardest times and how did you help yourself deal with it?*

Bibijan: Nothing. I could do nothing. My husband gave our 10-year-old daughter to his friend and took his friend's 20-year-old daughter for a second wife. After that, he beat me all the time because he got married to another woman. He never let me go out and all I did was work from morning to night.

It was also very hard when I just married. I was only 13 and still needed my mother. But when I married, I moved to a different village and my husband never let me visit her. He also never let me visit my daughter or see my grandson.

Peggy: Marriage swaps such as this allow both parties to avoid paying a bride price, which can be very expensive. If a boy grows up and is unhappy with his father's choice of bride, he will often take it out on his wife and later marry someone he chooses.

Bibijan's daughter didn't give birth until she was 17. In some cases when the bride is just a child, she will live like an adopted child until she reaches puberty. Other times the bride just doesn't get pregnant until she's older, sometimes due to malnutrition rather than abstention on her husband's part.

Peggy: *What wisdom do you have for us younger people?*

Bibi: I tell my brother's grandchildren to be good to their husbands and brothers and to be good under Islam. The one thing that helps me in Islam is never lying. When I pray, I feel I can see everything.

Peggy: *What is your situation now?*

Bibi: I didn't get married because I loved my brothers. When I was young I worked a lot in the fields with them. Now that I'm old, nobody likes me very much. I like my brother's son and he's good to me. I love him more than my other nephews.

Bibijan: After my husband had been married to his second wife for a while, I left him and went to live with my brother. I was 25 or 26 at the time and I had to work very hard to earn my keep. After five or six years, my husband's second wife died and he wanted me to come back, but I refused to go, so he went to live with his children from the other wife. Later, I lived with my daughter, but now I sometimes live with my nephew. Two years ago when my husband was very sick and about to die, his children didn't notify me to come and help. I didn't see him before he died.

Sakina: Now I am living in a tent with my husband and my three sons. Our camp has 15 families so it's very crowded. My husband is blind now so sometimes he sits on a corner and begs or sometimes he takes a bottle of shoe polish and sits on the street. He can earn A10-20 [20-40 cents] by polishing someone's shoes. Sometimes I do washing for people. [But] we Hazaras often get harassed by the Pashtuns because they're more powerful than we are and they are the majority in our camp.

Campaign posters for parliamentary candidates, 2010.

11/Parliamentary Women

King Amanullah gave women the vote in 1923, just three years after American women won that right. Unfortunately, he was overthrown six years later and women were again excluded from voting. **King Zahir Shah** established a new constitution in 1964 reinstituting women's suffrage as well as their right to political participation. A female Afghan representative was sent to the United Nations in 1958 and women joined the *Wolesi Jerga* in 1965.

Running for parliament or any public office requires courage and sTamima from anyone. Afghan women driven to run because they want to make changes in women's lives sometimes put themselves and their families in grave danger.

The 2001 Bonn Agreement[1] called for a 2002 emergency *Loya Jerga* and chose **Hamid Karzai** as President of the transitional administration. He won the national election in 2004. Candidates included Massouda Jalal, the first Afghan woman to run for president. Parliamentary election rules require that a minimum of 25% of Members be women. In fact, women won 28% of the seats in 2005 and 2010. In the September, 2010 elections, 400 of 2500 total candidates were women.

Many candidates for Parliament run independently of the eight major and twelve minor political parties. Each woman in this chapter ran independently because she wanted to be free from obligations to follow a party platform that would likely endorse an anti-women ideology.

Before I left Afghanistan in May, 2010, campaign posters of male and female candidates were again appearing on walls everywhere. All featured photographs of serious, dour-faced contenders. When I offered to photograph some women candidates as a donation to their campaigns, they also insisted on looking stern.

Malalai Joya
Former Member of Parliament, Farah Province

When Malalai began a 2006 speaking tour, I flew to California and met her for an interview. I knew she must have great internal fortitude to confront hardened warlords in front of 240 *Loya Jerga* members. She seemed a bit timid when we first met, but after speaking with me for a few moments, she warmed up and her inner passion burst forth.

I want to expose those enemies, those warlords who are against women's rights, against human rights, and against peace, security, and democracy... They may destroy a thousand flowers, but they can never stop the spring.

Malalai's family fled to camps in Iran and then Pakistan after a landmine blew off her father's leg during a *mujahidin* mission against the Soviets. Malalai studied in RAWA schools in a Pakistani refugee camp.[2] When she was 19, the Organization for Promoting Afghan Women's Capabilities (OPAWC)[3] hired her to set up underground schools in Herat, still under Taliban control. After the Taliban left, she was given responsibility for overseeing education and health programs in Herat, Farah, and Nimruz provinces. She became very well-known and respected, so she was easily elected to the Constitutional *Loya Jerga*, and later to Parliament. She now travels around the world speaking about conditions facing Afghan women. She co-authored a book about her experiences.[4]

Shinkai Karokhail

Member of Parliament, Kabul Province

Shinkai won a seat in Parliament in September, 2005, and was reelected in 2010. Her most important victory was amending the Shia Personal Status Law. Although it only applied to the Shia Muslim population, she knew that its un-amended passage would eventually affect all Afghan women. She is married and has four children.

I'm not fond of politics, but I agreed because I think we cannot do anything without politics. You have to be part of it. I don't belong to a political party, so I had to create my own political identity.

Sahera Sharif

Member of Parliament, Khost Province Member of Parliament,

Just going to see Sahera was an ordeal. The security guards at the Parliament compound examined and scrutinized me and my belongings multiple times. After all that, we couldn't find a suitable space for the interview, so we went to an office outside the compound. Two hours into our conversation it was lunch time. Some men set up platters of grilled chicken, rice, French fries, and a cucumber salad and invited us to enjoy the meal.

It is my opinion that the conservative male MPs are forced to work with women. They don't want to work with us. They only sit next to a woman because the government forces them. Their actions have changed but their ideas haven't. Those old mujahidin are conservative people who can't change their ideas.

Malalai   *Shinkai, 2010*   *Sahera*

Peggy: *What led to your running for Parliament?*

Sahera: When the time came for the parliamentary election, UNAMA [The UN Assistance Mission in Afghanistan] were worried that they didn't have any women to elect. So I decided to run and I encouraged other women. In the end, there were ten of us.

I had trained those women without thinking that I would be competing with them. I always thought that if I can't win, at least there should be other people to defend the rights of the women.

Shinkai Kaokhail: It wasn't my choice to run actually. My friends forced me to run.

Things are not going very well for women and sometimes you get the feeling that most people who say they are working for change are not very sincere. Many of them are only committed to themselves and how to secure their own personal future.

I decided to become a member of the budgeting committee because that is the best way to help the people of Afghanistan, especially the women. The budget controls everything. After a three-year struggle, last year I finally succeeded in putting one line in the budget for gender issues and to repeat that lump sum amount for gender promotion. It's not a huge amount of money, but it's a success and for me it was important.

I always try to remind our politicians, the ministers, and the government that women have a voice, and they can raise their voice and claim their rights. This was the reason I went to the budgeting committee. Otherwise, the budget is very boring. [She laughs.] Everyone is surprised that I'm not working for the Women's Affairs Commission, as if that is the only thing women can do. It's good to show them something different.

Malalai: I didn't want to run, but many people asked me to be a candidate. We saw how the warlords found their way into Parliament by cheating. They also used millions of dollars of foreign support, some of which they got from corruption. I thought, I am only one person, but the Parliament will be better if I am there. I also saw that I should expose these enemies [the warlords] and how they found their way into the Parliament.

Peggy: *Malalai, where did your name come from?*

Malalai: I was named after Malalai of Maiwan. She became a heroine of our country when we were fighting the second war against the British in 1880. She was at the front helping the wounded when the flag bearer was killed. She took up his flag and led the discouraged men back into battle. She was killed, but we won that battle.

My name gives me hope, strength, and inspiration. My people recognize my struggle and understand it. I put my life at risk for them and speak for those who have no power. I'm really proud of my parents, too, because they never compromised with the communists or the warlords.

Peggy: *And they taught you never to compromise...*

Malalai: Yes, and they support me because they saw that I chose the true path; there is no personal benefit for my family or for myself.

Peggy: Malalai became famous for speaking out against the warlords during the Constitutional *Loya Jerga*. She had been given three minutes to talk, but her microphone was cut off after a minute and a half. Pandemonium broke out among the members while she was asking, "How can we have a democracy when there are warlords and criminals in the government?"

The United Nations had called this *Loya Jerga* to ratify a new constitution and determine the future of Afghanistan. Malalai felt it very important to expose the elephant in the room that Afghans could already see. Her short speech was aimed at the people and organizations funding Afghanistan's reconstruction, making them publicly aware of just who was creating and controlling the new government. Her critique subsequently resulted in her being banned from addressing that gathering. She was elected to Parliament two years later, receiving the second-highest vote total of all candidates, male or female, in Farah Province, but Parliament eventually banned her from being an MP for her outspokenness.

Peggy: *What else did you say in your speech to the* Loya Jerga?

Malalai: I said that they had killed a lot of innocent people in our country and [had] turned our country into the nucleus of national and international wars.

Peggy: *It must have been scary to stand in front of those powerful men at the age of 24!*

Malalai   Shinkai, 2010   Sabera

Malalai: Yes, my heart was beating fast, but when I tell the truth I am never afraid. I am a freedom-loving woman. I want to serve my people. I will never compromise with warlords. After every speech or interview I receive many threats, but I also get lots of support from my people all around Afghanistan.

My life now is completely changed. After I gave that speech in the *Loya Jerga*, I have to wear a *burqa* whenever I go out. The fundamentalists attacked my office and they tried to kill me, but innocent people, mainly shopkeepers, neighbors, and some soldiers came and defended me. I get threats through my mobile phone and my website.[5] Sometimes they put letters on my door telling me that unless I stop struggling they will kidnap, rape, and kill me.

Shinkai: I am never afraid of people or politicians. Maybe it's not good, but I have that kind of nature. I'm not a very good politician. Even with the warlords, I just say openly what the Afghan women want.

Peggy: *What have been your legislative successes?*

Shinkai: After 18 months of work in Parliament and a demonstration, we changed 50 articles in the Shia Personal Status Law, and we got a line item for gender in the budget. We forced the President to introduce three women into the cabinet and we created the Parliamentary Women's Network so that women in Parliament can have a common voice. We struggled for three years and finally Karzai signed a law prohibiting violence against women. We did it.

But the problem is that it's only a law. If it is practiced in our country and people come to understand the strengths and weaknesses of it, then they will support it. If it is just imposed, the people won't follow it. I was once told that the courts aren't even using it. Some courts in Herat are, but most lawyers don't, not even defense lawyers. But if we publicize the law, slowly the courts will begin to implement it. If we don't, women will still think that it's their destiny or their husbands' right to beat, torture, or even kill them.

We have had some success and it reminds men inside or outside the Parliament that women are the reality of this country. Like it or not, they cannot go on without us. Maybe they won't like this, but finally they should accept it.

Peggy: *How many fundamentalists are in the Parliament?*

Shinkai: There are different types of people in the Parliament. Some are very traditional guys who don't know anything about religion, or they misunderstand our religion and believe that their understanding is the only correct one. Some don't want to lose their [female] servants and their power. Others are very selfish and cruel and not only want to have control, but also want to torture women… Believe me, we have some sick minds here. They want to return women to their homes. They will never agree with women who want to make their own choices. These people by nature don't want to support us.

Peggy: *So how much of Parliament consists of these kinds of guys?*

Shinkai: It depends. Sometimes 50%, sometimes 80%, and sometimes 20%, but in reality, they are the majority. Sometimes the illiterate guy,[6] the traditional guy, the commander, and the *mullah* all come together, but other times their interests differ. I'm sure that for women's issues we can find 40% of parliamentary men for our cause. Different women will work for themselves and we can't always count on their support, while some men help us a lot.

Peggy: *Why don't more women in Parliament support women's rights? Surely it affects their own well-being and that of their daughters.*

Shinkai: A big part of the answer lies in the election process. For one, it's difficult and expensive to run a parliamentary campaign. If a woman wants to win a seat, she often needs the support of a political party or a wealthy patron. Then, of course, she is not an independent agent, able to vote as she wishes, but must vote as her backers dictate.

There is a blacklist for elections to prohibit certain powerful men with abominable human rights records from running, but there is nothing prohibiting their wives from doing so. Of course, those wives vote as their husbands dictate.

Also, years of "divide and conquer" tactics used throughout all of the wars have left their mark even among women, creating suspicions between different ethnicities, social classes, and tribal groups.

When I first entered the Parliament, my expectations of women were very high. I was thinking that with unity among women, we could force some good changes. In fact, we were able to appoint one woman as a Deputy Speaker. But in the end, that same lady did a lot of damage by basing her actions on ethnicity.

Another time we were working on the structure of the government to improve gender issues inside the Ministry of Finance. When our proposal was rejected and one of the MPs began to insult me, the entire group of women got up and left. It was a good experience of solidarity. Now, we have formed the Parliamentary

Malalai   Shinkai, 2010   Sahera

Women's Network so that women can have a common voice, but in Parliament, men support my work more than the women do.

Peggy: *How do you think the rights of women can be preserved if or when members of the Taliban are in the government?*

Sahera: There will not be peace if we do not negotiate with the Taliban, so the question is really how can we preserve the rights of women through these negotiations? In the negotiations there must be one condition: that they accept the Constitution.

Our Constitution says a lot of things about the rights of women and men. If it didn't, the foreign people would not be with us. So even with their ideas against women, the Taliban can't do anything against us. They can carry out their ideas on their own women, but not on the country's women. Even though they cannot step on the faces of women, they will still try to oppress us.

Malalai: The thing our people need even more than water and food is security. When there is no security, how can we talk about women's rights, human rights, democracy, the Constitution, peace, or anything? Do you know why there is no fundamental change in the situation, not only for women, but for everyone? It's because of the warlords. Now the Northern Alliance is more powerful. But they are the brothers of the Taliban; they learned how to wear suits and ties and how to talk about democracy and women's rights. These warlords committed many crimes against humanity, but now they have changed their faces. They never believed in democracy.

Unfortunately, the US and their allies replaced the Taliban with the Northern Alliance; that is, with other criminals and warlords. With the Northern Alliance in power, we cannot bring peace and democracy. We cannot carry out the UN DDR program. [Disarmament, Demobilization and Reconstruction]. The warlords have a lot of guns and they have the support of our neighboring countries that have bloody hands in the history of Afghanistan.

Peggy: *Pakistan?*

Malalai: Yes, and Iran. Even now, some of their agents are here in Afghanistan and unfortunately, some are Afghans. They are being used. Those countries are against [Afghan] unity because they each want to dominate Afghanistan.

Peggy (in 2006): *If you could talk with US President George W. Bush, what would you say to him?*

Malalai: I would tell him to stop the support of criminals and tested warlords.[7] The warlords don't believe in democracy, and because the West has brought them to power, Afghans are suspicious of this "war on terrorism." Please change this policy.

I would also tell him, "You should think about the innocent people in Afghanistan who are tired of fighting. They hate guns and warlords, and they need security, education, and democracy. We need the help of foreign countries, but not by the way of warlords."

Peggy (in 2010): *What would you say to US President Barack Obama?*

Shinkai: First, do not deal with Afghanistan through Pakistan or through the eyes of Pakistanis. Don't ignore women. And I would tell him that he should ask the Afghan government how much money goes to women's issues. I'm not approving the mistakes that Americans have made in this country, but on the other hand, it's good for them to help protect this country from invasion by Iran and Pakistan.

Peggy: *So are you saying that you want America to have a long-term military involvement in Afghanistan?*

Shinkai: Yes, but not only to focus on and invest in bringing more troops. The cost of one American soldier is 70 times more than the cost of one Afghan soldier. Bring American soldiers only to help Afghan troops and help us develop our army with quality training and equipment. Aircraft and armed vehicles should be given to Afghans so fewer Americans would lose their lives in this territory and the Afghans can help themselves. So, for some time, the American presence is necessary, not only to help with security, but to help us develop our country.

Peggy: In Malalai's book[8] she wrote, "Often people say that when the foreign troops withdraw, a civil war will break out. [But] the longer they stay in Afghanistan doing what they are doing today, the worse that eventual civil war will be for the Afghan people.

"The biggest beneficiaries of the conflict have been the extremist groups who take advantage of the grievances against NATO. Rather than destroying these fundamentalist forces, the bombing and occupation of Afghanistan have added

Malalai   Shinkai, 2010   Sahera

fuel to their fire and swollen their ranks."

What kind of help do you believe Afghanistan needs?

Malalai: In our situation now, the people really need the help of the foreign community, not only the US, but also all countries that want to bring democracy to Afghanistan. But if they want to bring real democracy, they need to change their policies. If the warlords are disarmed and powerless, we will have everything. For example, after the domination of the Taliban, the foreigners spent about $12 billion for reconstruction. So why is there no fundamental change in Afghanistan? Because even though some ministers are democratic, most of the Karzai government is corrupt.

Our President doesn't have bloody hands in Afghanistan's history and he promised not to compromise with the warlords. Those were the main reasons why people wanted him. But now the London Conference[9] wants to raise $10 billion to give to this corrupt government. **Ramazan Bashardost**, the Minister of Planning, said that the government of Afghanistan and some "thief" NGOs receive money for reconstruction but pocket it themselves.

I tell the foreigners that they are wasting their money, that they should ask where the previous $12 billion went. Our people are dying because of poor nutrition and cold winter weather. With the warlords in control, we never get to use the money the foreigners give us to reconstruct and rebuild. Bashardost said that if the government of Afghanistan honestly used even $1 billion for rebuilding, it would change the future of our country.

Peggy: *What NGOs should Americans support? How can we be sure that the money we give will get into the right hands?*

Malalai: You need to look into the NGOs and see how they are working. Are they really working for people or do they just want to fill their pockets? You should ask questions and see where your money is being spent.

You should see what is going on in the provinces. In Kabul, there is some security, some women have jobs, and some women go outside without the *burqa*. Things have changed a lot for them since the Taliban left. But in the provinces where the warlords have power, women can't do anything. Some governors in the provinces have links with the opium mafia. The *New York Times* magazine exposed some of these drug mafia who have positions in the government.

So on one hand, the governors in certain provinces have links with the mafia, and on the other hand, the Afghan government tells the innocent farmers not to plant opium [poppies] and they even destroy it in their fields. That's good, they should destroy it, but they should pay something to these poor people when they destroy it. But really, is it ever possible to stop the opium trade when the governor has links with the mafia?

Peggy: When subsistence farmers lose their crops, for whatever reason, they often have to marry off their daughters so their family can survive with money from the bride price. Eradication needs to happen on all levels simultaneously so that farmers won't plant opium in the first place. Sometimes traffickers pressure farmers to plant opium poppies even at the expense of food crops for their families.

∐•◇•◇•∐

Peggy: *What are the most important things you will teach your future sons or daughters?*

Malalai: I will teach them to love their country and trust their people. They should serve their country, they should never compromise with their enemies, but instead they should expose them. I would tell my children that they should continue their education as well.

Peggy: *When you are training women, what advice do you give them to help them in difficult situations?*

Shinkai (in 2003): I tell them, "Don't be afraid." I help them feel successful even if they only accomplish ten percent. I always give them encouragement, and I lay the groundwork by writing letters or making contacts. I tell them, "Nobody can kill you or beat you." I pat them on the back and say, "Now I have a brave daughter."

Peggy: *How do you deal with discouragement?*

Malalai: Sometimes I struggle and get tired, but that doesn't mean that I become discouraged. My hopes and ideals give me more hope and courage. And when I see the many people who support me, it shows that the goals I have are worthwhile and that they are good for the future of Afghanistan. I'm sure that one day – I'm not sure if I will be alive or not – but I'm sure we will have a real democratic government in our country with peace and women's rights.

Malalai   Shinkai, 2010   Sabera

Peggy: *How do you deal with fear, so that you can do what you need to do anyway?*

Shinkai: First, you must have confidence. I never feel afraid or ashamed because I am working for a right cause. Second, I have a commitment to work with women. Of course you must have courage to do this work.

Peggy: *When you feel afraid, how do you typically react?*

Shinkai: I never show it. If you act afraid, the others will be more afraid. If you are a leader, you must be strong so they can depend on you. I say, "Don't worry, this is nothing, I am here, we will get support." I do this because they count on me. When I act strong and try to help others feel strong, I feel stronger myself.

Peggy (in 2010): *Shinkai, when I met you in 2003, you were running AWEC. Your parliament experience sounds even more challenging. How has being a Member of Parliament changed you?*

Shinkai: When I was managing AWEC, I was thinking of how to design a project, how to get funds, and how to provide work opportunities for people. I was happy doing that, but now the situation is different. I was forced to go to Parliament, and now I'm tired. But when I look at my achievements, even though they are small, achieving them is very important.

Then there is the politics of seeing how the region treats your country, and how the world treats your country, your politicians, and your President. When I see how much respect I am getting from my people, I see how important I am to the cause. This encourages me to keep going. I sometimes feel that I'm in danger and have to protect myself, not for me, but for the future generations. Now my world is much bigger than it was in my previous life. My strong rivals bring bigger challenges but I have to fight. I have no choice.

Peggy: *What are some of the biggest problems Afghanistan faces?*

Shinkai: People are looting this country and corrupting it. They are trying to secure their own lives, but they don't understand that securing this country is securing their life; otherwise you will see poverty [increase] and we cannot be secure.

Peggy: *What do you hope for Afghanistan's future?*

Malalai: My hope is this: that the freedom-loving people around the globe, countries, and organizations should not forget Afghanistan. Our people really need their help and support. Every kind of support.

Peggy: *What signs of hope do you see that makes you believe your dreams are possible?*

Malalai: When I stood up in the *Loya Jerga*, I saw that a lot of suffering people support me. It shows how aware our people are. They have nothing, but they know very well who their enemies and friends are. This gives me hope. Also, a lot of people participated in the election. In some provinces where the governor and warlords are committing crimes, the people have held some demonstrations against them. Even in Farah Province, some women went outside and defended me. This shows how our women are aware and how they hate the warlords. Another example is that there are lots of women who go to literacy courses because they want an education. It's a great hope for the future of Afghanistan.

Shinkai (in 2003): Many men have changed as well. They are becoming more educated and now they realize the value of it. Another positive thing is the traveling. Those who went to Pakistan or Iran or the West want a better and more modern life back in Afghanistan. Before, they only wanted education for their sons, but now I'm happy that they also want education for their daughters. The NGOs here have helped to change people's minds. Now we have the Ministry of Women's Affairs and women in the government. The men didn't agree at first, but now they have changed as they see that it is better. Women are even allowed to come to Kabul to participate in workshops.

Shinkai (in 2010): I see that there are still sincere and committed people in this country, and we still have some good supporters in the international community. Also, I'm hopeful for the new generation. They are very talented, strong people and I'm sure they will save this country. I'm also happy for the women's movement and I'm happy to see it getting stronger. I'm sure these women will stay very active and take care of this country. Nobody has counted on us before. Now they understand that women also can help their country.

Women wearing chadors. These are common in Herat.

Karima

Najia, my translator, and I walked around among the square brick buildings and tall pine trees at Kabul University until we found her friend, Karima, at our prearranged meeting place. Karima sat on the grass with the front of her *burqa* pulled back, framing her face.

Karima grew up in Kabul but lived in Pakistan for seven years during the civil war and Taliban era. She taught high school in Pakistan, and in 2003, when I met her, taught primary school in Kabul while pursuing a degree in education at the government teacher's college.

By 2011, Karima had graduated, married her boyfriend, given birth to a son, and was still teaching.

Peggy: *Is your family trying to get you married?*

Karima: Yes, but they can't choose for me. They have to wait for the boy's family to ask. So my boyfriend will ask his father, his father will ask my father, and my boyfriend and I will pretend that we've never met before.

We [female students] are five years behind and we feel bad since all the boys we went to school with have already graduated. Also, some of our girlfriends have gotten married or gone abroad to school. I miss my friends from before.

Peggy: *When you were a child, did you look forward to wearing a* burqa?

Karima: Never! I don't like it. Because I'm Tajik, I shouldn't wear a *burqa*. My father and brother don't make me wear one. I'm wearing it now because before I came here, I was with another girl who was wearing one. If we go out together and she is wearing one and I'm not, it's not good.

Peggy: This didn't make any sense to me. I often saw women in *burqas* walking with other women wearing only headscarves. In fact, the woman accompanying Karima was only wearing a scarf. Karima was so vehement about not liking *burqas* and not having to wear one that I wondered why she would voluntarily put it on.

Later, reflecting on this conversation with Najia, I learned that Karima sometimes converses with her boyfriend in public places under the cover of her *burqa*. If someone from her or her boyfriend's family were to see the couple, they might relay the information back home, and the possibility of marriage between them would evaporate. With the *burqa*, she can meet him with no one being the wiser.

With all the oppression of women in society, what are your feelings towards men?

Karima: Men should treat women based on their society and culture. If they are Tajik, they shouldn't put a lot of pressure on their women. If they are Pashtun, they can put pressure on women because their society is like that. I don't want men to put pressure on me.

Peggy: *What do you look forward to in your future?*

Karima: I want to be an experienced teacher and have a good independent life. I want to earn money and spend it. I will never ask my brother, husband, or father to give me money.

Peggy: *What do you think has the greatest power to transform Afghan society?*

Karima: Only one thing can change it: our entire nation has to come together. They should never separate into ethnic groups.

12/Refugees & Internally Displaced Women

Life in Kabul and other areas of Afghanistan became untenable for many during periods of heavy violence. Some families left even before the Soviet invasion because they had been involved in politics. These families knew they would be labeled enemies as competing communist factions struggled for dominance. The Soviets' mentality was, "You're either with us or you're against us," making life dangerous for people like Soraya Sobhrang, who would otherwise have stayed and aided Afghan women. Others stuck it out through the civil war but left during the Taliban's rule. Reasons for staying or going were as diverse as the people who had to choose.

The refugees left Afghanistan in waves. First, those who opposed the communists left. Many of them were very traditional. They included clerics or political dissidents and their families, as well as others who had been treated brutally by the Soviets or had their villages destroyed. The second wave left once the *mujahidin* overthrew Najibullah, the fourth and final communist leader, because those who had worked with the communists were in danger from the *mujahidin*. A third wave comprised those who fled the Taliban.

Habibba

Habibba was part of the second wave of refugees since she had worked for Najibullah's government.

During my interview with the jam-making businesswoman, we also talked of

her experiences in the refugee camp. When her camp's first-wave residents learned that Habibba had worked for Najibullah's government, they became prejudiced against her and suspicious of her actions.

Peggy: *Habibba, coming from your middle-class background, what was it like for you living in the camp?*

Habbiba: The living conditions there were so bad, especially for the new arrivals. It was really hard to adjust to that poor life.

I had a really nice life here in Afghanistan and had a position in the government. It was very hard for me to adjust to life in the camp. In part because it was very poor and dirty, and partly because the camp leaders were so conservative.

After we first arrived, my sister and I decided to gather all the kindergarten-aged kids and teach them how to behave, teach them not to throw things at people, generally teach them good behavior. The UNHCR [United Nations High Commission on Refugees] came to my tent and I suggested that they work with the students. They were quite happy to have me teach the children. But some of the other refugees were very mad and they asked, "Why are you doing such things? It's not necessary." They planned to kill my sister and me, but someone told me about their plan and we went to stay at our relative's house.

Peggy: *Why did they want to kill you?*

Habibba: The new refugees coming out of Afghanistan had a different perspective from the ones who had come earlier, beginning in 1978. Those old refugees had a leader with a big following who was always against the newcomers because we were more open-minded.

Peggy: *So did they kill each other often?*

Habibba: They didn't do that much killing, but they would warn and threaten people and scare them into not doing things.

Peggy: *So how long did you live in that camp?*

Habibba: I lived there for six months and in Pakistan for twelve years. After that first six months, I spent the day running my business selling things in the camp. When work was over around four in the afternoon, I'd go back to my house. I also worked with the UNHCR.

After talking with Habibba, I wanted to meet other refugees and hear their stories. A large cluster of plastic-covered ruins surrounded by apartment buildings lay along the main road out of town to Lake Qargha. During my time in Kabul, I often passed by such camps, as well as smaller ones with half a dozen tents, or just two or three tents in a vacant spot.

Nargis M, my 2010 translator, knew of a woman who helps people in one of the camps, so I asked if I could visit. She and others warned me that the camps are not safe. In addition, Nargis herself wasn't willing (or maybe not allowed) to accompany me into the camp, so we arranged to interview a group of internally displaced women in her home. (Since the camps are located inside Afghanistan, these refugees are technically referred to as "internally displaced people" or IDPs.)

All of the women in this and the following chapter had been refugees during the wars. In this chapter, all except Habbiba had returned to Afghanistan without resources and became economically displaced. The women I interviewed for this chapter had found space in informal squatter camps. Others in their situation took refuge in ruined buildings, often bricking or cementing up the broken walls for privacy and a modicum of security.

In 2010, Kabul was experiencing a building boom. Security had improved and many people had returned to claim title to abandoned or destroyed property.

Squatters were being displaced both from ruined buildings and the unused patches of land hosting informal camps.

I interviewed these women in Nargis M's home. They waited their turns in the servant's quarters. Although all were offered tea, sweets, and nuts, none partook.

A camp where economically displaced people squat.

Ghotai

Ghotai married her cousin at age 13. Her husband's family rented a house in Kabul but evacuated to a camp in Pakistan when she was 23 and the Taliban came to power. They returned to Afghanistan in 2002. Now she has four small boys. She really, *really* wants to live in a house with four walls and a roof.

Sometimes she gets work cleaning houses or doing other menial work, but since she is the main income earner, if she doesn't have work she begs or hangs out near a bakery, hoping that someone buying bread will give her a loaf.

In the winter it's so cold. I lost my son one winter due to the food shortage and cold when he was sick. When I woke in the morning, he was frozen solid.

Gita

Gita was five-years-old when her family fled to Pakistan. At first, her parents found temporary work making *tandoors* (large clay ovens) in exchange for room and board. Since they hadn't earned any money, when that job ended, their only recourse was to move into a refugee camp. Gita spent her next 14 years there. She

was forced to marry at 13 because her mother needed the dowry money to enable the family to survive. Although she never attended school, she learned to read a Dari translation of the *Quran.*

While the Taliban were still in Afghanistan, I came back to help take care of my in-laws. I'd never worn a burqa in Pakistan, and the Taliban beat me when I didn't wear one in Kabul. I decided that life in the camp in Pakistan was better than life under the Taliban, so when my mother-in-law died a year later, we went back to the camp in Pakistan.

Grayna

Grayna attended school until fifth grade when the Taliban stopped girls' education. Her family's poverty forced her to work at a young age. She and her family went to Pakistan soon after the Taliban arrived and returned to find their previous home destroyed. Since they had no savings and her father couldn't find work, they moved into the informal camp where she lives now. Eight years ago, a young man from the camp saw her and approached her family with a marriage proposal. They married soon after. She'd birthed the latest of their four children in the camp without help, and still suffered from medical issues related to the delivery.

My husband and I share one big tent with my in-laws, so there are eight people in our tent. The harassment of us Hazaras by the Pashtuns is the worst part of living in our camp. We have the same kinds of problems whether it's Pakistan or Kabul. The life in tents is really bad.

Laila W

Our biggest problem now is a shortage of water and food. Our tent is on ground that stays very wet when it rains. Our second problem is security.

Laila was 11 years old when her father died. She, her mother, and siblings went to live with her father's older brother. He wouldn't allow any of the women to work outside the home, but he also wouldn't give them much food. So when Laila was 14, her mother married her to a 45-year-old man. Laila had five children when we talked.

Nargis

The camps in Pakistan were much better than here. There we had the possibility of finding work so we could feed ourselves, but here there's no work. I can't find any jobs cleaning houses and my husband can't afford to buy things that he can sell in the streets.

Nargis' family left for Pakistan when she was five, soon after the Taliban came. At the age of 15 her mother married her, she told me, *to a man I never liked*. She lived in a tent in Kabul before moving to another tent in Pakistan. Eventually, the landowner of the camp decided to build there and evicted all of the squatters. By that time, the Karzai government had come into power in Afghanistan, so they returned to Kabul.

Freshta

Freshta's family fled Kabul to a Pakistani refugee camp when she was two. They returned to Afghanistan four years after the Taliban had gone. Her father died in 2007 when a bomb exploded in the government office where he had gone to get her brother an ID card. When we talked, she was 13.

Peggy: *Can you tell me about your experience of living in the camps?*

Freshta: While living in the refugee camp in Pakistan, sometimes we went outside and cleaned houses for Afghan families. But after 2001, those rich people began to return to Afghanistan and left us without work. The Pakistanis generally wouldn't ever pay enough for us to support ourselves. Sometimes they would harass us while we worked, calling us "worthless Afghans." My father sometimes got work, too, but my mother worked more.

Ghotai: The government gave our family three tents, but we do our cooking, washing, and

My biggest problem now is security. I can't use the latrine at night because of the boys in the camp.

I clean houses to help feed my family. When I clean the rooms of girls my age, it makes me wish that I could live like they do. But I can't because of our poverty.

sleeping in one. Our extended family uses the other two. We don't have *toshaks*, we just sleep on rugs. My mother and father-in-law died, but a sister lives with us, along with 13 kids between us.

| Ghotai | Gita | Grayna | Laila W | Narghis |

Security is a problem, and since my sons are small, sometimes people come from other camps and steal things from them.

Nargis: It was not safe in either of our camps. We would get harassed by Pakistanis and also by Afghans inside the camp. We had to stay in our tents because of rape and also to guard our things. If we left the tent unattended, people would come and steal everything.

Gita: Since I'm Tajik, I don't have any problem with the Pashtuns in the camp. But the problem is that we can't leave our tents at night to use the latrine because some men may come in the camp and rape us.

Peggy: *How often does that happen?*

Gita: After one 12-year-old girl was abducted and another woman was raped, the men began taking turns patrolling the camp.

Grayna: With eight of us living in one room it would help if we could go outside. But if we do, we get harassed. The kids are bullied whenever they play outside, but if they stay inside, it's hard for everyone.
Also, every year when it rains, my children get sick from the dampness.

Peggy: It tends to rain in the cooler months of the year, so it's not only dampness but cold that affects the displaced. The cold and dankness, coupled with poor nutrition and sanitation, leads to widespread illness.

Surely your camp is not the only one in Kabul. Are there other camps with more Hazaras or more Tajiks where you could live unmolested?

Grayna: Yes, there are other camps, but the people inside those camps won't let us live there. Once a person captures a place of their own, they will hold spaces for their families. Most of the camps are very crowded.

Freshta

Laila: Since I'm Tajik and married to a Pashtun man, I don't have any problems from men inside the camp. But our camp is near a factory, and the factory is near a certain place where men go to drink. It can be dangerous and we are afraid of those people. When they get drunk, sometimes they come into the camps around midnight and rape women. They are drunk and they don't know what they're doing.

Peggy: Alcohol is illegal for Afghans, so these "certain places" are like speakeasies during Alcohol Prohibition in the US. Foreigners can buy alcohol in special shops that Afghans can't enter and in restaurants catering to expatriates. I heard about a crackdown during my 2010 trip. Police stormed into several restaurants during the dinner hour and confiscated all of the liquor; they even grabbed glasses of wine out of patrons' hands as they drank.

Peggy: *How do you survive the winter?*

Ghotai: Some organizations come and help us, and sometimes the government opens some schools for us [as shelters] during the deadly cold times. [School classes are suspended in winter.] Also, we sit around a small table with a blanket over it and a heater underneath. That way our legs can be warm, but still our backs and heads are freezing.

Nargis: We also use those tables to keep warm. Sometimes the government or the Bayat Foundation[1] helps us.

Peggy: *What does the Bayat Foundation do for you?*

Nargis: Every two or three months they bring us one blanket per family and some food, mostly rice and cooking oil.

Peggy: *So you don't have any blankets to wrap around yourselves?*

Nargis: No, we don't.

Gita: When winter starts, we can't afford to buy anything to burn to keep warm, so my husband and I go through the garbage looking for plastic bottles.

Peggy: Several other people told me they collected empty water bottles to use as fuel for their heaters or cooking fires. Since plastic is made from petroleum, the

Ghotai

Gita

Grayna

Laila W

Narghis

bottles burn hotter and longer than wood, as well as being free. At least porous tent walls provide some ventilation for toxic fumes, but the plastic adds another noxious layer to Kabul's horrific air pollution.

How do you compare the camp in Pakistan to the one you live in now?

Freshta: There's not much difference. Here we have a harder time in winter because it's so cold, but in Pakistan we had a hard time with the sticky heat in summer. The poverty is the same.

Ghotai: It was much worse in Pakistan. The security was worse, the weather was so hot, and also our camp flooded. My daughter drowned in one flood 15 years ago in 1995.

The UN or somebody would come once a month and bring us a blanket and a package of biscuits [cookies]. When I could find work cleaning a house, I fed my children. Otherwise, we were hungry. In our camp here, there was a time when I couldn't find water to drink, but then they put in a well nearby.

Peggy: *What other issues do you face?*

Freshta: As a result of her hard work and stress, my mother became sick. She has diabetes and lung problems but we can't afford any medicine. My brother is only 11 and doesn't earn enough selling plastic bags to pay rent, so we have to live in a tent. He is the only one besides me who can work. I have six brothers and sisters. At 13, I'm the oldest. I usually clean houses every day, working for different people.

Peggy: *Does your 11-year-old brother boss you around, or try to restrict you?*

Freshta: No, we all guide ourselves.

Ghotai: We were also really poor when I was young. I used to go begging from different stores. I would also collect plastic bottles for my mother to burn when she cooked, and I send my children out to find them even now. If we have

Freshta

food, we eat, but if not, we just pretend that our stomachs are full and go to sleep. Usually we have rice once a week, and the other nights we just have a cup of tea with a little bread. Occasionally we can buy a few vegetables.

At one point, my husband had a job and we lived in a house for a few months. But then he got hurt and couldn't work, so we had to return to living in a tent. I was so disappointed. He had three operations, but he still has to use a wheelchair. He is a good man, though.

Peggy: *What about education?*

Freshta: I want to go to school but we can't afford it. But even if we could buy notebooks and pens, the girls inside the school would harass me because I live in a tent. And my family needs me to work.

Ghotai: I always wanted to go to school, but my family wouldn't let me. We also never had enough money. Now I don't have enough money to send my kids. Plus, the school is far from our camp and transportation would be a problem.

Peggy: Although there were still pockets of squatters as of 2010, some of the camps had been cleared out in 2009 and the people given land where they could build their own houses. There are many issues associated with this, such as breaking up communities that have formed among the IDPs, the distance of their land to possible jobs and schools, and the cost of building materials, especially roofing. Still, any of these women would prefer those difficulties to continued tent life.

People living in tents by the Kabul River. (2010)

The damaged building is open for business on the ground floor.

13/Voluntary Returnees

Afghans who left their country had entirely different experiences from those who stayed, and often, from one another. Women told me that those who went to Iran generally attained a better education and became more socially active than those who went to Pakistan; although wherever they went, those with the means to send their kids to private schools fared best. Generally, those who went to Pakistan had more opportunities to learn English, a language enabling many to work with Westerners in post-9/11 Afghanistan. Others went to European countries, Canada, or the US. When these refugees returned, they brought more Western outlooks along with their education and language skills.

Why, though, would anyone want to return to this wounded, governmentally-dysfunctional country? Iran, Pakistan, and the West all provided more freedom, amenities, and opportunities for female participation in society than Afghanistan. But exile is seldom simple. Iran, for instance, offered free education through high school and work opportunities to Afghan refugees. However, in 2004, due to internal politics and because it had been several years since the Taliban had been ousted, Mohammad Khatami, Iran's President at the time, revoked Afghan work permits and the right to study. He closed the refugee camps, forcing many to return to their homeland. Pakistan closed its camps around the same time. Still, many exiles found ways to stay abroad.

I spoke with several former refugees about why they had voluntarily returned to Afghanistan and their experience of living in a homeland that the younger ones among them had never known.

Marzia

I met Marzia at a dinner party in Kabul. Her mannerisms and accent led me to believe that she was Afghan-American, when in fact she had spent only two years in the US. We agreed to meet in her office the following week. On the wall at the head of the stairs hung a 1960s poster showing Afghan mountains with the word "serenity" scripted across it.

Marzia was born in Iran and earned her Bachelor's degree there. When she was 25, she visited Herat and fell in love with the city and with being in her own country. At that time in her life, she was very interested in exploring her roots, so she gave up her refugee ID and moved to Kabul alone. She worked there for a year, won a Fulbright scholarship, and spent two years getting a Master's degree in California. She returned to Kabul in 2008 and found an engineering job with a NGO.

The fact that people don't really love you and don't accept you as one of them really hurts. In Iran, you're not one of them and you come here and are not one of them. But I still believe things will get better.

Belgheis

My time in Bamyan felt like a vacation after Kabul, with its thick air pollution, heavy traffic, and overwhelming security. In Bamyam the air was crisp and cool, and the traffic sparse. I walked everywhere, sometimes cutting through fields along irrigation canals. Bamyan is considered a very safe area, so I was momentarily taken aback the one and only time I saw a machine gun. A big, burly, UN soldier was guarding his boss, who was shopping for souvenirs. I was amazed at how easily I'd become accustomed to an environment with guns everywhere in sight, and then to an environment with none.

In Bamyan, I first stayed in the extremely basic and dirty Zohak Hotel in the center of the bazaar, earning negative "stars" in my personal travel guide. My friend Shakila called and suggested that I stay with her friends Belgheis and Ali, who lived on the outskirts of Bamyan. Arrangements were made and I stayed a week with these lovely, welcoming newlyweds. Belgheis taught French to a few village children in her home, but she felt alone in the small town and was glad to have my company.

Iran was good. I like Iran. I love Iran, but we always felt like we were foreigners there and didn't have any rights.

Belgheis has three sisters and four brothers. She and her family left Dai Kundi, a remote province in Afghanistan's central highlands, when she was eight years old to live in Mashhad, Iran. She earned a Master's degree in French literature and met Ali at the university in Tehran. Five years later, her parents finally agreed to let them marry. Her father had wanted her husband to be from Dai Kundi, but now her family loves Ali. Ten days after their wedding, Ali left Mashhad for his new job in Bamyan. Belgheis followed eight months later. They'd been living there for two months when I visited.

In July 2010, they moved to Kabul, where Belgheis found employment as a French teacher at the Cultural Center of France, and Ali as an agricultural specialist. In June 2011, Belgheis was awarded a scholarship for a PhD program in Tours, France. Ali awaits her back in Kabul. In early 2012, they had a son.

Batool

In addition to Zainab R., whom I interviewed for the Women's Rights chapter, I met her daughter, Zahra, and Zahra's friend, Batool, when she was visiting Azdar Village near Bamyam. I interviewed Batool in the company of her husband. Both were outspoken in their critique of Afghan society.

Batool was born in 1982 in Mashhad, Iran. She graduated from the university there with a degree in philosophy. After she married, she and her husband found work in Bamyan and moved to a village nearby. She has a one-year-old son, Yashar, and works as an administrative finance officer.

I think in Afghanistan, the people who have been here forever don't see any other place. They have a small world. They don't know anything about the big world around us.

Shakila

I really enjoyed seeing Shakila in Kabul. I found her calm openness refreshing. She was so attentive and helpful, and was instrumental in connecting me to **SOLA** where I later stayed. She set me up with interviews for prospective translators and interview subjects. I got to see in practice what a warm, gracious, efficient, considerate, and accepting person she is.

When my father came back to Iran [after an exploratory trip to Afghanistan], he said the situation was not as bad as we thought, nor as bad as we heard on the news.

Touba

Touba is an amazing and complex mix of Eastern and Western cultures. Her powerful, independent personality shines through in her expressive hands and darting eyes.

Touba's father worked in **King Zahir Shah**'s government until the communists took power in 1974. The family left the country when Touba was five, and eventually made it to Canada. Once she earned her Master's degree in business administration, she began to feel the pull of Afghanistan. She returned to Kabul on her own and created a consulting business that helps girls get jobs in appropriate companies and grooms them for the business world.

I came back so I could learn about my culture, my history, where my ancestors lived, and why we were here. It's represented a lot of different things for me in many ways: socially, emotionally, financially, and culturally.

Peggy: *When did your family leave Afghanistan?*

Touba: By the time the Soviet war started, my immediate family was all that was left of our family there. My dad tried everything he could to get permission to leave his job at the Attorney General's office, but the government insisted on a guarantee that he would return. Since I was the oldest, I was the one left behind as that guarantee. I was only five! Since all our close relatives had gone, they found a really distant family member who took me in. A very, very distant family member. I was stuck here in Afghanistan for two and a half years with someone I didn't know in the middle of a war. I saw so many things that a child should never have seen: people burning and dying, rockets flying over the house and even hitting it.

Peggy: *You were too young to process it…*

Touba: And my parents hadn't explained anything to me. I had the impression that we were all leaving, but when the day came for us to go to the airport, my dad took me aside and said, "If anything happens, here's some money." He gave me an envelope with some money and showed me a safe place to hide it. He told me to only use it if I became sick. I was really confused. When we got to the door, my mom and the others were in tears, but they just took off and left me behind with the relative. It was really devastating for me to be here for those two and a half years, but if it hadn't happened, I wouldn't be who I am today.

My parents hired someone to smuggle me across the border, but those people turned out to be crooks. Finally, they brought me to India where my parents were waiting for me. My whole extended family had pitched in to help pay the millions of rupees they charged. When I got to Delhi, however, they refused to give me to my parents. They didn't hurt me or abuse me; they were just asking for more money. After two and a half years, I was so close to my family, but not close enough. My parents finally got more money to pay them and we were reunited and went to Canada.

Peggy: *What did you learn from those two and a half years? You said it made you who you are.*

Touba: Not good stuff. I was really traumatized from all sorts of war crimes. I guess the best thing was that it gave me my strength and independence. I have always been able to stand on my own and take care of those around me, even at a young age.

Living in Toronto was nice. Canada was a wonderful country, and I was honored to be there. I thank God that I had a chance to grow up in a normal society after what we endured. I have a younger sister and brother, so I had to be the leader; I had to pave the way for them. I felt really pressured.

My parents had left everything; my grandfather was the Minister of Transportation and my father was the Attorney General when they left for Canada. When he arrived there, my father started his own taxi business with five cabs while he went to school. Now, he's a lawyer.

We are Pashtun, so I was raised very strictly. Every day, my dad would drop me off at school and pick me up for lunch to bring me home. I never had that "normal Western" lifestyle, growing up with friends and peer pressure, especially during high school. Of course I resented it, but as I've grown older, I appreciate what my parents did. If they had been easier on me, I could've gone down a bad path. Despite my resistance, I earned a lot of respect from both of my parents. Now, when I decide what I want and what is right for me, my father says, "I trust you. I've done my job right. Go for it."

Peggy: *What made you decide to return or come to Afghanistan?*

Batool: I came here because my husband, Masti, got a job here in Bamyan. Also, I wanted to come because my good friend, Zahra, was moving here. I like Afghanistan very much, especially Bamyan. I never liked Iran because I always felt like an outsider there. I just miss my family because they are all in Iran, but I'm very happy to live here.

Touba: I have a strong sense of belonging to Afghanistan. That is one of the biggest reasons I'm here. In Canada, I had a great career, but at the end of the day, I felt like I was not contributing much to society as a whole. Here in Afghanistan, I feel that if I make a difference in one person's life and they can go back and support their family, then that's wonderful. If I can make a difference in one person's life, then I can do that in many more.

Before I left, my father asked me a question I couldn't answer. He said, "I am glad that you want to go back to Afghanistan and to carry on my legacy, but I worry for you." I told him that I would be totally secure and have guards. He replied, "Fine, but with the war and everything, if something bad happens, who are you going to call, 9-1-1?" When he said that, I got really scared. I wondered, who *could* I call on? The government? The police? The security manager? My guard? Who would I go to? How could I trust any of them? Then I told myself that something bad could happen to me anywhere. Maybe it was a little more dangerous over here, but my contribution would be that much more as well. I'm willing to take risks in my life. I don't want to have regrets. That's been my motto.

Shakila: We had to come back, since the Iranian government wouldn't let us work or go to school anymore. There was no life left for us there. I was sad to leave.

Marzia: I was living in Iran as a refugee and felt that I had no roots. Moving to Afghanistan was a big decision, especially since giving up my refugee card meant I wouldn't be able move back if it didn't work out. I can't believe I did it, because I didn't know anyone here in Kabul. I only knew a friend of a friend who let me stay with her for a month.

I made the final decision to come when I was 25. I visited Herat for two days and I was so excited just to be there! I walked around the city and went to bookstores. The weather was great and I was totally enamored.

I came here because I had always wanted to know about my homeland. I was isolated from my heritage, save for my relationships with my immediate family. We barely had anything in common with Afghans in Iran, and Iranians treated me as an Afghan [that is, badly] because I didn't have an Iranian passport. I thought I was part of the crowd, but I was not; I really didn't belong.

The one thing that tied me to Afghanistan was my mother. My father never talked about Afghanistan, but Mother would tell us stories about when she was a child living in Kabul. She told us about sugar cane and farms and the people. It made me very curious to see it. My mother painted us a nice image, but when I came here, I didn't find it to be true.

My mother told me that Afghans are the best people in the world. I don't believe she lied, but I think that the war changed everything a lot. She was talking about 30 years ago when she said Afghans were like this. She told me that everyone goes to school and people are very open-minded. She talked about the festivals she went to and this wonderful park in Shar-e Now [a district of Kabul]. I went to the park, but it wasn't nice at all.

Yet, I still like it here. I went to my family compound and met my aunt. She and her family were living in our old house. She took me to some really small rooms where you could touch the ceiling, and she told me that my father was born there and she used to take care of him. I love my dad's house because it takes

me back to where I'm from. There are a lot of things I don't like about living here, but the feeling that I belong to this place means a lot because for 25 years, I didn't belong anywhere. Even if I don't like it here now, I know where I'm from and I don't live in a vacuum.

Peggy: *What surprised you most about living in Afghanistan?*

Shakila: I remember very clearly the first time I saw meat hanging in the butcher shop windows. I was shocked because I'd never seen that before. It took me a while to get used to it.

Peggy: That's funny, because the first time I saw meat hanging over the sidewalks was when I went to Iran. But that was in the early 1970s and in the south.

Shakila: At first, I compared everything to Iran. One thing that was harder to adjust to was that the people here seemed more aggressive. Now, I see that it's just their mannerisms and their way of talking. But at first I was afraid because I thought they might hurt me. It's just how they are; if they are happy, they shout and they speak louder. I found these differences to be exciting, too.

Touba: A while ago, I read a UN Office on Drugs and Crime (UNODC) survey about corruption in Afghanistan. They found that the majority of people in Afghanistan thought that giving bribes to the government was the only way to get things done. Seventy percent of people from all over the country thought it was normal! I was shocked; how could people think that? It made me realize that it happens so much that it's just *become* normal.

Marzia: I got my Afghan ID card the third day I was in Kabul. It made me feel very Afghan! That same afternoon, I heard about a job. I was interviewed and hired the next day. I worked there for three months and really loved it. At the end of that job, I visited Iran. I encouraged my brother, who had just completed medical school, to come, and we lived together in my father's old house.

Batool: I think life in Afghanistan is a little bit hard, especially in Bamyan, because we don't have many amenities, but it's good for me because of Masti. Even though he is my husband, he's also my good friend. I can adjust to everything and everywhere with him. The other thing is that my friends are here, too, like Zahra and her mother, Zainab [R]. They were a big help.

Belghais: It's good here in Bamyan. The air is good and fresh and I love having nature around us. It's very quiet and I can study at home. My problem is that I can't find a job.

Peggy: *What was the best part of your life in Afghanistan when you came back?*

Shakila: It turned out that in Afghanistan, I had a lot more freedom than I did in Iran. I could communicate with more diverse people. I learned new ways to function in the workplace. All of this provided a bigger picture of the world. I also understood that learning another language was important for my career. Reading English books became a window into the world and I got to see many new things.

Peggy: *Were more books available to you in Afghanistan than Iran?*

Shakila: In Kabul, there are some very good English-language bookstores, and I could find some books that weren't available in Farsi or in Iran. I never saw foreigners when I lived in Iran, but in Afghanistan I worked with them, as well as with Afghans who had lived in other countries.

Peggy: *How are relations between those who never left and those who did?*

Marzia: Actually, I feel like an outsider all the time, except when I'm at home with my siblings. When I'm with Americans, I'm not American; I'm someone from the East. I'm Afghan, but I always see myself as Middle Eastern because I grew up in Iran. In daily life, I feel like an outsider because I have a different accent and I wear different clothes. I try to blend in, but everywhere I go, people ask me whether I'm Afghan or a foreigner who speaks Dari. Foreigners notice that I don't seem very Afghan. When I came here, I could hardly speak or understand the Dari accent. I constantly had trouble in the office for the first month. From the beginning, I tried to learn the words and made myself a small notebook of expressions. Even now I have a hard time speaking without my accent. That's fine, but on a daily basis I still get the feeling that I don't belong.

Marzia   Belgheis   Batool   Shakila   Tonba

Peggy: *When I met you, I thought you had grown up in the US.*

Marzia: People assume that about me all the time and are surprised that I was only there for two years. I think part of it was from growing up in Iran. People in Iran are very Westernized even though they don't speak much English. I had a lot of foreign friends, too. In addition, my parents were very open-minded and independent. A lot of my mother's relatives went to the US. For example, my great grand-uncle went to the US on a scholarship in 1935. I have a great-uncle and aunt who were both very well-educated. My mother didn't have a chance for an education because her parents passed away when she was young, but my father always told me about the older relatives and said that he wanted me to be like them.

My father had told me how to find his old house. I went there, but my relatives didn't believe I was my father's daughter. They were worried that maybe I was scamming them into giving up their home. It was my right to have it because it belonged to my father, but they said, "We've been living in this house for 30 years." Finally my brother came, and since he looks exactly like my father did 30 years ago, they were very happy and let us live upstairs with our cousins.

I always felt I couldn't live in a place where water and electricity were scarce. But what is harder is the fact that my family doesn't really love me and doesn't accept me as one of them. People who stayed here resent those who left. My relatives told me, "When you were in Iran having a good time, we were here with rockets trying to protect your house. We had a hard time and didn't have enough food while you were in Iran living the good life." I had been in a good place, but it doesn't mean I had a great life. My father was the only breadwinner, so money was always tight. I wish that people would understand that life is hard everywhere.

My mother had it really hard when we went to Iran, but she always gave herself hope. I think that's the only reason she survived all those years raising seven kids in a country where she didn't know anybody. She was on her own all the time because my father was always at work. I guess I learned how to stay positive from her because that's what I have been doing the whole time, too.

Belgheis: I don't have any friends here and it's difficult to find new ones. There aren't any other girls or women who came from outside. I think those who stayed had a difficult experience, and because of that we are separated. I was in Iran and now they look at me as a person who didn't suffer and who can't understand them. I don't think I can be close to them.

Peggy: Opportunities for women to connect with others outside their extended families are limited to school or work, especially for a shy person such as Belgheis. Her few friends are the wives of Ali's friends.

Touba: Even though I grew up in Canada, I have my parents' values. So here I am in Afghanistan trying to be Afghan, yet everyone sees me as a foreigner. One reason I came was to have more of a sense of belonging, but no, it didn't happen. Now I call myself a world citizen, and I think that's how we should all be.

However, my biggest challenge is to be accepted as an independent woman. It's very chauvinistic here and there are so many societal rules about women. I'm a trendsetter, so I'm not going to just follow the norms that have been imposed on me. I really want to be myself, but I have to make sure that I'm part of society as well; that is my biggest challenge. It's very masculine-driven here, and women are not given opportunities. As soon as people see a professional woman, they think that she must be bad; she's willing to do anything.

Peggy: *Can you talk about your work experiences?*

Marzia: I work for a foreign NGO and the Afghan women are not given enough opportunities there, simply for being Afghan, female, and young.

Peggy: *You mean, even the foreigners discriminate?*

Marzia: Yes, although there's a lot I can do at work, my boss is criticized daily for giving me certain assignments because I'm an Afghan girl, even though my engineering Master's degree is from an American university. I've found more resistance to increasing my authority and responsibility from white American men than from Afghan men. Afghan men listen to what I say and accept my opinion. Honestly, I thought only Afghan men didn't accept the value of Afghan women, but I see it more with the Western men in my office. The foreigners always assume that if I'm working in a NGO office, then I'm definitely a computer operator or an English translator. They just cannot see us doing technical work.

NGOs say they can't find enough women, but there are plenty of good women who are very competent and qualified. They just need to look for them. Yes, we have to change the Afghan people's mentality, but we also need to change that of the foreigners who come here.

| Marzia | Belgheis | Batool | Shakila | Touba |

Shakila: I got a job at Bamyan Hospital as a nurse. Before I left Kabul, people really pitied me. Everyone told me that Bamyan was a very remote area. They said, "You will be depressed there because you won't be able to find many people with common interests. It will be boring." Someone even told me that Bamyan was like Guantanamo prison! He said that because I wouldn't have a connection to other cities, it would be like living on an island. But he had lived there a long time ago.

I went there and found it to be totally different. At Bamyan Hospital, I found many international staff members mixed with Afghans who had never left Bamyan, and still others who had come from Pakistan and Iran. We also had some Indian staff. I found this mixture very interesting because I could talk with different kinds of people.

Peggy: *What are some challenges you've faced living and working in Afghanistan.*

Batool: The biggest issue facing Bamyan is that there aren't many jobs. The security here is good, so it's a good place to build factories or industries. Most things we have here are imported. The general infrastructure here isn't very good, though. For example, there is no working internet for the public, and in our village, we don't even have electricity. We also need better education and ways to raise people's awareness.

Peggy: In Bamyan, electricity only comes on for a few hours during the evening, but in Belgheis' suburb there was none at all. They had a solar panel that charged two batteries, providing enough energy to power their computers and lights in the evening.

Batool's village has a primary school for girls, but for high school, students must walk two hours to Bamyan. Most parents won't allow their girls to walk that far.

How do you personally deal with challenges?

Touba: First of all, it takes tremendous patience to be in Afghanistan. Every night before bed, I pray, "God, bless me with more patience than yesterday." It's patience that keeps me going. I've had major setbacks and many disappointments. One time, I had a breakdown because there was so much; it was not just one wall, but many all around me and I just felt like they were closing in on me. I asked myself, "How can I deal with this?" I do a lot of things: I meditate and I'm very spiritual in my own way. I just talk and pray for guidance and ask God to show me the right way. I have my trust and faith and I know that whatever happens, it's always in my best interest.

Shakila: When I'm feeling bad, I write. I write down all of my feelings and it helps me see them more clearly; then I feel better. Sometimes I read Nathaniel Branden's book, *The Six Pillars of Self-Esteem.*[1] He has a chapter on self-acceptance, and said that writing down one's feelings will help. For me, this has really worked.

Also, society supports some values, but they aren't necessarily absolutely right. There are deeper values, important ones, but society puts other things in front to secure them. Those things themselves aren't important; they are only protecting what's important. When I understood that, I became more flexible. I really try to respect society's values, but sometimes they create an unnecessary limitation.

Marzia: When I first stepped foot here, I didn't know anyone and everything was so new. It was the hardest and most exciting time of my life. It was hope that brought me here in the first place despite my worries. I just kept thinking that things would get better after some time, and they have.

I've always done things to try to improve myself. In Iran nobody spoke good English, but when I came here my English was very good. Sometimes my dad would give me $20 and he would say, "Okay, with this $20 you could buy new clothes or you could go to an English course." I chose the English courses.

Belgheis: When I'm feeling lonely or depressed, I work on translating a novel from French to Farsi. I also study English and write letters to my family and friends in Iran. Sometimes I read poetry and play uplifting music. Walking in the clean air here makes me feel better, too.

Peggy: *What effect did living outside of Afghanistan have on you?*

Marzia: I had a much easier time adjusting to university life in America after having lived in Iran because Iran is very westernized. In America, I got used to all of the tall buildings, and when I came back, I felt like I'd come to the middle of nowhere. It took me a month to get used to Kabul again, but now I am. I've found that humans are very adaptable.

Marzia *Belgheis* *Batool* *Shakila* *Touba*

Shakila: The Hazara people were never treated very well by other ethnic groups, so we mostly live in our own area in the central highlands, the *Hazarajat*. When the Hazaras went to live in the cities, they were usually given menial jobs because they were mostly uneducated. When the Soviets invaded, our family went to Iran. Because there was no work in the countryside there, we went to the city. In Afghanistan we had lived in a small village, and I would have grown up without education and married young. In Iran, school was free until university; then we had to pay. Since my father and brother could work, they paid my school fees. There are women in villages all over the country who have the same potential as I do, if only they could go to school. Think of what Afghanistan is missing...

Working with foreigners has had a great effect on me. I learned that I should listen to others and consider their ideas. Before, I thought that my ideas and lifestyle were the best. Maybe they were better, but really, they were all I knew. When I was dealing with foreign people or other Afghans who had lived in Pakistan or other countries, I found that they also had interesting ideas and I should respect and learn from them. This was the best part of that experience. I came to understand that when we interact and talk with other people, it's not a bad thing as we've been taught, but it improves your way of life.

When I first returned to Afghanistan, I thought how bad it was that we have four major ethnic groups, different religions, and two languages, Pashtu and Dari. I was looking for similarities and thought they would create unity for Afghanistan. After living here for five years, I see how beautiful it is that we have these different ethnicities and languages, and understand how they enrich Afghanistan. If we try to get to know each other, we can see how beneficial it is to be different, to listen to each other, and learn from each other.

Marzia: I find it very hard to connect with Afghans. When I talk with Afghan girls, it's like I'm talking with my mother. What they talk about is not exactly interesting to me. Another thing is that Afghan girls are not really allowed to have a life after work, so I can never have the experience of going out to dinner or shopping with them because of their restrictions. There are a few girls that I hang out with who studied in the US, but even they have to make special arrangements with their families just to go out for dinner. If they can go, we still have to finish very early. It's just hard for me.

On the other hand, it's totally impossible to hang out with men! First, I haven't found the men here interesting. They will talk to me, but they think I'm not a good person because I'm not conservative. I have some very open-minded friends, but they didn't grow up here. I feel that I live in a fantasy world, not the "real" Afghanistan. I mean, it's real, but not very. I spend a lot of time in the office or I hang out with my expat foreign friends. The problem with them is that I can't make many long-lasting relationships, because they come and go.

My life would be more "Afghan" if I spent more time with my relatives, but that's painful. I hate to say it, but that's how I feel.

Batool: We live in a village nearby called Sarat Siah. I talked with a neighbor who is originally from there, and I came to see that the village women have the mentality of someone from 20 or 30 years ago. They have strange beliefs that I don't accept or understand. I think Afghans who have been here forever don't see anything outside their own experiences. They don't know anything about the big world around us.

Let me tell you a story about a girl who is 24 years old. She lives in my village and she has never seen the bazaar in Bamyan. For her entire life, she has stayed in her own compound in her own village. First, she lived in her parents' house, and then in her husband's. She never went out of her yard, except occasionally to a few other homes in the village. She never met any of her husband's friends. She would send her daughter into the living room to bring them tea.

That is her life; it shocks me. This woman told me, "I remember when I was sick, I was put into a car. I had to lie down and I just saw some wires." Electric wires and poles was her view of the world! Her brother is the decision-maker, and he got a satellite dish. So now she watches TV and can see life halfway around the world, but she's not allowed outside of her home.

Touba: It is a big challenge to be an Afghan girl who has grown up in the West. For example, it's not "normal" for women to talk with their hands or have facial expressions. Of course, physical contact is totally forbidden. Sometimes when I'm giving a training, depending on my audience, I have to remember how to conduct myself. I put my hands in my pocket or hold them together to keep them still. I have to adapt myself to the culture and the mentality.

Peggy: *Your face is so expressive, too…*

Touba: Yes, my facial expressions help me keep people awake! It's a big challenge to change this part of me. I try to express myself in moderation; I talk with my

Marzia   Belgheis   Batool   Shakila   Touba

hands only when I'm very serious and I want to make a point. I've learned to develop myself as a trainer, but I still have a long way to go.

Peggy: *When I'm in America, I call someone and directly state my business. I know that in Eastern cultures, there is a lot of polite talk you must have first. How is this for you here?*

Touba: With my friends, being straight-forward is very normal, and the same is true for Afghans who've lived abroad. For the ones who have always lived in the region, though, you have to be very polite. It's more family-oriented here. For example, my uncle nearly chopped off his finger and I had to take care of him and call him several times a day to check up on him. I did it so that he can feel special about it. This is how we bond. It's not just the connection between two individuals, it's bringing our families closer. It took me a while to get used to that, but now I really enjoy it.

Peggy: *How do you deal with the frustrations of living here in Kabul?*

Touba: I have run into walls; not walls but mountains, but they say there's always a path around the edge of the mountain to the top. After being here for five years, it's difficult to keep sane after a while, but I'm content. I've met so many interesting people, but they all come and go. I have a sense of responsibility about this place. I have to work here because I am part of Afghanistan. There are so many great minds and people who are here making an effort. I'm really proud of them, but it's still sad that most of these wonderful people come for a while and then leave.

Peggy: *Do you maintain contact with them?*

Touba: Well, it's difficult. I'm a business owner, and every week, I meet about 15 new people; sometimes at meetings, sometimes randomly here and there. I can't keep in touch with all of them. On the other hand, there are others who I just have a bond with, a special connection. So, I stay in touch with them even though we may be out of contact for six months. I know that they are there, and they know that we can always reconnect.

Peggy: *What do you see for your future?*

Shakila: Right now, working at American University also allows me to take some classes. I love psychology because it helps me view things in a new way. I also love teaching and have thought about teaching psychology. Now that I'm working with 10,000 Women, I've decided that I want to go into business. Afghanistan needs more businesses to create more jobs.

Belgheis: I would like to go to France and earn my PhD, then get a job I like here in Afghanistan. I hope Afghanistan will be more secure than it is now, and that corruption in the media and government will be less.

Peggy: *What do you see for the future of Afghanistan?*

Marzia: I think to change ordinary people's minds, you have to work slowly and not shock them. You have to understand people's mentality, so it will take long-term work. NGOs need to look for strategies to help move women towards a better life.

There are some programs available that send Afghans abroad. These are very good and we need more of these programs. I've seen Afghan women before and after going to the US. There's a big difference in what they can do.

I've also met many members of the younger generation, and even though they don't know a lot, they are very hard-working. Many of them go to school at five am, go to work from eight am until five pm, then take some courses. When they get home from those, they have homework to do. I think this sort of spirit exists in the young. In 20 or 25 years, they and their children will make Afghanistan a different country. This is my main hope.

What scares me is not having the international community support Afghanistan. What will our country be like if nobody is around here in five years? Our economy is very dependent on donor money. In my work with the government and the Treasury, on a daily basis I can see how dependent we are. While I don't want us to be dependent, I think we need to transition to independence gradually. A sudden withdrawal of support really frightens me. I think it would bring trouble. It's good to find ways to make us sustainable by developing industry. I was working in mining and energy, but I observed that we are like a startup company, and it will

Marzia   *Belgheis*   *Batool*   *Shakila*   *Touba*

be a while before we can survive on our own. If the venture capitalists bail out, our economy will fail. This is what inspires both hope and fear within me.

Belgheis: I see a lot of people who work hard to create a good life for themselves and others. That encourages me to do the same. I think that while there is hope, we should stay in Afghanistan and work. I think this country has a lot of potential. If we have a good government, good governors in the provinces, and engaged intellectuals, the country can grow and advance. I hope things will change, but I know it will not be quick. The changes will be very small, but are better than nothing. I think we should work for the children, for the future generation. Maybe they will make a good situation in the country without war and disaster. Regardless, in the meantime we all should stay here and work patiently and responsibly, because we have something to give to others.

Peggy: *What things can help bring peace?*

Shakila: We have four major ethnicities and maybe a dozen smaller ones. I think that to live together peacefully, it is good for them to be in touch with each other and become friends. That way, they won't be afraid of each other.

Peggy: Before the wars, there wasn't much animosity between the ethnic groups, and intermarriage was fairly common. However, the wars accentuated differences, and divide-and-conquer strategies led to inter-ethnic atrocities and subsequent hatred and fear.

Shakila: When different groups get to know each other as individuals, it inspires trust. Afghan security must be based on building trust, not building walls or making separate neighborhoods here in Kabul. When children mix in school, adults in the workplace, or people in their neighborhoods, it can create trust and we can rebuild the country.

Peggy: *In Kabul, are the different ethnic groups in separate neighborhoods or are they mixed?*

Shakila: Actually, most groups have their own neighborhoods, but sometimes there is some mixing. The good thing is that even though they might live in different areas, parents send their kids to the famously best schools, and those schools are mixed. It's the same with the universities.

Peggy: *What would you like to say to people in the West?*

Shakila: I want to say that Afghanistan is not a horrible place. It's not all about terrorism and war. There are many, many good things about it. It's not just about escaping from the problems there. There are women who want to stay and face the challenges; that can be a beautiful thing. It's hard, but it's part of life, too.

I would like to suggest to President Obama that he should emphasize education more and war less.

Belgheis: I want to invite people to think more deeply about Afghanistan, Islam, and Iran. What the media says is only one side of reality. It's always better to doubt and ask questions. If we ask ourselves and think about whether the things we see or read are true or not, maybe we can make better judgments. When we blindly accept what the media tells us, we can't view others elsewhere accurately.

What remains of the Musalla Complex commissioned by Queen Goharshad in the 13th century. The dome covers her tomb.

Old Soviet weapons still lie in place. This one is aiming toward the village where **Ahmed Shah Massoud** lived in Panshir.

14/Tajwar Kakar

Tajwar was working as an educational consultant for the **International Rescue Committee** (IRC) when I met her in 2003. We sat across from each other at a battered wooden table in an unadorned, hot, dusty office.

I opened the interview with, "Tell me the story of your life." Two hours later, I was finally able to ask my second question. Tajwar's life is the story of the Afghan resistance. She told me that she was merely one of thousands of brave, freedom-fighting women sharing similarly fascinating stories.

Tajwar and some others who supported the *mujahidin* always referred to the Afghans who fought the Soviets as "freedom fighters." This is accurate since they were fighting for the ability to run their own country free from foreign domination.

Life has two faces: a good face and a dangerous face. The good face is easy; everybody can handle it. With the bad face, it's necessary to fight and find the way. I thought that if somebody doesn't know how to swim and they go in the water, they have two choices: drown or try to get out, learn to swim, learn how to stay alive, and find a good way.

Tajwar: My father, Ghulam Mohammad Kakar, was the son of an Afghan general who fought against the British. My father was Commissioner of the Border between the Soviet Union and Afghanistan in 1948. Russian soldiers had taken control of the Amu Darya River, the northern border of Afghanistan. They were trying establish the border on the Afghan side of the river so they could deprive our country of access to water and passage. My father didn't let them. Afghans tried to negotiate a mid-river border six times previously, but failed. King Zahir Shah brought my father to lead the new delegation.

Before my father left, my grandmother told him that my mother was pregnant with their first child. He told my mother, "It doesn't matter whether this child is a girl or a boy, but if I get the river from Russia, then it will be a lucky child for me. If I lose this river and Russia creates the border inside Afghanistan, the child will be bad luck and I will never want to see its face."

So, every time my grandmother prayed, she would say, "*Allah*, please help that man. This is an innocent child. When he says he will do this, he will, because he's a very strong Pashtun." My grandmother prayed every day that my father would get the river back. On the same day I was born, he won back the river.

Upon my father's arrival at the river, he called to his people and told them to bring his child to the border. More than 5000 people followed. When I arrived, my father put me in his boat and we went out into the river where he gave me the name Tajwar, meaning "crown."

When he returned to Kabul, my father warned the King about Russia's intention to invade Afghanistan. He also warned that the King's treacherous cousin, Daoud, intended to help make this happen. My father was ignored, and his anti-communist views became known within the palace. Shortly after that, he was arrested.

When he was let out of prison, we moved to Kunduz. I was nine. Two years later, Daoud's people poisoned my father because he didn't support the Russians.

My mother arranged my marriage when I was 12. I was married at 14 and delivered my first child when I was 15. My husband, Aminullah Rahim, is Uzbek, which means that Uzbek was his first language and he had many customs that I didn't know. He was twice my age and I was his second wife. He was a very powerful man and always invited guests over. Every other night, I had to prepare large dinners for him and his friends, keep up with my school work, and take care of my children. I never had any help. I did all the work myself. All of my life, I never slept more than three or four hours.

Tajwar and two of her children.
photo by Jackie Davidson, 1968

Before the government changed, I had a normal, happy life. I finished my schooling and taught in Kunduz High School for five years before becoming headmaster. Soon after Daoud took over the government [1973], just as my father had warned, they began registering people in the Communist Party. My husband's entire family signed up. They especially wanted me to join because my father had been so powerful and popular, but I rejected it.

Even before Russia invaded, the government had become communist. As headmaster and Pashtu instructor at my school, I began to organize women to fight against the Russians. In 1978, we experienced the first effects of the government change in Kunduz when government forces began attacking people and their homes. They arrested the leaders of the tribes and some rich people.

The communists called me to Kabul and asked me to join them. I was the first woman to be fired because I refused. After three months at home, they assigned me to another school where they watched me very closely so that I couldn't contact my friends. A year later, they sent me to Kabul, and every subsequent year, they placed me in a different school and gave me different subjects to teach. They hoped that I would not make friends but really, they gave me a good opportunity. I found a lot of my friends, teachers, and previous students, and we carried out some activities.

Every week, they came into my classroom and pushed me to join the Communist Party. They promised to give me a good position if I would do so. They offered to send me to Russia or Poland to get my Master's degree, but I kept refusing.

The Russians thought that Afghan women needed to become like Western women, that we needed freedom like Western women. They wanted us to have the freedom to divorce and to choose our own husbands. This is something like poison in Afghanistan. Our religion is different, our customs are different. The foreign people coming now are pushing the same thing.

One night after the Russians killed many of our soldiers, we wrote a night letter[1] telling people to stand in their compounds and say, "*Allahu Akbar*" [God is Great] the following evening. When we started chanting, you would have thought that the whole world was saying *Allahu Akbar*. It was so loud that the walls shook and it made the Russians afraid. We chanted it all night.

Peggy: After returning from Afghanistan, I heard this story: One evening a foreigner was sitting on her second floor balcony in Kabul when she noticed a rumbling in the distance. Thinking that she was hearing more Soviet tanks rolling into her part of the city, she braced herself for a new onslaught.

As the sound grew closer, she realized she wasn't hearing tanks rumbling, but instead, chants of "*Allahu Akbar*," growing stronger and closer until the sound surrounded and embraced her. She looked down into the neighboring courtyard and saw the family members standing outside, shouting their defiance from the safety of their compound.

Tajwar: Another time, I wrote a night letter telling those who opposed Russia not to go to work or go shopping. For three days all of the shops were closed. We did this just to find out how much support we had. But distributing the night letters was very dangerous. Once, a woman we knew poured boiling water on our heads. All the communists knew me and tried to watch my every move.

We also disrupted the May Day parade.[2] I talked with certain students at the school and told them to collect wasps in tiny boxes. On May Day, the Russians organized a big parade with tanks and rows and rows of soldiers marching with their rifles. A large crowd gathered to watch them. At a signal, our supporters in the back of the crowd begin pushing everyone toward the parade. When they got close enough, at another signal, the kids started going crazy, weaving in and out of the lines of soldiers; stooping low while they opened their boxes. You should have seen it! The wasps flew up the soldiers' pant legs and into their shirts. They dropped their banners and rifles as they began swatting at the wasps. The whole parade was disrupted and then disbanded. We collected 25 rifles and small arms that day, showing the Russians our power.

We also decided to disrupt the celebration of the first anniversary of the communist regime. Teachers were forced to bring their students to watch the parade. We gave the kids some balloons and toy explosives. When the parade started, the kids began popping the balloons and setting off the firecrackers.

Women in the crowd shouted, "The *mujahadin* are coming!" The communists in the parade ran for cover and the rest of the ceremony was canceled. These were the kinds of things we women did.

Throughout these four years, the authorities were arresting people twice a month. They arrested me in 1980. At that time, my oldest child was 14 and my youngest, five. That same year, whenever the communists saw any young men, they conscripted them and sent them to war. At one point, they arrested 150 men and asked each of them who was leading the women's resistance. Three men gave my name.

At first they put me in Shashdarak, a **KGB** jail, to perform an "inquiry." A lot of people died in there. I was tortured with electric shock and other things.[3] After that, they put me in another prison. I refused to give any names or information the whole time. I was released after a year. Afterwards, I went to visit some of my friends who had been in jail. Some of those women had broken down, others had lost their memory. The single women would never be able to find husbands because it was assumed they had been raped. Even my own husband asked me some very hard questions. He had divorced his first wife five years before, but remarried her while I was in prison. My personal property then belonged to his wife, since she was a "good communist." That was another punishment for me. They had also punished my children by telling them lies about me.

Friends began telling me how the Afghan communists were attacking villages, raping women, and killing their husbands and children. My brother, the leader of the University Union at the time, and my brother-in-law were killed as well. What could I do? I knew that one day I would die, but in the meantime, I promised myself that I would do something for the freedom of my country. I became a freedom fighter leader in the city.

The communists suspected that I was working against them, so they got my family to watch me. My husband's other wife reported my every move: when I left the house, what I wore, everything. Her two sons worked for the KGB, but she was an uneducated woman.

To do my work, I needed to go to my friends' villages to talk with people. Thousands of freedom fighters came to visit me. Once, a popular commander came from Herat and another from Mazar-e Sharif. Everyone was watching me, so I couldn't travel to the meeting by bus. Instead, I left home wearing a *burqa*. I went to different freedom fighter friends' houses, changed into peasant clothing, and covered myself with a different *burqa*. All of the roads had checkpoints, but I went by donkey and was ignored.

When I was seven months pregnant, I couldn't travel by donkey anymore. Sometimes the Russians would bomb villages, and because I couldn't run in my condition, I stopped going to the villages. Instead, I just worked at home and waited for my child. When I was nearly due, the communists wouldn't let me visit the doctor, even though after ten months the child still hadn't come. Finally, I gave birth alone at home.

When this baby, my seventh, was born, the communists planned to arrest me again and give electric shocks to my child in order to get me to talk. That baby is now in Australia at the university studying journalism. A week after the birth, I heard that they would arrest us. So, at midnight that very night, my husband, my six other children, and I with the newborn child began walking over the mountains to Kabul. On roads not guarded by Russian soldiers, we rode buses and cars. When we came to checkpoints, we got out and walked in the mountains. The trip took us a week.[4]

In that year, 1984, they[5] raped an especially large number of women and killed many children. At one point, we got on a bus that was full of escapees. When we arrived in Taloqan, a man jumped on board and told the driver that the Russians had blocked the road and they were looking for one woman. I understood that they were looking for me.

I told the driver to wait. There were a lot of women and children riding the bus without their men, so I told my husband to bring them all some water. The bus driver was irritated and asked, "Why are you changing my schedule?" I asked him to please wait for 30 minutes while my husband fetched water. When we finally left, another bus had taken our turn in the convoy. The Russians rocketed that bus, killing all the people on board. In the line of 70 vehicles, only our bus and three people from another bus remained unharmed. When I left, I didn't take my gold or anything else; I just took my holy *Quran*. When they tried to shoot our bus, they missed. One Hindu lady, whose family was on the other bus, came covered in blood. I took her inside to sit with us. When she saw the *Quran*, she said that they couldn't shoot this bus because I opened the *Quran* for *Allah* to save us.

Only our bus arrived in Kabul safely. Friends there told us that the Russians had put pictures of me everywhere, and a price was on my head. They warned us that my life was in danger, so we decided to flee to Pakistan. After a week, some men came from Ghazni to guide us. We bought wedding party dresses at the bazaar and sent my brother to buy the bus tickets. He told everyone that we were going to a wedding party in Kandahar, but we got off the bus early and made our way to Ghazni. When the way was safe, we continued to Pakistan.

When I arrived in Peshawar,[6] I thought that the seven *mujahidin* leaders would invite me to work with them. While I was still in Afghanistan, they had sent me a letter calling me Sultana, or "queen." Tajwar means "crown." So, they were calling me "Crown of the Queen." Naturally, I thought they would come asking for me, but seven months passed and no one came. We spent all of our money. My husband and children lived with me in a tiny apartment. Our life was poor and very difficult. On the streets, men wore long beards and turbans, and some of the few women seen wore the black *burqa* and covered their faces. I got nervous.

I spent the next year knocking on doors, talking with the *mujahidin* leaders about women's rights, and asking why women didn't have rights. I told them that girls needed education, but no one listened. Finally, I knocked on the IRC's door. When the Afghan guards saw me, they said, "You are a woman, what are you doing here?"

I told them, "I am Afghan and the IRC is a foreign NGO working for the freedom fighters. I came to talk with them." They didn't admit me. The next day, I got a very strong *mujahidin* commander to go with me and then they let me in. I told the director, "Afghan women are also freedom fighters and have spent time in jail. The IRC needs to work for women and girls, too, and make schools for them."

The director told me, "Afghans have never wanted their girls to go to school [they had only ever asked men, of course], so what can we do?" He gave me some forms and told me to conduct a survey of 300 families on the issue. I went to the most fundamentalist areas, and after two weeks I brought 1000 completed forms from people who wanted schools for their girls. They gave me a job and I set to work planning the new schools. The IRC employees had very nice offices, but I was locked in a garage office with only a chair and an old table because they were afraid of the fundamentalists. That was my first office.

To begin, I knocked door-to-door to find Afghan women teachers, but many refused to work. They told me, "Stop it! Don't talk like that!" because in Afghanistan the teachers endured a lot. The communists arrested many of them and killed others. When they were released from jail, they were afraid and very quiet. For some married women, the entire country had become a jail. Their husbands' families were their jailers. Other women had been divorced by their husbands when they were released.

Before I went to Pakistan, I thought that the freedom fighter leaders were helping women. Once there, I saw that they were not. In fact, they were trying to keep women at home and away from education.

In May, 1987, I became part of the freedom fighter delegation in Paris. The Russian [USSR] president, Mikhail Gorbachev, had come to Paris to get support for the communist government in Afghanistan. There were two rooms for the press conference, one for Afghans, the other for Russians. Local TV stations, plus BBC and Voice of America (VOA) radio, were broadcasting everything.

In Afghanistan, the Communist Party controlled all the TV and radio stations. We could only get real news from the BBC and VOA. Some wealthy and middle-class people in the cities had televisions, but most homes throughout the country had radios.

The Russians talked about how they were bringing education and freedom for women in Afghanistan. I talked about how the Russians had put thousands of educated women in prison.

Then one of our "freedom fighter" leaders said, "Women don't need rights because they can wear a gold necklace and stay at home."

I got very upset and replied, "When the Russians leave Afghanistan, I will buy a gold necklace for that man and *he* can stay at home!" I said to Afghan women listeners, "If you don't have rights, if your husbands are abusing you, stop supporting them. Don't cook their food. Don't wash their clothes. Don't care for their injured. Don't support them. *Stop*. And don't start again until I tell you."

And so the women stopped. I arrived back in Pakistan two days later and the entire next week commanders kept coming and pleading with me. Mr. **Rabbani** came also and said, "Sister, what did you do? All the leaders are dying."

"From what?" I asked.

"We've received thousands and thousands of letters from freedom fighters in Afghanistan saying, 'We don't have food and nobody is washing our clothes, nobody is caring for our injured.' What did you do? We will lose our position and power. Please help us."

He told me to hold another interview and tell the women to help. I said, "Women have the Soviets abusing us and our husbands abusing us. What is the difference? No, I will not tell them to stop until you give women their rights and stop abusing them. When you men went to prison you talked, under torture or out of fear. That's how I got caught. Women in prison had a very hard time. They received electric shocks, they were raped, but they still wouldn't give any names. When the men were released from prison, they were given a good position and salary from their leaders. Why did you say those men were brave just because they went to jail? Why was the same thing shameful for women? Women were freedom fighters. Women went to jail, too, but when they got out, there was nothing for them. Their families only said they were shameful. Now we are showing you the power of women."

No one heard from those individual women, but every woman heard from me.

After that press conference, different leaders came ten times a day to apologize. After two days, I was convinced that the men would change, so I announced that the problem was finished and that the women should resume helping the freedom fighters. After that, no one called us shameful.

I opened 22 schools in Afghanistan for girls and boys with the help of the **Swedish Committee**. The IRC helped me open a school in a refugee camp and set up English courses there for girls. Conditions in the camps were uncomfortable and unhealthy. The children were bored and traumatized, and the men had nothing useful to do.

I began to get offers for good positions from some *mujahidin* leaders, but only if I supported them. I told them, "I'm sorry, but I can't support you because you did nothing for women. I support the return of King Zahir Shah."

During the King's rule, Afghan women held Cabinet and Parliamentary positions, unlike women in neighboring countries. They wore stockings and skirts. The war changed everything. We were Muslim, we loved our country, and we loved our freedom. We had democracy. Our country was very peaceful. Nobody said this person is Tajik; that one is Pashtun, or Hazara, or Uzbek. Not once when I was growing up under King Zahir Shah did I hear that somebody had killed someone.

Peggy: Just because Tajwar never heard of a murder, doesn't mean they didn't happen. There would still have been honor killings, and personal disagreements that led to the death of one or more participants. Zahir Shah was widely popular, but he also had his detractors and his secret police. Additionally, local leaders would have controlled much of the countryside. Still, her statement says a lot about how peaceful Afghanistan was.

Tajwar: It began to get dangerous for me in Pakistan. Once when I returned from a conference in Geneva, my husband asked, "What were you doing in Geneva? Every time you leave, a lot of threatening letters come. You are making problems for yourself. They will kill you and one day, they will kill me because I'm your husband."

A few days later, I saw one of my friends, Dr. Ludi. He owned a childcare center. He told me, "Tajwar, you know the fundamentalists are killing us. They already hired a professional killer to kill you and me."

I asked, "What did I do wrong that they want to kill me?"

He replied, "You rejected them for the future of Afghanistan."

"That is good. I do reject them. They can do nothing for Afghanistan."

"But they are going to kill you." He left and returned two hours later saying that he had [hired] six gunmen; three for him and three for me.

I asked, "For what?"

"For security."

I refused them. "I just need security from *Allah*. Because my faith is very strong, *Allah* has saved me. I don't need security guards."

"OK," he said, "I will pray. If they kill me, I'm not worried. *Allah* will save you, because Afghan women need you, and you are important for Afghanistan." Those were his last words to me. They killed him that night.

The next day, Mr. Tom, my boss, told me that he had received a message saying, "If Tajwar continues working for the IRC, we will bomb your office."

"What do you think?" he asked.

I told him, "I know they are very dangerous people, so I will leave." I resigned, then went home. Two hours later, a car came from the Afghan Commissioner of Pakistan and police arrested me. They accused me of being an un-Muslim woman.

I asked, "Why? I'm a complete Muslim woman and a real Afghan."

"Then why are you talking about women's rights?"

I asked, "How did Aisha, the Prophet's wife, teach Mohammad's followers if nobody believed women could be teachers?"

He asked again, "Why are you talking about women's rights?"

I asked my interrogator, "Is Islam the same for the whole world or is it different for Iran, Pakistan, or Afghanistan?"

He replied, "No, it's all the same."

I said, "Look. If Islam is the same everywhere, then why is Benazir Bhutto your Prime Minister? She is a woman."

The official became very upset and demanded, "You will leave Pakistan within 24 hours or we will arrest you and leave you on the border for the communists." The next day, the Norwegian Embassy held a press conference for me, but within ten minutes of my arrival, I saw that their demeanor had changed. They whisked me away to another house, and after an hour, they moved me again. I was taken house to house, and our last stop was the IRC office. When I saw my children and husband, I was so relieved.

When I asked them what was going on, they told me that they had received word that I would be killed that night. So we rented taxis, and one by one my children went to Islamabad. We stayed in a hotel there for 18 days until it could be arranged for us all to go to Australia. I lived there for 15 years and their government gave me good support.

⊰⊱◈○◈◈○◈⊰⊱

In Australia, I was diagnosed with cancer. I had developed the disease during my time in prison. After 12 operations, I was cured. I returned to Pakistan in 1994 for a year to research women's conditions.

I discovered that they weren't letting girls go to the mosque to study. While I was in Pakistan, I talked to various religious leaders about women's rights and girls' education. Some open-minded *mullahs* wrote letters to **Mullah Omar**. As a result, we got 70% of woman's rights[7] from *mullahs* in Quetta and Peshawar.

Two years later when the Taliban Prime Minister came to Islamabad, I went to speak with him. His secretary asked me, "Why are you here?"

I told him, "Because I'm an Afghan, I am a woman, and I have rights. One day, the Prophet started education for men, and a lady asked Mohammad, 'Are you a prophet just for men or for men and women?' He said, 'For both of them.' She asked, 'Then why aren't you starting education for us?' The Prophet replied that he would start education for women as well. Now I'm here and I'm using those same words for the Prime Minister of the Taliban. Is he the Prime Minister only for men? If he is, I will leave. If the population is twice that of men, then please, I have some questions."

After that, he let me in. I had an hour-long discussion with the Prime Minister about women's rights and *jihad*. I also said to him, "Islam is the first religion that gives rights to women. Education is part of Islam. Why are you stopping it?"

He said, "Fine. Come to the cabinet meeting in Kabul and ask your questions. If you can convince them, we will do what you want for women." After that, somebody called my youngest son and told him that if his mother went to Afghanistan, they would kill her.

Later that year, I learned that my mother had suffered a heart attack, so I returned to Australia. When my mother recovered, the first words out of her mouth were, "Stop yourself, my daughter. You are a woman. Why don't you understand? A woman can do nothing. You must stay with your children. Your father did a lot of things for his country and he lost his life. You, too, will lose your life."

I said, "Mother, how did I become a strong freedom fighter? It was because all the people knew who my father was and they supported me. My father did nothing wrong and I am proud of him, but he didn't finish his job, so I will."

In 1998, I went to the Taliban Foreign Ministry in Kandahar to discuss women's rights and sat in front of six *mullahs*. I couldn't talk with them while wearing my *burqa*. I said, "I have a question for the Taliban. Please don't become upset. Men grew long mustaches and sold our country to Russia. Later, men grew long beards and sold our *jihad*.[8] Then you put women in *burqas*. What did we do that you put us in *burqas*? We are not ashamed. We did nothing wrong. We should not have to hide our faces."

I took off my *burqa* and said, "I'm not wearing this. The *burqa* is not Afghan. Some Mogul families brought it to Afghanistan and it became stylish. Traditionally, Afghan women never wore *burqas*. In Islam, it says that the women must wear long sleeves and cover their heads. All of my clothes are Islamic clothes, so why should I wear the *burqa*? The Pashtuns never wore the *burqa*. They have their own traditional clothes." The *mullahs* didn't reply, but they were very upset.

Peggy: Toward the end of my trip in 2003, I met with an NGO director who had attended one of Tajwar's meetings with the Taliban. He described how she stood up in front of a room full of big-turbaned, black-bearded, scowling Taliban and boldly declared that women shouldn't have to wear *burqas* and that Afghanistan can never rebuild unless its people are educated, both boys and girls. Eventually, Mullah Omar gave permission for her to open a school for boys and told her that if that school succeeded, he would give permission to open one for girls later.

Tajwar: In 1999, King Zahir Shah invited me to Italy, where he lived then, for a *Loya Jerga*. Everyone was saying "The Taliban are dangerous. How will we face them? They take hostages."

I told them, "If you consider Afghanistan to be your country and you are not going there, then you are not facing the problem. Who else is going to solve it?" Some suggested bombing the Taliban, but who can support that? It would kill both the guilty and innocent.

I told them, "We must go there to educate the people and use our power to change the government."

Other people said, "She's talking like that, but she can't go anywhere in Afghanistan." That was a challenge for me, but I didn't have a way [to finance the journey.]

In early 2000, I received a call from an NGO inquiring whether I would be interested in opening a boys' school in Kabul. They promised me that if the Taliban didn't close that school for six months, then they would finance the opening of a girls' school.

Before I opened the school, I spent three months meeting with various Taliban. The Taliban Minister of Women's Rights told me, "You don't know how much I'm upset with this situation. All of my family is educated. My mother, my sister, everyone. Why are you fighting with me? Go fight with Mullah Omar."

I came back to Kabul in 2000 and opened my school. It was called Omid School, The School of Hope. All of the students were boys and the teachers were men. I only worked in the office. Every week, one of the Taliban officers would come to check the school. On June 1, 2001, I got special permission from the Taliban to open a girls' school, but the NGO that had agreed to finance it backed out.

When I tried to take a break to be with my children back in Australia, I got more than 15 anonymous phone calls telling me not to give up, not to leave.

Those callers who were working in the government never shared their names; I only understood that I had a lot of people on my side.

Once a man told me, "We [Taliban] are fighting with **Massoud** but he can do nothing. He can't take one meter of land from us. But you come fighting and you've broken all the boundaries. Why are you working in an office? Why are you working in a school? Why don't you wear a *burqa*? Every week you're going to one of the ministries to fight with them. Maybe in one year you can finish the Taliban government. Why is the Taliban quiet? Why aren't they stopping you?"

When the American bombing stopped and Mr. [Hamid] **Karzai's** government came, I returned to Kabul the next day. My school was the first to re-open, and I registered girls as well as boys. All of the businesses along the road to my school had been looted, but in my school nobody had taken anything. When I asked why, people told me that every night, my students' parents had taken turns guarding the school.

On the same day I opened the school, the US bombed the *Aljazeera* [news organization] office next door. My students were taking their placement exams. The parents came running to the school crying and looking for their children. A student's father, Mohammad, came, and when he saw the fire and broken windows, he told his son to come quickly, to get away from there. But his son said, "No, I have exams and my principal will get upset and go to Australia if I stop." My students were like that. They always came to school.

When the new government took charge, they appointed me Deputy Minister for Women's Affairs but I was fired after I questioned where $2,000,000 had gone that had been given to our ministry to help widows. After that, I continued working for my school and I also worked as a special advisor to the IRC.

Peggy: *What are your children doing now?*

Tajwar: I am very happy that my children were part of the *jihad*. My oldest daughter was 14 years old when I went to prison. She took care of the entire family. When I was in Australia, I started an organization and school for Afghans. Now, my oldest daughter runs that school. Every Saturday and Sunday, we teach the children Dari, the national Afghan language, religion, and history. All of my children received a good education in Australia and they all are trying to come back to Afghanistan, but their children need a good school. My youngest daughter was eight days old when she left Afghanistan. Now she is 18 and comes back during her school holidays to learn Pashtu and Dari and teach Afghan history. She's studying journalism.

One day, I turned on her computer and read a story she had written about a "bad luck woman." I realized that the story was about me. I asked her to explain who this unlucky woman was.

She said, "You've had a very hard personal life, living with your husband's family and fighting in the war."

I said, "Look, I am a very lucky woman. I am still alive and I'm still fighting. I finished my education and I support myself." She was quiet.

Once, I got very sick and she came from Australia to help me. She said, "Now that you have established your school, you can come back and live with us."

We visited the school together, and the students came and kissed me; they told me they were afraid that I was going back to Australia. I saw my daughter crying and asked her why. She said, "I can see how much these children really need you. I will never tell you to return to Australia again."

Peggy: *What is the most important thing for the improvement of Afghanistan?*

Tajwar: Many educated women went to live in foreign countries during the wars and the Taliban. Now Afghanistan has peace and those people need to come back home. Our country is like our mother. She is sick and has suffered many injuries. If her children don't look after our mother, what will we say to *Allah*? Our mother needs her children.

We must forgive what was in the past. I don't blame the people who became part of the communists. Some of them joined by themselves, some were just afraid. Now Russia is gone and everyone knows that she did nothing for them. Some of them became *talibs* and we understand that. Somebody made them *talib*, and the Taliban did nothing for their mother. These people need to come home and help their mother.

We need educated women, too, because we lost so many educated people during the war. The Russians imprisoned 25,000 educated people. Nobody knows what happened to them. My brother was in jail at that time and we don't know where he is or if he's even alive. Those Afghans living abroad need to come home. The foreign countries don't need them; they have their own educated people, but Afghanistan does need them. If all of our people come back and help, the country will be rebuilt.

Peggy: *What can women in America do to help?*

Tajwar: We need help for our widows, especially the freedom fighter widows and children. Together, we can make a center for widows. I can help, but can't do it alone, because many doors are closed to me. I can't get in to see Mr. Karzai so he can hear the truth. He can't get an honest picture of what is going on outside.

People who have access to him tell him nice things, but outside the palace is another reality. We have freedom, but not total freedom. I understand that one day my enemies will kill me. I have lost 29 members of my family and more than 2000 people from my tribe. We aren't crazy because we love our freedom. America shouldn't forget their friends or their longtime enemy, Russia.

Peggy: *Who would be a good leader for Afghanistan?*

Tajwar: There are a lot of groups, but still, everyone who has power only helps his own party. Look at our ministries. If the minister belongs to a certain tribe, all the people in that ministry belong to that tribe. That is not democracy. That is "gun-ocracy." Before, all the ministers had one car. Now they each have five or six. Where did they come from? Many people are begging in the street. How many ministers took their land? Why don't they give land for widows and orphans? They gave me land for my school, but I have to build on it quickly or the ministers will take it.

Peggy: *Is there anyone in Afghanistan who has the heart to be a good leader?*

Tajwar: We have two choices. One choice is an old man, King Zahir Shah, who has experience and, like a father, knows all of his children. If the country needs a younger man, we must find someone who is not afraid of being killed. If he can be brave, he can make a real democracy in Afghanistan. He must be someone who will give rights to all the people.

Afghanistan needs an army, too, because an army is like a roof; if you don't have one, everything will come inside. Karzai could have made an army very easily. He could have invited all the tribal leaders to send their top freedom fighters. Just among the Pashtuns, we have 160 tribes. Each leader could send one general who could bring 100 fighters for the national army. The tribes would send good soldiers because it would be shameful to send bad ones. This would make a strong army because the freedom fighters understand how to fight. They only need training in modern warfare. Why didn't he do that? Now he has no power. If he has power, why does he use Americans for his security?

Why did Mr. Karzai say he would give rights to women, but did not appoint two or three women ministers? Women have minds. In their personal lives and in their political lives, men ask their wives for advice. Why doesn't Mr. Karzai listen to people who tell him the truth? I'm afraid for him.

The foreigners are taking guns from the freedom fighters, which is a big mistake.[9] A better way is to send *mullahs* to each tribe and have them talk with the leaders about when Islam says to keep the gun and when to drop the gun. My brother-in-law, the former KGB agent, says, "If the freedom fighters don't give up their guns, we report them to the American military saying that they are al Qaeda, and then the Americans kill them. It is better for us if America kills all the freedom fighters."

Tajwar, 2010

Peggy: By 2010, modernization of the Afghan phone system had rendered all old numbers obsolete. It was only at the end of my trip that year that I was able to find Tajwar.

This time, we met at her apartment and drank tea on her enclosed porch. A taxi dropped me off on the street outside her five-story apartment complex. Since she lived alone and hadn't yet returned from work, she had arranged for two young men to meet me, guide me to her apartment, and wait with me until she arrived. I could hear great respect and admiration in their voices as they spoke of her as "*Hajai Sultana.*"[10]

After seven years her hair was somewhat grayer, but her face showed the same authority and determination I'd noted in 2003. Even after a long workday, she climbed the five flights of stairs without becoming winded and talked with me for over two hours. At 61, Tajwar is still a pillar of strength.

I brought some photographs of her to share that my friend Jackie Davidson had taken in 1968, when she was a Peace Corps volunteer, giving smallpox vaccinations throughout rural Afghanistan. Jackie was based in Kunduz, where Tajwar lived at the time, and the two had become good friends. Jackie, a professional hairdresser, had cut Tajwar's hair stylishly short; a radical move for a provincial Afghan. Tajwar, however, was a modern woman. She also wore knee-length dresses.

A modern woman.
photo by Jackie Davidson, 1968

By 2010, Tajwar no longer worked for the IRC. She had been working for four years as Senior Parliamentary Liaison Advisor for the USAID-funded Afghanistan Parliamentary Assistance Project (APAP). Her job was to establish and maintain good working relations between APAP and the Parliament, and to help the parliamentary committees implement their projects.

Tajwar: I enjoyed my work when I returned to Afghanistan. I kept close contact with the religious people, the *mujahidin,* and leaders of Taliban because I knew how to talk with them.

Peggy: *Does your work involve education? I know how passionate you are about that.*

Tajwar: Education for me is like fish in water, but this job is not about education. I used to have hope for the role of education in Afghanistan, but now I'm discouraged because the system is not good. Afghanistan needs a new system for education. The communist regime pushed children to join the communist educational system, but they didn't like it and went to the *jihad.* Now, they are adults without any education, jobs, or any way to earn a living. When I visited

Mr. Karzai, I told him, "The young men who joined the *jihad* fought against Russia, and now they have families who need food, clothes, and housing. What programs do you have for them? Their lives are very hard without an education." He never answered.

Peggy: *What do you think about the conditions of Afghanistan now, compared to when I saw you in 2003?*

Tajwar: The conditions have improved greatly here in Kabul. For example, there are female members of Parliament and some women ministers. Most girls in Kabul go to school. Many private schools and universities provide a good education. Girls have the freedom to walk in the street. On the other hand, security is very poor. People are fighting for power in Parliament and not accomplishing much. Nobody can stop the war, especially when they're just working for personal benefit.

During the *jihad,* a lot of people abandoned their homes and lived as refugees in Pakistan, Iran, or other countries. Those who stayed took the refugees' land and belongings. I lost my house in Kunduz like that. When we talked with the government about this, they didn't support our claim.

For example, one man told me, "When Mr. **Dostom** left Afghanistan, we had good security, but when he returned, he took my land. I came here to tell Mr. Karzai, but he did nothing." This is a big problem because if the government won't help them they will choose another path, perhaps joining the Taliban.

Corruption has also gotten worse in many ways. Government officials demand bribes in order to do their jobs. In another kind of corruption, officials or gunmen kidnap a person's wives and children. Nobody punishes the criminals, so what will the people do? They will join the enemy.

My son lived here with me for nine years. They attacked him twice. The first time he was working with a Dutch NGO. When he woke up from a coma, he said they told him to tell me to resign from my job [as Deputy Minister of Women's Affairs]. The second time, someone had pushed his car off the road. I sent my son away a year and a half ago to avoid his being killed.

When the *mujahidin* had power, why didn't they rebuild Afghanistan? Why were they fighting? Why did they destroy Kabul? Now they have changed one thing: their looks. They're clean-shaven and wear suits now, but their mentality is the same. That is the danger of the Taliban. They say, "I want Islam like this," and I like everything they tell me, but it's just another face. I feel it is better to bring good, educated people into the government from outside Afghanistan. Karzai has had a long time to bring good people into the government, but he is always making deals with the warlords.

Somebody asked me earlier if I was planning to run for Parliament in September. I said I didn't think so. I have had many people call me from Kunduz, and especially from Kandahar, asking me to run. However, many MPs receive support from powerful people. They come from **Rabbani's** side, Karzai's side, the *masjid* side, and some from Dostom's side. All of them have their affiliations. If their leaders say, "Do this," then they do it. If they say, "Don't do this," then they don't. So when people asked if I was going to run, I replied that I didn't have a chance; I wasn't a puppet backed by a powerful man.[11]

Peggy: *Has anything good come out of the Parliament?*

Tajwar: Honestly, I will say that when Mr. Karzai ran for president in the first election, I campaigned for him because I knew him from Pakistan.

When I was a member of the Cabinet, at one meeting I asked the ministers about the money they received from foreign countries. I asked them, one-by-one, "What did you do with the money? In one week, how much money did you spend?" They all gave me dirty looks and no answers. Another time, I said to Mr. Karzai, "Two ministers are dead, who killed them? Please authorize me to do an inquiry. I will find out who killed them in one week." But he just gave me a bad look.

I also raised the question of why they took my school away from me. A few years ago, I went to Bonn, Germany, with the rest of the Cabinet, Karzai, and NGO leaders from all over Afghanistan. I asked the NGOs in front of everybody, "How much money did you give to Afghanistan, who did you give it to, and for what? You are losing your money." When I came back, they took my school and they attacked my son. Now the school focuses on educating the children of the wealthy.

Never in Afghanistan's history has so much money come to help the country, but look at all the people begging in the streets. The ministers are not working for the people. It would have been easy to solve the housing shortage, but the ministers took the government's money, government lands, and even private land for themselves.

The second time I went to Mr. Karzai, he told me that when I talk with him, he gets upset and angry. I said, "Mr. Karzai, I am older than you, I am like a big sister to you. I will not be sweet-talking you. You promised that you would not become upset with me and I promised that I will always tell you the truth."

He promised me that things would be different but he did nothing. He is like a child. When you talk to him he says, "Yes, yes," but when you leave, he does something different. He follows the people who have power and honestly, in this last election, I did not give him my vote. If the people tell Karzai that this or that minister is bad, Karzai will just transfer them to another ministry. If the ministries had good ministers, the government could work well. I don't know why Karzai is working like a servant.

Today, we have women's rights. We have a Women's Ministry and the head is a woman. But, what have they really done for women? It is not right for women to have to go to men to ask for permission, help, and support. A woman is a human. That minister [of women's affairs] goes door to door, seeking help [from powerful men] so she can keep her position.

They made that woman a minister so she would be in their pocket. I am a woman and I am Afghan. Never will I be in anyone's pocket. This country belongs to me and I belong to my country. I work and don't need support from my husband or anyone.

Peggy: *In fact, during the* jihad *you had to work around his family because your husband was a communist, right?*

Tajwar: My husband's family was communist. Not long after we were married he divorced his first wife, but he remarried her while I was in prison. And now he is in Kunduz living with her again. We are still married, but he signed over all of his things to her and gave me nothing. I worked very hard and I bought this apartment myself.

Peggy: *He didn't divorce you?*

Tajwar: No, I'm technically still married, but now he says that it's shameful that I went to prison. When he was in Pakistan, he didn't talk like that, and when we went to Australia, he never mentioned it; but now he asks me, "Why did you go to jail? It's a shame that you went to jail." He hurt me a lot. He is still with his wife, and I'm happy to live here alone. My children are grown and I've done my job. Now, I'm looking for my own life and my own voice. My country needs me now and I am free to do my work. That is my life now; I don't worry about husbands. When you are young your husband comes panting like a dog. Sometimes they come like a lion. I don't like that. Now life is easy, and I am very happy.

Peggy: *So, what hope do you see for Afghanistan?*

Tajwar: *Allah* knows. We have more women than men in Afghanistan, but every time, they keep putting us down. They don't give us a chance because they're afraid of us.

The Afghans trusted the foreign people, but now they've lost hope. They say openly to me, "The foreigners brought back those warlords and now we are hostages." Really, I don't know what's happening, but I know we are not losing hope from *Allah*. We had a very hard time when the Russian soldiers came and *Allah* helped us. I just trust that *Allah* will find a way this time around.

That is my life story.

Peggy: In March, 2011, the Ministry of Education in Uruzgan Province hired Tajwar as an advisor. Her mandate is to improve educational quality and enhance the overall literacy rate. She is working on a book about the many remarkable women of the Afghan resistance.

A traditional, middle class living and sleeping room. Heavy quilts are stored behind the curtain and extra mattresses (*toshaks*) are piled up on the left.

15/Suraia Perlika

I met Suraia in her small office in one of the five Soviet-built Macrorayan subdivisions in Kabul. The now shabby, bullet-pocked, four-and-five-story walkup apartment blocks were considered good housing by middle-class Afghans when I visited in 2003 because the utilities and toilets were working.

Suraia is an activist intellectual who has lived in and around Kabul her whole life. When she speaks of conditions of women or conditions overall, she's speaking of conditions in Kabul.

Suraia: I was born in a village about half an hour outside of Kabul in 1944. My father was an educated intellectual, and although my mother was illiterate, she was very enlightened. I grew

Witnessing all of these atrocities compelled me to stay here and resist. My country needed me to defend the rights of the people.

up with a lot of freedom. My parents saw my brothers and me as equals. Both of my parents exemplified compassion and always encouraged me to help others. I wondered about the discrimination I saw in society between the poor and wealthy, between men and women.

During my senior year at Kabul University, different student movements sprang up, from Islamist to communist groups. Six of my friends and I started the Democratic Association of Women (DAW). The Afghan Constitution had given women the right to vote in 1964 and indeed, one of our members won a seat in Parliament. We enjoyed complete freedom back then. We were free to do whatever we wanted.

Peggy: Suraia is speaking for herself and her educated urban friends. The government gave Afghan women their rights legally, but the real power to give and take these rights lay then and still lies within the family unit. Progressive laws are beneficial but unless the people, especially in rural areas, become aware of them and buy into them, they mean little.

Suraia: At first, our association focused on raising awareness. We encouraged women to use their rights and vote, especially for the women running for Parliament. Kabul was much smaller then, having no more than 500,000 people, so we could be active in every part of the city. We canvassed neighborhoods and knocked on doors to promote our candidates. Now, with 5,000,000 people, that is nearly impossible.

Only a few women wore the *burqa* in the late 1960s. Many women exercised their rights, ran for Parliament, and worked outside the home. Due to our activism, four women won seats in Parliament. In response, some men in Parliament presented an amendment to the Constitution requiring women traveling to other countries to have a male relative as an escort. This was designed to stop women from studying abroad. As soon as we heard this news, our association decided to demonstrate. We gathered at the Parliament Building daily, from morning to night, until they decided to drop the law. Male students also marched with us for the entire 40 days it took for them to withdraw the amendment. The demonstration put us way behind in our classes.

I took advantage of our big success. After I received my Bachelor's degree, I studied for my Master's in Kiev. In 1978, I graduated, returned to teach at Kabul University, and was elected president of the DAW.

When we were only raising awareness, the communists supported us, but when they began forcing their agendas on Afghan society, we spoke out for human rights. As a result, they threw my six co-founders and me into the infamous Pul-e Charki Prison for a year and a half.

Peggy: The communists Suraia speaks of consisted of rival factions. So, depending on which group was in power at any one time, she was helped or tortured. Speaking out against them in favor of human rights brought condemnation from all sides.

Suraia: First they brought me to a detention center where they tortured me with electric shocks. This was not an interrogation; they asked me no questions, they were only punishing me for my resistance.

Once I was transferred to Pul-e Charki, I was relieved to see my six friends as I was led past their cell on the way to mine. My own cellmates hadn't been tortured, because they hadn't resisted. They were imprisoned because their husbands or fathers had opposed the regime.

When the guards realized that I was spreading our ideas among the other prisoners, they moved us seven DAW members into one cell and began abusing us. They broke my hand, my nose, and my head, and they put a cloth in my mouth. They pulled out my fingernails, and my fingers continued to bleed even after I got out of prison. I had been so proud of my beautiful long nails during my university years! They still bother me. After I was released from prison, I had ten or twelve operations to correct the problems my torturers had caused.

As time passed, intrigues and infighting weakened the government. Opposition parties grew stronger, more active, and numerous. Prison conditions changed as well. We were transferred upstairs to a large room with many other prisoners. When President **Amin** was killed, people outside began shooting at the prison, trying to break down the walls, and resisting prisoners inside clashed more and more. Someone even fired a rocket into our previous cell, trying to kill us.

The prison commander began releasing prisoners who had opposed Amin once his rival, **Karmal**, assumed power. One night, a group of Russians entered our room asking for someone to translate for the *mujahidin* and their families. Since I knew Russian, I learned about Amin's overthrow and that the next day we would be set free. Everyone rejoiced at the news.

The earlier rocket attack worried the prison officials that the attackers would return to kill us. The morning after Karmal overthrew Amin, two other women, four men, and I were released. Early the following morning, I returned to the prison to negotiate the release of the other DAW women. It took about seven or eight days to empty the entire prison. Finally, the doors of Pul-e Charki were opened and all of the prisoners were freed.

Peggy: Suraia was set free in the early hours of the Soviet invasion, along with 600 other prisoners. On January 6, 1980 about 2000 more were freed.[1]

Suraia: Before going to prison, I was head of the DAW. After we were freed, I was elected leader again.

During the communist governments before and during the Soviet war, we decided to start daycare for working women. Because of our efforts, this became compulsory for offices and factories. No one opposed us when we suggested that during the last three months of pregnancy, and for three months after giving birth, women should have the right to maternity leave with their full salary. Our organization proposed these things and the government implemented them.

Women were using their rights to be equal to men. Thousands of women received scholarships to study abroad. In every way, women received as much support in their jobs as men. We had equality, even under Islam.

Women were driving and women's organizations existed in all of the provinces. There were more female doctors and educated elite than males. I also proposed a law saying that no one in Afghanistan would have the right to take a second wife. In Islam, men have the right to have four wives, but I wanted to change that. The *Quran* says that if a man has four wives, he has to treat them equally. I told them that is impossible therefore, it is not fair to the women.

Dr. **Najibullah**, the president at the time, told me that this idea was not feasible because there were *mujahidin* who would never agree. He suggested that only those people belonging to political parties or working in the government be prohibited from marrying more than one woman. As a result, ministers with more than one wife were fired. After firing two or three of them, other such men didn't dare take a second wife. Women who had office jobs usually only had two or three children, and they were left in daycare. Mothers enjoyed the right to visit their children every three hours. In addition to earning a salary, the workers received basic foods like sugar, oil, salt, and tea. These were part of their meager salary, and it alleviated poverty.

Unemployed people didn't receive these foods, but their distribution to the workers resulted in lower prices for everyone else. Right now prices are increasing daily, and people have to take corruption money or embezzle in order to feed their families. Much less corruption existed at that time.

In 1986, I was appointed President and Secretary General of the **Red Crescent Society of Afghanistan** and I helped set up their office here in Kabul. Getting permission for the Red Crescent to examine prisoners was difficult but we managed to do so. We arranged for war-injured children to get treatments in other countries. I also started working with a de-mining organization, **Halo Trust**, that is still here removing land mines.

After the Soviets left and the *mujahidin* came to power, there were abductions, rapes, forced marriages, and all kinds of violence against women. We had seven parties with seven leaders, each fighting the others to control Afghanistan. Throughout all of this, we kept working for our rights.

Peggy: In 1992, Professor **Mojaddidi**, a man trusted by all of the *mujahidin* groups, was elected President of the Islamic Interim Government of Afghanistan. Two months later, as agreed, he stepped down in favor of the newly constructed, power-sharing government of **Rabbani**, with other *mujahidin* leaders filling key government roles. These positions were to rotate every four months. However, Rabbani called a conference excluding certain key members. Then, in violation of the rule to check their weapons at the city gates, **Hekmatyar** and his troops entered, fully armed, from a side gate. The resulting skirmishes expanded into civil war.

Suraia: This building we are in now was fought over by the forces of Rabbani, Hekmatyar, and **Dostom** as they killed each other and anyone in their line of fire. Our water was cut off. The situation got so bad that no one could go outside. Those who did venture out to buy food or get water were fired upon. One day, a young boy who tried to open a door to this apartment building was killed. He was a relative of a family living here and had come to check up on them, to see whether they were alive or not. The boy knocked on the door, but no one heard him. When the fighters came, he was shot. The fighting raged so intensely that nobody could open the door to bring his body inside the house or bury him. Finally, after two days, there was a cease-fire for a few hours and the family was able to lay him to rest. They left the country that very day.

Peggy: Kabul lies on a high plateau surrounded by hills. Warring factions positioned themselves on the hills surrounding the capital and fired rockets across the city at each other. Most landed inside the city. Hekmatyar also fired rockets on civilian targets to punish the people of the city for having supported the communists; of course, only some had done so. In August, 1992, Hekmatyar, again shelling the capital, killed as many as 1800 people in a single barrage of rockets.[2] In addition, bands of militias battled each other in and among the buildings and apartment complexes. The factional infighting from 1992 – 1996 caused an estimated 50,000 deaths.[3]

Suraia: They were firing from all different sides, killing many innocent people. Now, those leaders are still alive and some of them are working in the government.

In every part of the city, there were different groups of *mujahidin* fighting each other. It wasn't just one soldier here and another there. They went as a group into any area that they wanted. The people had to stay inside their houses, or else they might be killed. They were even firing on people who were going up on their roofs, and they shot at each other, rooftop to rooftop. Without exception, all of these *mujahidin* groups killed random civilians. Whatever they could do, they did: killed, raped, gang-raped. Sometimes they removed women's clothes so they could see how children were born.

A young girl whom one of these *mujahidin* groups had raped lived across the courtyard from here. Her apartment was on the sixth floor and she jumped to her death because she couldn't live with the humiliation and pain. Her body lay in front of the entrance and nobody could take it inside because of all the fighting. There were parents who killed themselves and their children with rat poison because the situation was so bad.

If these *mujahidin* wanted to marry a girl they saw, but her father didn't agree, they would kill him. One girl in this situation told them, "You can come tomorrow and I will marry you. Don't kill my father." The night after she agreed to get married, she killed herself. When the *mujahidin* came and asked where the girl was, her father took them to see her body.

Another woman was about to deliver a baby. While she was in labor, some *mujahidin* saw her. Four of them gang-raped and then killed her. Her seven-year-old son witnessed it all.

8>◆IOI◆ ◆IOI◆<8

My country needed me to defend the rights of the people, so I started a new union of women from all over Afghanistan, the **All Afghan Women's Union** (AAWU). The DAW had disbanded when the communists left. Some of the members had been killed, or became depressed and hopeless. A few killed themselves. I made this new union for women to give them hope for the future.

My full name is Suraia Suraia but because I'm so well-known for my past activities, I realized that women might encounter problems by associating with me. Therefore, I decided to start the union under an alias and created the name "Perlika." I am the only one in Afghanistan who has this name. In Dari the first part, "per," means the "feather of a bird." "Li" means "writing" in Pashtu, and "ka" means "Afghanistan" So, my name means "Afghanistan's writing quill."

During the *mujahidin* time, there were some schools, but people were afraid to venture outside and walk the distance to get there. There weren't many teachers who would brave the bullets, either. It was a very nerve-wracking and depressing time. Many, many people were killed, leaving their families crying and fearful. Our union members went to visit their friends and encourage those women to be active and think about the future.

We suggested that if any of them were teachers, they could start classes in their homes by gathering some students from their neighborhoods. That's how the home schools started. When we started them, we thought that it would only be a way for children to keep up with their studies. The home schools were good for everybody, though, because they gave people something to do and the teachers could earn income. The secret schools under the Taliban started from this.

Under the Soviets, we had a center where women could gather and discuss issues. When the *mujahidin* were killing each other, attendance dropped because of all the threats from rockets and bombs. That's when we began to diffuse our ideas through speaking to people at funerals. There were many funerals in those days. We used them as an opportunity to talk with women and raise their level of awareness. After we offered our condolences, we would talk about classes and handicrafts like knitting and carpet weaving, and things like that.

Peggy: In Afghanistan, the deceased are buried within 24 hours of death, either in graveyards or in the place they died, if no family member comes to claim them. For the next 40 days, the family will sit at home to receive those who come to give condolences and companionship. Suraia and her cohorts made use of this long mourning period to spread their ideas.

Suraia: We didn't have any expenses. We only visited our friends and got them to visit their friends. In this way, the movement expanded. It even spread around the country as members evacuated to different areas and began women's unions there.

Once the Taliban came, violence and crimes against women continued, but there wasn't as much killing as there was from the rockets and skirmishes, because the Taliban were only one group. The seven *mujahidin* leaders reunited to fight them. Under the Taliban, women were prohibited from going outside uncovered, so there were fewer forced marriages since the women couldn't be seen. Women were a bit safer, but our activities were very limited.

During the Taliban, there weren't as many funerals, so we created other ways to gather. We used *nazr*, a religious custom, to help women connect. For example, we'd get eight loaves of flatbread or eight nuts – something small – and invite eight women to our house. We would ask them if they had any special goal, desire, or prayer. While they were thinking about their desire, I gave them a nut or piece of flatbread. They would come every week for seven weeks. Either naturally, spontaneously, or by the will of God, their wishes were sometimes fulfilled. After a while, women began gathering regularly, often at mosques, and we spread our ideas among them.

Since *nazr* is a custom we already have and since it's tied to our religion, it was well-accepted. It spreads easily since, if the woman gets her wish, she would be obligated in turn to purchase eight nuts or breads and invite eight other people who would, in turn, spread it to eight more.

Peggy: *Wasn't walking to the mosque dangerous during the Taliban?*

Suraia: Not so much, because we would wear *burqas*. Maybe it was dangerous, but it was a process by which women could get together. We already had a network from the *mujahidin* times and we expanded it even more during the Taliban.

During both times, powerful men demanded to marry the girls they wanted. We trained the women on how to deal with this. We told them to tell their husbands not to resist when the Taliban came demanding their daughter. Just agree with them and ask for some money and jewelry as the bride price. Usually they would bring that within 20 days or a month. Once it had been paid, everyone would leave the house, one-by-one, and move to another area of town. When those powerful people came to get the girl, no one would be there. When they would ask around, the neighbors would only say they had been there yesterday, "but now no one's there."

We also used a second kind of *nazr*. We told the women to cook a traditional sweet religious dish. The women would make it and then invite several neighbors to partake. It was important that this be done at a time when there were no men or children at home so that what was discussed would be kept secret. Women would come and eat the dish in hopes that their wishes would be granted. We told them that if they shared anything that was said at the meeting, God would not grant their desires. After we ate, we discussed the plans for our activities.

As our activities increased, the number of suicides and attacks on women decreased. Because of the *burqa*, we were also able to go outside more. In general, women didn't wear the *burqa* during the *mujahidin* regime; rather, it started during the Taliban. I started wearing one from the beginning of the *mujahidin* fighting because I could be hidden. Nobody could recognize me or see where I went so they left me alone. If the *mujahidin* saw a beautiful, stylish, or modern girl, they would often rape her or force a marriage with her. Under the *burqa*, we were safely hidden. Throughout this time, all of our activities increased until the Taliban were gone.

Within two days of the Taliban's overthrow, I held a meeting at my house. One hundred and twenty active women came to discuss our next action. We formed the AAWU and they elected me president. Our first activity was to encourage teachers and students who had been studying in their homes to go back to the schools. Many older girls were behind in their studies because they had been prohibited from attending school. We began special classes and tests for them so they could advance more quickly, without being taught with younger children.

Many journalists flocked to Kabul after the Taliban left, so we decided to hold a gathering for 20,000 women in 2002. We hoped this would garner the attention of the international community and give us the support to go before the UN to talk about women's rights. Of course, there was no place to gather 20,000 women together, so we decided to meet in different places around the city simultaneously, in spite of soldiers and other people trying to prevent us.

The meeting that I led was in a park near here, with 2700 women in attendance! It was also like that in other parks. A few *burqas* were burned in front of the UN building, but that wasn't part of my plan; it was their own idea.

Kofi Annan, then Secretary General of the UN, chose 21 people to make up the preliminary *Loya Jerga*. I was one of three women in that group. Our job was to create a procedure for the election of delegates who would set up a transitional government. It took us six months to create the procedure and another six months of travel throughout the provinces to make people aware of it and teach them how to choose their representatives. In 17 days, I met with 15,000 refugees. They came up with a list of 300 people and we helped them select ten to participate in the *Loya Jerga*. After the transitional government was set up, I ran for the Constitutional *Loya Jerga* and won the highest number of votes cast for women in Kabul.

The new constitution said that all citizens have equal rights. It also said that citizens should spend two or three years in National Service. I reasoned that if all citizens were equal, the constitution would say that both men and women should join the military. I understood that people would assume that only the males were citizens under the constitution unless we spelled it out.

Peggy: This seems like splitting hairs until we remember that in the US Constitution, "We the People" originally meant only property-owning white men; women were excluded from public office until 1916, from voting until 1920 and did not become full-fledged members of the US military until 1943. Women now serve in the Afghan military and in 2010, 29 women graduated as second lieutenants after completing an officer candidate program. These women will carry out culturally sensitive tasks such as entering houses when women are present and carrying out body searches.[4]

Suraia: It was also my idea to reserve two seats in Parliament for women from every district because otherwise, men would take those positions for themselves. By explicitly stating "men and women" in the Constitution, it obliged everyone to accept women as equals.

My suggestions weren't accepted by the *Loya Jerga*. I told Mr. Azra Ibrahimi of the UN that if he didn't implement my suggestions, not only would I leave the *Loya Jerga* and take many of the other women with me, but also many women would demonstrate, making him look bad. I explained how these little words seemed insignificant, but in fact [the situation] was very serious, because if "men and women" was not specified, men would take all the power.

We told Mr. Karzai the same thing: he must persuade some of the *mujahidin* to accept these ideas or we'd demonstrate. So, Mr. Ibrahimi and Mr. Karzai convinced the *Loya Jerga* to accept our proposals. Afterwards, I was threatened and some people came to my house to kill me. When they shot at me, I went to stay with my neighbor. They searched my house and took my money, but I was elsewhere. They broke into my office and stole all of my papers and pictures. Because of this, many women wouldn't officially join us for fear that the soldiers would come again, even now.

After seven other attacks, we moved our office here to Macrorayon. We still weren't safe as they even broke into this apartment-office. That's why we put bars on the windows. Several years ago when I ran for Parliament, the opposition broke into our homes and offices to steal things and destroy our records, making it impossible to continue our campaign. Now, I'm only working with the AAWU, increasing the awareness of both men and women about gender violence, human rights, and the law as it affects women. I wrote some booklets about how women are victims of the media because they don't give us access.

I believe that women must participate in the economic and other important sectors of society or our country will never develop. Women must hold [responsible] positions and be able to make independent decisions. Without women involved, we won't have a true democracy. Until we eradicate dire poverty, there won't be any peace. Without full equality among citizens, there won't be justice and therefore, no peace.

Peggy: Suraia was nominated for a Nobel Peace Prize in 2005.

16/The Taliban

Media demonization of the Taliban has led many Westerners to associate them with unmitigated evil. Their acts of terrorism, horrific treatment of women and men, inhumane punishments, mangling of Islam for their own purposes, and destruction of civil society deserve condemnation. However, misinformation and overly-broad generalizations can only inhibit our ability to deal with them effectively.

Najia: I studied nursing in Jalalabad a year before the Taliban came and then worked as a midwife in the hospital there. The Taliban made us do our work wearing a *burqa*, even though there were no men with us in the hospital. Occasionally, they would come and beat the doctors and us. We had to cut our fingernails short. I worked there from 1996 - 1998, until our NGO's funding lapsed. Then I joined my sister and her husband who were working in the village of Alingar. After that, I went back to Kabul for a year, where I found a job as a pharmacy counselor in another NGO's clinic. My job was to read the prescriptions and explain the medicine to the patient. After two years, the Taliban Director of Health, who knew nothing about medicine, stopped me. He had finished high school and then become director of all the doctors in the city. He started asking why "these two women" were working there. He shouted at me because I was explaining to men how to take their TB medication. I got the janitor to explain everything to the men, but he was illiterate and couldn't do a good job. Then I came back to Kabul and began working for an American NGO doing health education. For this job, I had to tell women how to boil water and care for their children. We did our work in secret because the Taliban hadn't approved the American NGO. After that I worked for them as a midwife until the Taliban were kicked out.

Ramzia: During Taliban we worked for a Swiss NGO in a poor village, Alingar, which was very far from the city. It was so remote that the people didn't even know what a car was. We worked very hard there and when the Taliban left, we came back to Kabul. I had chosen to work in a village because maybe there would be fewer Taliban.

Peggy: Ramzia, Najia's elder sister and a doctor, was allowed to work because her husband was also a doctor in the same clinic. Since Najia was a relative, she was allowed to work with them.

Meena of Macrorayan: My worst experience was when I was a young girl and the Taliban had just taken over Kabul. I was living in this same apartment we are in now. One day, I went outside into the garden and the Taliban saw me, caught me, and cut my hair.

The second worst experience of my life was when I went outside without a *burqa*. They caught me, slapped me, and hit me with a stick. They would regularly hit women like this.

 **Homaira of Macrorayan:** We lived near a clinic during the Taliban times. One day I looked out and saw a woman who had brought her little baby to get a vaccination. I saw the Taliban coming. This woman was completely covered with the *burqa*, but she was wearing sandals with bare feet. They jumped out of their truck and started hitting her. The worst part was that the woman was just trying to save her baby when their rope was hitting her. Watching this was the worst experience of my whole life.

Peggy: *Did you ever go outside during the Taliban era?*

Homaira: Yes. I used to go outside completely covered, including socks. It was so dangerous that when a person called out, "Taliban!" everyone, both men and women, would run from the streets and try to hide from them. If people were inside the house they would close the curtains. When people watched television, they put up thick curtains so that the sound wouldn't go outside, because television was banned, as well.

Peggy: *Could you still get television signals?*

Homaira: No, there were no stations, but we would watch videos.

Peggy: *And you'd watch the same videos over and over?*

Homaira: Yes. We used to buy the films secretly in some bookshops. Behind the books they would have videos.

Peggy: *I guess everyone knew which shops were selling videos. How did the Taliban not know?*

Homaira: They didn't know because they all had come from other places. But if the shopkeeper got caught, he would be tortured and given the hardest punishment. And you know what? Those Taliban would watch the same films on the TVs they confiscated!

Peggy: *Do you have any other stories you would like to tell?*

Homaira: Since schools were banned, some of the houses had secret schools. I was coming from one of those schools when the Taliban saw me. I was only wearing a shirt [not the required knee-length dress] over my pants underneath my *burqa*, and I think somehow they knew. There were two other girls with me, but the Taliban only followed me. I ran to a house and the neighbor opened the door and let me in. The Taliban came and knocked at their door, but I had opened a back window and escaped. After that, I stayed home and didn't go out anymore.

My friend's mother sent her young son out to buy some food, but when he left the house, she realized that she'd forgotten to give him the envelope of money. She went out on the balcony, called to her son, and tossed the money down to the boy. The Taliban saw this and asked the boy why he was talking to that woman. They took him away.

Do you want to hear another story? When the Taliban would punish people, they would make an announcement calling for people to come to the stadium to see the punishment. One time, I went to that place with my neighbors and some other women. They made the women to be punished sit in front of the crowd. We watched while they shot a woman in the head. After seeing that, none of us could eat for an entire week. We couldn't relax. One of my neighbors was so sick from watching the violence that she almost died.

Peggy: *Were people forced to go there?*

Homaira: No, we were not forced, but they announced that everyone should go. On Fridays, they would cut off the hands of people who committed crimes. After they cut off the person's hands, they would cover him up completely so no one would know who he was. Then they would hold up the hand and show everyone.

Freshta of Macrorayan: The Taliban were the worst regime in Afghanistan. I want a government that will kill all of them.

Peggy: My long interview with Tajwar Kakar had included her experiences with the Taliban.

Tajwar: When I began talking with the Taliban about women's rights, one of the members told me that women had rights during the communist regime when **Karmal** was president and Karmal brought Russia into Afghanistan. I asked, "Who was Barbarak Karmal? Was he a man or a woman? Who was **Amin**? Who was **Taraki**?"
The Talib answered, "They were men."

I said, "Okay, you be the judge. If women brought Russia into Afghanistan, then women should stay at home. But if men brought Russia, then the men should stay at home. Also, why do you separate women from the *Quran*? In Islam, the first Muslims were women. Khadija, Mohammad's first wife, was the first to believe in him. She had the right to spend the money in their family. The first *shahid* was a woman. Men were the ones who fought against and within Islam. So, why do you keep girls from going to school? In Pakistan I had a group of *mullahs* who helped me open a school for girls." I asked these Talibs, "Where does it say that girls can go to the mosque but not to school?" They couldn't tell me.

After my school was opened, three religious police came to my office one day demanding to see "the room where you put pictures." I opened a door and showed them two walls of photographs, one group showing the city before the war and the other showing the destroyed city.

"Look," I said, "Who destroyed our country? Who made you poor? Who made you uneducated? Before the war, people had a good life. It is not your responsibility to take your stick and punish women. Now you should build up your country. Here are books. If you need to understand your religion, these books will answer you. If you need to understand your history, those books will answer you. If you need to understand geography and what lands belong to Afghanistan, the books will answer you. What are you doing here, have you come to punish me?"

One said, "You did nothing wrong." I asked them how old they were.

"I'm 18."

"I'm 19."

"I'm 20."

"How much did you study? How will you rebuild Afghanistan with that stick you are carrying? If you punish women, remember you are punishing your mother. If you punish women you are making enemies. Islam doesn't teach you to punish women."

Then they asked me, "Is it possible for you to teach us every day for half-an-hour?" They had come to punish me, but now they wanted to study. But that was my work. I try to help my people.

When I came back to Afghanistan under the Taliban, I saw that my people were walking like zombies. I know my people. When the Russian soldiers came, the Afghans had not been so afraid. When I returned, I promised myself that it didn't matter if the Taliban killed or punished me, I would face all the problems. I had 160 children in my school. The community supported 100 of them and my family supported 60.

In the beginning, the children walked in the street begging, shining shoes, or whatever. You would never see them shout or play, but I brought a ball to school and played with them. Every day at 6:00 am I went to the school and we exercised.

I also started one hour of singing traditional songs but someone reported me and the religious police came.

They asked, "What are you doing?" I invited them in and they saw the kids singing but they did nothing. After three months, I took my children into the streets to march as they sang. Opposite our school was an apartment building with all of the windows covered. Whenever I blew my whistle, the kids would change their song. The first day, I could see people peeking out from behind their curtains to watch the kids. After three days, they took down the curtains. In the second week they opened their windows. By the third week, they came down and clapped for my children. The singing children helped the people become brave again.

One day a Minister came telling me not to take my children into the streets to sing. I told him, "But that is my job." When my children sang and walked, the Taliban walked along with them. They looked so sad. I saw their faces and saw how much they needed help, how much they needed education.

One day one of my children came up to me crying. I asked him what was wrong. He told me that a *talib* had stopped him, saying, "You lucky boy, you are going to school. You tell your headmaster to make a school for us."

I asked the child, "Why are you afraid?"

"My mother said that they are very dangerous people, they are killer people."

I said, "Do not hate them, those *talib* boys are orphans. Their fathers were freedom fighters and they grew up in the refugee camps, closed off from everything. Now they look at you, enjoying yourself, and they forget their responsibility."

My school was very crowded. It was a model school built for 100 students, but we had 160. When we'd have an assembly in the courtyard, there was no place for all of the children to sit, there were so many of them. Every day, there would be knocks at the gate from children pleading to be allowed into my school. One day the knocking was more persistent than usual. Finally the guard answered and a *talib* with a Kalashnikov stood there. He wanted to trade his gun for books and admission. The guard explained to him that the school was already over-full.

The boy shoved his gun into the guard's hands and said, "If you won't let me into the school, then you might as well shoot me."

The guard brought him in to me. I told him, "You can see how crowded this school is and we don't have room for even one more. But I promise you that next term we will make a space for you."

Peggy: As the clock winds down on the international military presence in Afghanistan, with a September, 2014 target date for US withdrawal, Afghanistan remains intensely divided. Negotiating with the Taliban is a controversial issue.

If they are brought into the government to share power, what will happen to the gains that women have made? Indeed, women are already losing their rights in anticipation of a settlement with the Taliban. If the Taliban see that they have no chance of having at least a share of power, they will never stop fighting. As this book goes to press, it doesn't seem to be an issue of *if* but of *when* the Taliban participate in the government. Already we are seeing chilling effects on women's liberties, as Karzai supports legislation and other measures conducive to the interests of the Taliban, like signing the Shia Personal Status Law, and his lack of support for women's participation at the London Conference and 2010 Peace *Jerga*.

There was controversy among activists over whether it was most strategic for women to boycott or to attend the 2010 Peace *Jerga*. The **Afghan Women's Network** had submitted a list of bold, outspoken women whom they wanted to have attend, but the government invited others who would be more likely to be compliant. Boycott supporters contended that women needed to constitute a critical mass, at minimum one-third of the participants, in order to have any influence. Because most of the actual work at these conferences is done in committees, when only one or two women sit in these smaller groups, it is even more likely for them to be intimidated into agreement or silence; indeed, that was the result.

Alyssa J. Rubin, the *New York Times* Kabul Bureau Chief, said in a September 8, 2011, interview on "Fresh Air"[1] that she believes that if the Taliban come back into power, it will be somewhat different this time around because they have changed. Certainly there would be fewer women in most jobs than today, she opined, but today's Taliban is more open to having girls learn to read and go to school, at least in the primary grades. They now recognize the need for female teachers. Even during their previous reign, they tolerated having some women doctors for their wives and daughters, as evidenced by Najia and her sister Ramzia's experiences.

When I asked women about reconciliation with the Taliban, opinions diverged. Many activists, highly educated women, and those involved in the government said that as long as the Taliban would agree to abide by the Constitution, there would be no problems. They say that their constitution guarantees women their rights and will protect them. They think negotiating with the Taliban is necessary to bring about peace. This viewpoint made sense to me, but I was chilled later when I read an article stating that the **Haqqani Network**, a terrorist group with ties to the Taliban and al Qaeda, would gladly participate in the government. When they gained a majority, they would rewrite the constitution along their own lines. Perhaps the Taliban have similar ideas.

The majority of women with whom I spoke said that they would never want to live under a Taliban regime again, let alone negotiate with them to participate in the government.

Who makes up the Taliban today? Professor Akram, Director of the National Independent Peace and Reconciliation Commission,[2] divides them into three groups. He says that about 10% are Taliban ideologues, 20% are hard-line Pakistani Taliban, and the rest are Afghans who joined for various reasons. These include the fear of not joining, the ability to earn a living, to avenge family members or friends killed by foreign troops, or simply because the Taliban are the *de facto* government in their area. The Reconciliation Commission is trying to coax the latter type back into mainstream Afghan society.

But even among the Taliban "moderates," with whom would one negotiate? According to CNN,[3] after a January, 2010 suicide bombing in Kabul, several different Taliban groups all claimed credit for the attack. If one faction were to reach agreement with the government, would the rest join in? This seems unlikely. Additionally, there are smugglers, warlords, and criminal groups that operate under the banner of Taliban but have different agendas.

I've been hearing talk about bringing the Taliban into the government, and I wonder what you think about that?

Shinkai: Taliban is one of the realities of this country. Whether you want it or not, it exists. Whether Afghanistan has the capacity to extend and sustain the war and whether continuing the war will make the Taliban tired, I don't know. But I don't think the government has much capacity to deal with them, and I don't think the friends of Afghanistan have enough patience to continue to support the war.

Also, we are very unlucky to have neighbors like Pakistan and Iran that are not very sincere in helping us. Maybe our government has denied its support for our neighbors' involvement, but I'm sure there are certain groups in this country who encourage it, who support the Taliban movement, and who want to take over Afghanistan.

If the Taliban are interested in coming into the government, they need to change. They cannot ignore the female half of the population and they cannot abuse our rights. We must put these conditions and strong expectations into the negotiations, and our government and president must not compromise on the rights of women. The Taliban are already not respecting our Constitution and if they don't respect that, how can they be a part of this country?

Honestly, in my heart, I don't have much fear. I'm optimistic that they won't demand such things but if they do, the government will not compromise because the international community would not accept it. We can't run this country without being a part of the international community.

Finally, how can women like me ever keep quiet in this country? Many, many women will raise their voices and object to such negotiations. That's why I don't think that they will go back to such an idealized government like they wanted, like they had before.

I don't think the people, that is, the youth groups, women's movement, the civil society, and this big political mafia[4] or economic mafia will accept them back. I'm sure Americans will make their government accountable and ask themselves, "Why have we lost so many Americans in Afghanistan when in the end we have only brought back the same extremism so that the women of Afghanistan must suffer again as they did before?"

Nasrine: I don't think it will be useful [to negotiate with the Taliban]. In the past, the Taliban didn't let women study, they forced people. Even though they were not bad in the beginning, they became worse. I believe that if we invite the Taliban into our society and they promise to behave the same as other people, it's not beneficial. I believe that again they will trick the women of Afghanistan. For one or two years they will follow the Constitution, but after three or four years, again they will be the same as before.

Maihan: Everybody has his or her own opinions about the Taliban, but the most important thing is that they would not let us go to school or play basketball as we're doing right now. We don't want to be faced with the same problems with the Taliban we had before in the future, right? So if they agree to be good people and act differently, it would be okay. But how can we have a guarantee that they're going to be good? If someone is like them from the first step of their life, then it will be hard to change them in a short period of time. Also, I cannot trust them.

Tajwar: I don't know. The Taliban might be different this time. If they stop the war, that will be good. We have to stop the war.

Peggy: It baffles many Westerners that some Afghans choose to side with the Taliban rather than strive for a more permissive state based on personal freedom. Even among those who hate the Taliban, in conservative areas of the country, disaffection is more about the Taliban's methods than their ideology. This issue is well-illustrated in Joel Hafvensten's *Opium Season*,[5] a chronicle of his time managing a cash-for-work program in southwestern Afghanistan. One co-worker, Raz, a passionately devout young man, worked as Chemonic's[6] paymaster. In spite of his ultra-conservative convictions, he hated the Taliban. During his medical studies at Kandahar University, he had been harassed over small infractions of the Taliban code. Raz and many other conservative Pashtuns have no complaint against the Taliban's stark, demanding interpretation of Islamic laws. The Pashtun's complaint centers on whether enforcement should be loving or punitive. They want strict laws, but they want enforcement to be merciful rather than cruel. These Afghans love freedom, but to them that means, "freedom from violent coercion, not a society where anyone could do whatever they desired."

Once when I asked why the Taliban are so popular in certain areas, I was told the following story:

A village girl in northeastern Afghanistan was raped by the son of the local warlord. When she told her father, he was so angry that he traveled all the way to Kabul for justice. He went to different ministries, lawyers, and courts, but no one wanted to touch a case against this warlord. After a month, he went home discouraged and empty-handed. The next morning he explained his situation to the local Taliban commander. By evening, they had caught the rapist and were beating him within an inch of his life. They didn't kill him, but warned him never to do anything like that again.

Vigilante justice is based on a religious/military commander's authority rather than the rule of law. It is not good for Afghanistan nor the rights of women. But to be successful, the Afghan government must be able to stand up to the warlords and protect its citizens from outlawry. In the case above, the rights of the woman were served and the Taliban were enforcing their own rule of law, however inhumane some of those laws were. One of many other issues is that the accused has no recourse and no way to defend him or herself.

A story reported in the Western media concerned Aisha,[7] an 18-year-old woman who was mutilated as retribution for running away from her inhumane marriage. This article blamed Aisha's disfigurement on the Taliban because a Taliban commander ordered her punishment. Although it was a Taliban commander who ordered her horrific punishment, it was her husband who held her down.

Aisha was a victim of *baad*, a human rights abuse that takes the form of reparation in a legal dispute and has been practiced in Afghanistan since before recorded history. To hold the fabric of society together in the aftermath of serious crimes, the family of the perpetrator may give a daughter in marriage to a man from the wronged family. In Aisha's case, she and her sister were given to atone for her uncle having killed someone. Women married under these terms are generally treated as slaves and subjected to all kinds of abuse from their husbands, mothers-in-law, and other new family members. Aisha's tormentors were Taliban but they didn't abuse her because they were Taliban. Even completely eradicating the Taliban wouldn't end this brutal practice.

Changing these and other abusive traditions, and improving human rights for the long run, requires education in rural areas like Aisha's village. As crucial as it is to educate girls, human rights education is also important for boys who will ideally grow up to share power with women.

The best, most sustainable way for this to happen is via Afghan-run NGOs. Not only are they often more cost-effective than international ones, but they are also more likely to be accepted by local people and able to foster genuine change.

An article from April, 2011,[8] reports that in Khost Province, the governor convinced village elders that certain traditions: *baad*, high bride prices, and lavish weddings were dysfunctional. The elders saw his logic and agreed. Changes like this need to be agreeable to and enforced by local *shuras* to be effective.

Candace Rondeaux, senior analyst in Kabul for the International Crisis Group,[9] has said, "Instead of spinning its wheels on cutting deals, the US and its allies need to throw their backs into a whole-of-government approach that engages Afghans on all levels – not just a handful of powerful men. No amount of dealmaking will erase 30 years of entrenched conflict. Ensuring that the Afghan public is fully engaged in the peace process from start to finish is the only thing that will prevent the next civil war."[10]

I would add that to be successful, the process must include women in significant numbers.

Girls play with a soccer ball at a school sponsored by
Afghans for Tomorrow.

Girls and boys play on a neighborhood slide.

17/ Youth

Youth under 14 years of age comprise 42% of the Afghan population.[1] People under age 35 constitute 76%.[2] The median age is 18, and anyone under 30 is considered a "youth."

The young women in this chapter are a select group. All but one participated in the US State Department's Youth, Exchange, and Study (YES)[3] program; one other also studied in the US. Participants in the YES program received scholarships to attend a year of high school in the US "to learn about American society and values, acquire leadership skills, and help educate Americans about their countries and cultures." YES students lived with host families and participated in a wide variety of high school activities. The young women I met had become fluent in English. This fluency made them eligible for jobs with foreigners in Afghanistan and contributed to their future eligibility for scholarships at American universities. As this book is readied for publication, two of the women I interviewed are pursuing more education in the US to better prepare themselves for leadership positions in Afghanistan.

However, in 2011, the YES program stopped accepting applications from Afghans, after more than half of the 2010 group illegally overstayed their visas or fled to Canada. The State Department decided that rather than aiding the rebuilding of Afghanistan by its own citizens, YES was contributing to Afghanistan's brain drain.

This brain drain is very real as violence continues with no real end in sight. It is understandable that people would choose to flee seemingly endless violence and chronic dysfunction rather than stay and continue to work for a possibly better future. Several Afghan professional women told me that in their offices, conversations often revolve around exit plans, or "Plan B," should security deteriorate beyond a certain point. But how can Afghanistan realize its potential without these home-grown leaders?

The younger generation, boys as well as girls, is often more open to the reform of dysfunctional traditional practices than their elders. Often, their minds are opened by their time in exile, either in other areas of Afghanistan and/or outside the country. Change is happening within the family unit as well, because educated, wage-earning sons and daughters now command more respect and authority.

Even though much of the money donated by foreign governments has been wasted through sub-contracting and corruption, there have been significant improvements in educational prospects throughout the country as well. Most of these opportunities have been in Kabul, many in provincial cities, some in rural locales, and a few in remote areas. Not only will education and its embedded messages of human rights and ethnic harmony make a critical difference, but they will aid in the country's further development.

I began my interviews by asking these women to tell me their ethnicity. Several said, "I'm Afghan." When I pressed, they'd tell me how seeing themselves as Afghan is a very important step in rebuilding ethnic harmony within their country. This attitude was unheard of previously. Traditionally, when in Afghanistan, Afghans identified with their family first, then their tribe, then their ethnic group, and lastly their nationality. Another impact of the years of exile has been the increased mixing of ethnic groups. Host populations viewed all of them as Afghans, subject to the same stereotypes and prejudices. It is difficult for non-Afghans to see the differences Afghans see among themselves.

Educated urban youth from different backgrounds increasingly contribute to both public and private spheres. They influence the media, government bureaucracies, and civil society. Social media[4] is having a large impact as internet cafes spring up in towns and cities. People tweet and text with their cell phones. Lima Sahar, a woman from Kandahar, was voted the third place winner on the television program *Afghan Star* with hundreds of thousands of texted votes.

Very few in Afghanistan have internet access in their homes. Families often forbid women to enter mixed gender cafes. In Kabul, **Young Women for Change** has opened a women-only internet cafe which has become a center for women's activism. Still, only four percent of Afghanistan's 30 million people have internet access. But, as of 2011, 17 million Afghans use mobile phones.

Meena

Meena was the financial officer for **SOLA**, the organization I stayed with during most of my time in Kabul in 2010. Although only 20 years old, her presence and the quality of her work was that of an older and more experienced person. She would come to work nearly every day in a somber black scarf. She also had a lighter side that I saw when she giggled with her girlfriends and at times during her interview.

Meena was born in Kabul, but became a refugee in Pakistan when she was three. After ten years, she and her family moved back to Afghanistan, where she and her brother finished high school. In tenth grade, she was chosen to attend a festival in Japan, and as a high school junior, to participate in the YES program. When she returned and graduated high school, Meena began working with the American Council as an office assistant. Shortly thereafter, she was promoted and trained first as an accountant, and then a finance officer. After two years, she came to work at SOLA.

I was supposed to give presentations. In order to present my country better, I had to learn many more things. That's why going to America helped me learn a lot of good things about my own country and about Islam.

Nasrine

I met Nasrine at American University in Kabul and was struck by her clear way of speaking and her thoughtful comments.

Nasrine was born in Bamyan, but fled to Iran during the war. She has six sisters. Just before she was about to enter the university, Iran withdrew its educational support for Afghans. When they returned, her family opted to settle in Kabul rather than go back to the scarce opportunities available in Bamyan. At Kabul University, she has been harassed frequently for studying veterinary medicine, a field dominated by men. Her schedule was overloaded; she was a full-time student, teaching in a private school, and working as a program coordinator for Good Neighbors International's Education and Cultural Center for Women.

I'm not living for myself. I want my parents to have a good life. My father and mother are old, so now they need to rest and it's my turn to help them.

Rabia

Rabia was a soft-spoken, independent woman who often had lunch with us at SOLA. She exuded determination and compassion.

Rabia was born in Kabul and is the second youngest of five children. Her father is a retired professor and her mother hasn't been to school. Her older siblings are all university graduates. Rabia spent her sophomore year in the YES program and after high school was accepted into Kabul University Medical School where, in 2010, she was in her second year.

I want to help women in places that don't have doctors. I want to be a person who can bring change in someone's life. If there's someone suffering, I want to do something to change the situation.

Anisa

After our interview, when Anisa told her family about being in my book, they refused permission. They had taken "tremendous, disastrous risks" by allowing her to go to the US, and if her identity were to be made known by this book, it would make their lives harder. At the very least, it would increase their feelings of insecurity. Anisa's story is quite compelling, and she's such a shining example of Afghan youth that I couldn't bear to leave her out. To protect her identity, I omitted her photograph, and changed her name and all identifying circumstances in her story.

Whether you are an angel or the worst person in the world, people will talk about you. So just be yourself. Do whatever you think is good for yourself. When you get somewhere and get to be someone, then they will understand what you were doing.

Anisa attended a photography class I taught and became one of my most ardent students. She worked harder than many due to her intense desire to be the best. When she was assigned to be the official photographer for her company's annual dinner, she especially enjoyed telling her superiors how and where to stand, always following my advice to do it with a smile.

Anisa's family fled Afghanistan in the early days of the Soviet war. She and her siblings were all born in Iran. They were educated there and came to Kabul in 2004. In 2006, she was accepted into the YES program.

Peggy: By mid-2003, the number of registered Afghans in Iran was 2.3 million[5] in a total Iranian population of 68 million. Bowing to domestic political pressure over unemployment problems, Iran encouraged Afghans to return home. The issue in Iran was one all refugee populations and their hosts face: hungry exiles are forced to scramble for work wherever they can, often for lower wages than the nationals will accept. Lower wages anger the nationals, who become hostile to the refugees. Those who arrive illegally are additionally at risk for exploitation and abuse. Some women I met said they were discriminated against and made to feel unwelcome, while others said they were well-accepted.

Although it seems cruel that Iran stopped allowing education, the fact that they not only allowed, but encouraged and often paid for it at all was very generous. Work permits were freely available during certain times, as well. Pakistan didn't offer free schooling until late 2007. I believe Iran did Afghanistan a big favor by educating many who could thus contribute back to their own society. It was also a smart political move, since Iran would like more influence in Afghanistan.

Talk about your time in exile.

Anisa: Our school in Iran wasn't free, so my father worked two shifts in order to pay our expenses. Many people told my father that he was crazy to work so hard to educate his girls, but he was determined. Do you know why? When my grandfather had cancer, my grandmother was also very sick at the time. Before he died, my grandfather told my father that his future would be much easier if he'd had a sister to help him. When my grandfather died, my father was only 12 and had to quit school to support his family. He had been a good student and he missed school terribly. Because of that, he vowed to educate all of his own kids, and because of his struggles to do that, we all take our studies very seriously.

Despite my father's two jobs, we were very poor when we lived in Iran. For example, we tried to study as much as we could before sunset so we'd use less electricity. We didn't have heat in our house during the cold winters. Iranians treated us badly and discriminated against us. They complained because, since Afghans like my father would accept a low wage, we took jobs away from Iranians. We worked harder in school and so got better grades. The Iranians were jealous, so they treated us badly.

I had an incident at school once when a boy told me, "Go away, Afghan!"

I went home and cried about it to my sister. She said, "I'm glad this happened to you."

"What? What did you just say? What are you talking about?"

She went on, "If you really want to be the person you say you want to be and if you want to repay Dad for all his hard work, then you have to forget about

Meena   Rabia   Nasrine   Anisa

discrimination. You have to study even harder. Instead of being in second place, you have to be first. You have to get more involved in school activities." After that, I became more active outside of class and my grades were only 100's. It really made me proud and made people discriminate against me less.

Meena: We faced a lot of difficulties in Pakistan. Both of my parents worked full-time and taught us at home. My parents, brother, sister, uncle, and paralyzed grandmother all lived together in one room.

Peggy: *How was it to leave Iran and live in Afghanistan?*

Anisa: When I came, I didn't know any Afghan traditions, so I had to adjust to many things. Also, we were very poor at that time. Our expenses were high because of our schooling, rent, and food.

Peggy: *How have you dealt with the hard times in your life?*

Anisa: Whenever I would start something, I would tell myself that, no matter what, I could do it. I would tell myself, "I want to do this because of my family or friends or just for myself. If I don't, bad things might happen."

My neighbors talk about me because I have a job. Proving that I'm not a bad person even though I work in an office and talk with men is kind of hard. So instead, I watch out for myself and make strong goals. Then I can care less about what people say.

When I was young, I was the first one to encourage my younger sister when she was afraid. I had to be positive so she would be positive. I was an advisor and a young "mama" for her. I would watch my older sisters to see what they were doing and how they would act, and then teach that to my younger sister. I would also teach her how to think things through so she could make her own decisions.

Nasrine: I have a lot of stress because the veterinary faculty is very difficult and there is heavy competition. I also have two jobs, but I believe that God helps me through. I don't have enough time to study, so I listen to my professor very, very carefully. When I go to work, I use every free minute for studying. I take a five- or ten-minute lunch break and study the rest of the time. Also, I have a very efficient method for handling my schedule.

Meena: First of all, I usually share my problems with my sister and mom because they are closest to me. They advise me well because they know more than I do about society and the community. If there's some kind of problem that would hurt my family, I just try to hide it from them so they don't have to worry about it. I sit by myself and think about it, and then I find a resolution.

Peggy: *What do you do if someone tries to keep you from what you want to do?*

Meena: When I'm faced with someone telling me, "No, you can't do this," I try to convince them that I can. If I really want to do something and I have strength and confidence in myself and I really want to show that I can do it, I can usually succeed. Even if they don't agree, if I'm still confident that it is the right thing, I will do it anyway, and see how it ends up.

Peggy: *What hardships have you encountered at school?*

Nasrine: I had a teacher from Panshir in my first year. I was the top student in the class. If I could pass that semester with good grades, I would be eligible for a scholarship to study in South Korea. I don't know what happened, but this professor failed me. Actually, when I reviewed an exam I took, I saw that everything was correct, but the professor didn't accept it. I complained to the department and university deans, but one of my female teachers said it was better for me to stay quiet because this was Afghanistan, and if I complained, it may prove dangerous for me. That meant that the professor might decide to pay someone to catch me in the street and hurt me. So I stopped.

Peggy: *What advice do you have for your sisters?*

Nasrine: I would say the most important thing is that our studying and working is not for ourselves. I am always thinking about my parents and how I can make them happy. I study hard so I can be a successful person and make my parents proud. I would tell my sisters to think positively, target their goals, be serious about their lives, and help people. First, they should ask for help from God and then try to do their best. There is nothing that humans can't do if they think deeply.

Meena   *Rabia*   *Nasrine*   *Anisa*

Peggy: *What do you think is the most important thing for female students to learn besides their subjects?*

Nasrine: The women of Afghanistan are always thinking about rights, rights, rights. However, they think about rights in the wrong way. Men in Afghanistan are very sensitive about the words "women's rights." When we say "rights," they say, very roughly, "You're right, you're right, everything is your right." That's because the women of Afghanistan don't think about the rights of others in their family.

Most organizations that try to help Afghan women don't realize the problems they are creating by not talking about the responsibilities that go with having rights and that *everyone* has rights. Most Afghan women are illiterate. Some of them don't have a television or any access to the media. When you're talking with illiterate women and say, "This is *your* right," they think that their husbands don't have any rights. This is a mistake. I think female university students should understand that in Afghanistan, if the women are working outside, that's fine, but their husband still needs to eat. Some Afghan women have this idea that when they are studying, they shouldn't have to work at home or take care of their children.

If women really want to be successful and don't want their husbands to complain, then they should pay attention to their housework and children in addition to their studies. In that case, the man will encourage his wife to study more. We should think about and perform well in all of our roles, from mother to student to daughter.

Peggy: *When you're afraid or get angry, how do you typically react?*

Anisa: I speak out. Sometimes it's very forceful and my face will instantly become angry. Afterwards, when I reflect on it, I realize that maybe I was out of place to talk that way with people older than me. Then, I go back and apologize and make my point again in a gentler way.

Rabia: Sometimes my uncles will tell me that girls shouldn't study, but I've gotten used to it and just ignore it. I say, "You don't know what it means to study and help people. If you knew that, you would not have stopped your girls from going to school." I never get violent or show that I'm angry. I just tell them over and over, "You have to send your daughters to school. Nothing bad will happen when they study. Maybe they will be doctors. Maybe your wife will get sick and can't be sent to a male doctor, so your daughter could care for her. If you don't let your female relatives go to school, who will be the doctors for women in the future? Who will be the teachers? Where will we find the kinds of people we need to work in our society? Afghanistan will be left behind. Other countries are moving forward because they send their girls to school. Girls make up half of society, and if half of the society is not doing anything, then the country is going to drown." I keep trying to tell them this. Maybe some people I know can understand. With those who don't understand, I say it anyway and then drop it. Maybe after they hear it many times, their minds will change.

Meena: I just sit quietly at first, then I get really mad at myself. "Why didn't I say something to that person?" When other people hear bad things said to them, usually they become mad, but in that situation I just sit quietly. There's a saying in Dari, "The answer to people who do bad to you is silence." My mother always said that it's better to be quiet than to say something bad.

Peggy: *What do you want to study?*

Meena: I would be like to go back to the States to get my higher education. I would study international relations and political science. That would help me serve my country better.

Anisa: I really wanted to study journalism, but now the situation is not good for journalists, especially for women journalists, whether they are a reporter or an announcer. But I think I have a real talent. My family was not happy with my decision to be a journalist. And really, my family has a big part in my decisions because they are the people who raised me to this stage. They are the people who will hold me if I fall. They are always there for me, so I respect that.

One day my sister asked me, "Why don't you want to be the person the journalists will want to interview?" So I thought more and decided to study political science. What I really want is to be an ambassador to the US or the UN.

Rabia: I had never thought about what I wanted to be until I was at my uncle's house in Ghazni Province. My mother and I were walking one day when we heard horrible screams coming from the back of a truck. When we got closer, I saw a crowd of ladies surrounding it. They told us that a lady was having problems trying to

| Meena | Rabia | Nasrine | Anisa |

deliver her baby. There was no hospital or even a doctor to help her. The lady's screams were so desperate and I felt useless because I was only a child. I could feel her pain. After a few days, I found that she and her baby had died. That's when I decided to be a doctor. No matter what happens, I want to be a doctor, maybe a gynecologist. There are people who don't allow their women to go to male doctors and there are places without any doctors, male or female.

I'm working on getting a scholarship to the US, because I know that if I study in Afghanistan, I can become a doctor but not a very good one, because the facilities here aren't good. There are too many restrictions.

Peggy: *How are you different after studying in the US?*

Anisa: Before I went, I only thought about my family and the people around me and very little about what was going on in Afghanistan. When I came back, I was more open-minded. I now think that if I, as a person who was so poor, got to where I am today; I think everyone in the world can and should have the ability to do something with their lives. Seeing this in myself makes me want to help other people, not only Afghans, but the whole world. However, Afghans are my priority, because they're members of my own country.

Peggy: *When you were in United States, what effect do you think your presence there had on Americans?*

Anisa: I was only 12 when I went. I told them that I was almost 14 and I look that old, so I got away with it. It was the first time that I had to make my own decisions. My host family saw me as a mature person. I tried to participate in the things American kids did, but I knew very little English, so it was hard. I always wanted to help around the house because that's what I would do at home. I always obeyed the host parents. I showed them that Afghan kids have good manners. You could really see the difference between Afghan children and American kids.

Peggy: *If you were to have lunch with President Obama, what would you advise him?*

Anisa: I would tell Mr. Obama that I want to meet the ambassador so I can tell him that he should work with the locals here. I'd ask the ambassador to live in a normal place in Afghanistan, meet with normal people, and listen to them. I know security is a challenge, but what he or she would learn is important. When diplomats visit, they stay at the Serena Hotel [a five-star hotel in Kabul]. When someone goes inside there, they forget the rest of Afghanistan and what the rest of the country is going through. If they only go to these fancy places, how can they understand?

Meena: I would tell Mr. Obama that all the money he spends for soldiers would be much better spent if he built different kinds of factories. So many people are jobless here. They sit in the streets waiting for work, then go home with no money. If you went home with them, you'd see the sadness in their faces.

Nasrine: It's been eight years since the Taliban left Afghanistan and we have more than 50 countries working here. If each country were to take care of one province, Afghanistan would be something like the United States.

The Taliban are powerful, but not stronger than the United States, NATO, or other countries. So I would ask him, "What is your policy?" We can see that women have their rights and are more satisfied than under the Taliban. But when I talk with people, they don't see any bright future.

Security is not good here, and the Taliban have weakened us. I'd ask Mr. Obama to work more seriously on our problems, because we are tired of the current situation. Sometimes they work in Iraq or Iran. I would ask him to please first help the problems of Afghanistan.

Peggy: *What do you think has the greatest potential to transform Afghanistan?*

Meena: Education. When we get higher education and go to different countries, we can learn from them. We can get ideas about how to make our country function better. Someone going to the university in a foreign country will learn more about how to be a good leader, how to perform jobs better; or like Rabia, how to be a better doctor.

Peggy: *What do you see as your role in the future of Afghanistan?*

Meena: Actually, I see myself as an ambassador, whether here or elsewhere.

Meena Rabia Nasrine Anisa

Peggy: *What gives you hope for Afghanistan?*

Nasrine: When I see all the students interested in studying, it makes me more hopeful about Afghanistan's future. I have experienced that those who studied in Iran have the top positions in their classes. Afghans who only studied here may have the talent, but the schools and teachers here are not so good. We need to help them get a good education. I am also encouraged when I see that the people are really tired of war and of being refugees.

Peggy: *What do you think about your own future? Do you plan to stay in Kabul, or will you go back to Bamyan or Herat where you say there is a better quality of life?*

Nasrine: To be honest, if the security gets worse, I don't want to stay in Afghanistan. I told you, I don't study for myself, I don't work for myself. Everything that I have is for my family. I live with my parents. When I look at security, I see that this is not a safe country for a family, especially since I have no brothers. When people see that my father is alone and doesn't have any sons, they will force him to do things. Even now, people are rude to him and don't pay him attention. When I see these things it makes me suffer. My father is too old and weak to stand up for himself. Once he told me, "I'm alone, and if they do something, what can I do?"

That's our problem, so if I have a chance to leave Afghanistan, I will go and take my family with me. My parents are old and they need to rest. It's my turn to help them now. I'm really grateful that they allowed my sisters and me to study and work, and I want them to finish their lives peacefully.

Peggy: *What would you like to say to the American people?*

Meena: I want to go there myself and represent my country and tell them how we are here in Afghanistan. As you've seen in the news, they always show poor people and bad situations. I had this experience when I went to the US. People didn't know anything about Afghanistan. People were asking me if we had TV, if we ate pizza and fried chicken. We do have TV, we have educated people, and we eat these kinds of foods.

I would really like to show how Afghanistan is. I don't want them only to see politics and war. I want them to see the normal life that people have, how Afghan girls and boys want to get higher education, and how much we want to build relationships with other countries. As far as I have seen, other people who come here just emphasize the negative points.

Anisa: I want the people who get involved with Afghanistan to learn about Afghan traditions and culture before they come. That way, they can adjust themselves more easily to our way of thinking and it will make their work more effective. The most effective people stay longer than a year or two and build connections. Then they find that a lot of people support them.

Peggy: *How would you have foreigners adjust their thinking?*

Anisa: They have to accept the differences, like we did when we lived in the US. They have to be more in touch with normal people, their situations and problems. They need to appreciate the Afghan way.

Peggy: *How would someone appreciating the Afghan way behave?*

Anisa: Foreigners always say "thanks" and "please" but we never say it. If they give us a notebook, tomorrow we will do something great with that notebook, even if we didn't say "thanks." Afghans give their reaction by *doing*, not just *saying*.

Girls in the Mini Mobile Children's Circus perform for schoolchildren.

Frequently Asked Questions

These questions from my lecture audiences raise additional relevant issues.

What did you wear when you were in Afghanistan? Did you wear a burqa?

When I went out in public I wore a headscarf, loose pants, and long-sleeved, mid-thigh-length shirts similar to tunics. In 2003 I bought a *burqa* so I could share the feeling of wearing one with people here. I decided that I should give myself the experience of walking in it in public so I put on Afghan shoes, enveloped myself in my portable tent, and set out on a short walk. I was surprised at how well I could see looking straight out, but my peripheral vision was cut off. I couldn't see my feet (and things I might stumble on) unless I held the *burqa* to my chest and tilted my head down. Due to the weight of the gathered fabric in back, the garment tends to ride upward, so it was necessary to hold onto the front to keep the screened grid over my eyes.

At one point along a shaded, mostly deserted street, as I approached, a guard stood up from his chair and began walking towards me with his arms extended in a friendly greeting. Immediately afterward, another man came from behind me and embraced him. It was unsettling because I never heard the second man coming, and I would have with my ears uncovered. Being invisible took some getting used to.

Were people receptive to your taking pictures and asking questions?

What surprised me most was how much women really wanted to tell their stories. In one case, my translator had arranged an interview with one of her maid's friends, but when I pulled out my camera, the woman said she couldn't be photographed. I told her that without a picture, I could only do a short interview rather than the regular longer one. Immediately, she sent her child to her husband's workplace to ask permission, which he granted. Afghans are very sensitive about the fact that most of the news coming out of Afghanistan is negative and focuses on war and social problems. When people learned that the Afghan Women's Project's purpose is to share a balanced picture of their country, they were very grateful and receptive. I was always treated respectfully.

One aspect of my success in finding people willing to talk with me was that

I was always introduced to the women, I didn't just go up to them to ask for an interview. Being associated with someone trusted and respected is critical to success in any endeavor in Afghanistan.

Who were your local contacts and what were the ethnic origins of your translators?

In 2003, my translators were Pashtun and Tajik, and in 2010 they were Hazara, Pashtun, and Tajik. This is an important point. When journalists and aid organizations come to a country, they see things through the lenses of their guides and translators. This is one reason I chose a variety of translators. It's important to be aware of the biases that translators and guides bring to the endeavor. One good example is when the director of the **IRC** told Tajwar Kakar that he had already asked the Afghans working for him (men) if they wanted schools for their girls. They told him they did not, but Tajwar was able to collect over 1000 signatures from conservative areas requesting girls' schools.

What are some of the most interesting things that you didn't know before you went and that the average Westerner wouldn't know?

I have a serious personality. Before I went to Afghanistan in 2010, I believed that aid and development work had to be serious to deal with the very critical problems the country faces. Then I visited the Mini Mobile Children's Circus (MMCC). As I walked around the colorful compound, adorned with fanciful papier-mache animals made by the participants, and watched laughing kids zipping by on skates, I couldn't help but feel happy and hopeful. I came to understand that MMCC, Clowns Without Borders International, No Strings Puppet Theater, and Skatestan[1] all play a more important role than just giving kids relief from the stresses of their lives. These fun physical activities also help heal trauma, develop confidence and leadership, and give young people a vision of possibilities for the society they will one day be called on to help create.

Girls and boys who use their bodies to develop physical talents in addition to mental ones gain confidence, as well as an increased physical capacity to carry out their lives.

What are some lesser-known effects of the foreign presence in Afghanistan?

Foreigners have provided employment for many educated, and especially English-speaking Afghans. Providing foreigners' food, transportation, and other needs has increased local economies. If the foreigners leave along with the military, the economy of Kabul, especially, will be badly affected.

On the other hand, foreigners' housing and office needs have contributed to the shortage of properties available to Afghans, resulting in exorbitant housing prices in addition to general inflation. I asked Ramzia how foreigners renting housing and offices built to Western standards created a shortage for poor and middle-class people. She explained that the landlords for the NGOs get wealthy, buy up smaller houses, then raise those rents. The shortage trickles down from weathy, to middle-class, to poor as Afghans rent what they can afford or squat in broken buildings and informal camps.

By 2010, the picture had changed somewhat as new apartment complexes were being built on the outskirts of Kabul and damaged buildings were cleared of squatters and rebuilt. But the new buildings are for middle- and upper-middle-class families. Not much is being built for the poor.

What is the difference between Shia and Sunni Islam?

Sunnis and Shias share basic Islamic beliefs. Differences between them arose from the issue of succession after Mohammad died. The Sunnis believed that the new leader should be selected from those best qualified for the job. The Shia believed that the new leader should come from the lineage of the Prophet. Since then, different practices and beliefs have arisen between the groups.

You interviewed Krayba, whose creditor would take her daughter if she missed a payment. Why doesn't she, or anyone in an abusive relationship, just run away and go live in another city?

Although running away is not a crime in Afghanistan, women who do so are routinely suspected of *zina,* or sex outside of marriage, and often labeled "bad." This makes them much more vulnerable to rape and other abuses. If Krayba moved across town or even to another city to live with relatives, her Kabul relatives would know where she went and might inform her creditor of her whereabouts, especially if the creditor put pressure on them or if they disapproved of her. Going to a new city without a man is also problematic if a woman doesn't know someone there who can give her a place to stay while she looks for housing. It is difficult for a woman not to be taken advantage of in negotiating a rental agreement. Doing so may also leave her vulnerable if the landlord decides to enter her home to "do anything he wants," knowing that there is no man to come to her rescue. In a communal society such as Afghanistan's, living away from one's support network would be very painful and risky.

With so much money being given to Afghanistan, why hasn't the country developed more? Even considering the corruption, it seems that such huge sums of money should have made a bigger difference.

One of the reasons why the huge sums haven't been more effective is that development work is very expensive. Agencies pay exorbitant salaries to attract high-level people to work in uncomfortable and sometimes dangerous environments away from their societies and families. Housing standards that include consistent electricity, running hot water, and internet become outrageously expensive in cities with a large UN and foreign worker presence. It has been estimated that 40% of money given to Afghanistan winds up back in the US as salaries deposited in US banks. Stipulations that materials used be bought from American sources may help persuade the US Congress to fund a project, but raise its cost significantly while doing nothing for the local Afghan economy. Sometimes specialized American products are needed, but often materials could have been purchased locally for a fraction of the price. Security for projects done in dangerous areas or perceived dangerous areas is also very expensive.

Another issue is the concept of "burn rate." This refers to the amount of money an organization must spend during its yearly budget cycle. To qualify for funding for subsequent budgets, the agency must show that it was able to spend what was already given. This leads to projects whose quality and sustainability are secondary to statistics and showy claims. Producing results in the short term becomes paramount, irrelevant of how effective or ineffective they might be over time.

Wherever large sums of money are involved, the potential for thievery, nepotism, and corruption increases. When organizations don't understand the local culture, or when the corporate cultures clash with local culture, mis-management and misunderstandings are inevitable.

The answer to this is not to cut our spending, but to approve projects based on their sustainability that focus on the longer term. Also, agencies should develop local talent as an important component of their mission. Aid projects are often designed around a donor's preconceived ideas and needs. For example, there is plenty of support for building schools. Newly constructed buildings offer visual proof of the accomplishments of an organization. However, what Afghanistan needs even more than schools is qualified teachers trained in updated methods. Creating teacher training institutes would be far more effective long-term than putting up another school building.

Another way to make aid more cost-effective and sustainable is to support Afghan-initiated projects that are already working. Supporting expansion of their efforts will require ensuring transparency, monitoring accountability, and helping them bring their efforts up to the required scale.

FAQ

What is the best way to help Afghan women?

Social change in Afghanistan (or anywhere) is only sustainable when there is a large grassroots consensus. Foreigners should avoid pushing agendas that we deem important, such as unveiling, but instead ask Afghan women what their real needs are, and work to fulfill those. External assistance is important, but for sustainability, it must be integrated into Afghan solutions only as needed and in ways compatible with Afghan culture.

In the same vein, Rostom-Povey states, "Muslim and Western conceptions of feminism and women's rights need to intermingle and learn from one another, to construct a more inclusive, global vision of feminism that people can use in their struggle for their rights in the context of their own identities and communities."[2] The most successful way to begin is with common goals that people all across society want. One example is access to health care. Another is primary education. Most Afghan families want their children, including girls, to be educated. Certain barriers keep them from participating. Issues such as the girls' safety during sometimes hours-long walks to their classrooms; a lack of female teachers for girls; and the cost, if not of tuition, of clothes, shoes, notebooks, pens, and the income lost when children give up their petty entrepreneurship to go to school, override their desire for education. Organizations that build schools must address these issues as well.

One reason Afghans have been suspicious of education, especially when it's funded or influenced by foreigners, is because of how it was coerced during the Soviet era. Girls were forcibly taken from their families and subjected to pro-Soviet propaganda. Education is never free from indoctrination; indeed, that is part of its purpose, but instruction provided under the aegis of Islam by Afghans, or by already-trusted NGOs, can aid its acceptance and diminish the propagation of dysfunctional traditional practices such as *baad* or early marriage.

With all of the depressing news and the Taliban gaining more of a foothold, what hope is there for Afghan women?

Hope for Afghan women lies in their own resilience and resourcefulness. Hope lies in awakening women (and men) to their own talent and power. It lies in the idealism of the youth and their dedication to developing their country. Their hope also lies in people like us supporting their efforts. News from that region does look very discouraging. In late 2012, it's looking like Afghan women and Afghans in general may be in for some tough years, maybe even some tough decades. A helpful approach to development strategies is to ask, "What will life be like for Afghan women in 20 or even 50 years? In particular, what will life be like in a village if several young adults can become teachers and midwives there?" They would be able to create an educated core of people in the village, and elevate the quality of life for their community. What will be the impact in 20 years, in 50 years, of the 275,000 students (boys and girls) who are currently being educated in the Mazar-e Sharif area by **Ayni**'s Journey with an Afghan School programs? In addition to building schools, this program pairs American and Afghan students and, through citizen diplomacy, creates good will and increased understanding on both sides.

Even in the worst case scenario, if schools were to be shut down within the next five years, what will the effect of education already received be on those kids' willingness to be used as terrorists? Or their ability (they already have the passion) to rebuild their country? To ease the suffering of their fellow Afghans? Whether their future looks bleak to our eyes or not, the more appropriate and carefully given support we can contribute and the sooner we can give it, the better prospects they will have for a decent future, whatever the political situation.

I didn't really understand the full implications of literacy until I went to Afghanistan. I remember what a struggle it was for me to learn to read as a child. I used to wonder, if I were illiterate, would it really be worth all that effort if I would never get to the point of being able to read as easily as I do now, or wouldn't have access to interesting materials?

That perspective changed for me after reading a chapter in *With All Our Strength.*[3] Ann Brodsky relates the story of a middle-aged woman who was encouraged to join a literacy class. She was very embarrassed to be in this class where everyone else was the age of her daughters. She sat in the back and her daughters helped her complete her homework. One day, the teacher called her to the front of the class to write the letter *alef,* our "A" on the board. *Alef* is written with one downward stroke, like the number one. The woman's fingers fumbled with the chalk. Her hands trembled. She couldn't do it. Then the teacher put her hand over the woman's and helped her draw that simple line. After that everything changed for her. She began doing her own homework. She began learning to read numbers as well as letters and then words. By the end of the story, I didn't have the impression that the woman could read well enough to enjoy newspapers or books, but when talking about her transformation, she said that now she could read signs and numbers and avoid being cheated in the market. Becoming even semi-literate changed this woman's life and gave her the confidence to be active in her community, until eventually, she became one of **RAWA**'s more active members in that region.

The brain gets rewired when one learns to read. Reading is a symbolic act, the letters being only symbols for the "real" thing. Literacy is one step towards more abstract thinking which leads to better decision-making.

All of this is to say that if the situation for Afghan women is poised to get worse, then it is even more important for us now to support the shining lights that will lead their people up and out of a possibly dark future.

These days, more and more women are networking and becoming active in claiming their rights, whether clandestinely, in small groups, or publicly. Whatever happens in the greater political sphere, these local, often informal networks are one of Afghanistan's most reliable sources of long-lasting change. Their strength is that they consist of Afghans implementing changes they consider important into their own culture. They need our support, but not our domination.

Don't you get discouraged with the way the war is going, with the fundamentalists taking over the country, the corruption and seemingly insurmountable problems?

Yes, I do get discouraged. At times it seems hopeless. But one recent event made me remember that the discouraging things we see are not the whole picture, and that behind the scenes and below the surface, there are stabilizing forces which sometimes bring results one can't foresee by watching the news. In February, 2011, the Afghan Parliament passed a bill to put all of the country's battered women's shelters under the auspices of the Ministry of Women's Affairs (MOWA), claiming that the shelters were "hotbeds of prostitution." The shelters were being run by several foreign NGOs. If they were put under MOWA, they would be underfunded, their secret locations would be leaked, and they would have to abide by new regulations that would put sheltered women in prison-like conditions and jeopardize their safety. Petitions went around the US opposing this measure, but I reasoned that the Afghan Parliament wasn't going to pay attention to the internet petitions of infidel feminist foreigners.

But guess what? On February 24th, the takeover plan was officially dropped! It was not because the anti-women elements of Parliament had a change of heart, it was because **Women for Afghan Women** (WAW) had collected so many petition signatures that ultimately caused President Karzai to nix the bill. Pressure on Karzai wasn't only coming from the US government and Western feminists, but also from elements of Afghan civil society working behind the scenes. These countermanding influences aren't ones we can necessarily see. And even when we see some of them, we can never see them all, especially as events unfold.

So, take heart, fight for what you believe in, and don't give up. A lot of people have commented on how brave the Afghan women are to be able to endure the difficulties of their lives and their often risky work. Yes, these women are very brave and strong. I believe that the same potential lives in us, as well. If we can't see it, it's only because we haven't been put to the test.

Satellite dishes and solar panels in Jaroo Kashan
Village near Band-e Amir National Park.

Epilogue

Ominous news reports telling of women's rights reversals and increased terrorism directed at both male and female leaders who are working for a stable and just Afghanistan worry and sadden me. Many fear that when the Allied troops withdraw, the country will revert to civil war.

There is nothing you or I can do to change this big picture. What we can do is take steps to help Afghans, and especially Afghan women, weather the coming changes. What can we do that will help them persevere and emerge on the other side, equipped to help create the kind of society that will allow them to blossom?

Political changes are important but can be swept away by new regimes. Social acceptance of women's constitutional rights is necessary for those changes to last. This is primarily an educational and economic issue. The force of repressive traditions and outlooks diminishes as people learn of their rights and responsibilities under Islam. Women gain power and respect as they contribute to their family's economy, lessening the necessity for "solutions" that commodify daughters.

Networking will play a big role in women's well-being in the upcoming years. Women's networks, such as those developed and matured since their inception during the Soviet war, civil war, and Taliban era, have grown exponentially since those times. **The Afghan Women's Network** was founded in 1995 and has grown from a fledgling network to an advocacy group that represents the interests of over 65 member organizations.

This growth is in part due to the proliferation of technology. In 2011, there were 17,000,000 cell phones in Afghanistan. Television is very popular throughout Afghanistan for anyone who can receive it and afford it. Three houses had satellite TV dishes on their roofs in Jaroo Kashan, the village where I stayed in Band-e Amir National Park. Jaroo Kashan had been electrified two years previously, but the power was only turned on in the evening to run light bulbs and the few TVs. In more remote villages without electricity, car batteries or a generator might power a wealthy person's TV. The midwife in Jaroo Kashan had a computer but no internet. Cell phone reception was limited to a hill outside the village. Even in Kabul, very few people have internet at home, but go online at their offices or in cafes. Small cities like Bamyan and larger ones like Herat have internet at the universities, in cafes, and some offices. Bamyan had one wired public cafe, but the internet was down during my entire two-week stay. If infrastructure can catch up with demand, Afghans will have access to a whole world of ideas and information.

Long-term stability is not only a political or military condition. Civil society also plays a major role. With the withdrawal of foreign troops, governments have begun backing away from "nation building" endeavors. The 2011 USAID budget for Afghanistan was cut by nearly one-third from 2010 levels. The 2013 budget will be even smaller. That leaves it to us, the supporters of Afghan women around the world, to make up the difference. Recent scandals within the aid community make choosing an organization to support more difficult than ever. Donors must conduct due diligence before pledging money to ensure that it does what the donor intended.

The American Institute of Philanthropy, (AIP) helps donors make informed giving decisions. It rates charities and shares information on those it doesn't recommend. The AIP lists groups that help children in Afghanistan and Pakistan. That said, some organizations that I personally know are effective and well-run are not listed, such as **AIL** and **WAW.** As AIP states, "Omission of charities from the Charity Rating Guide or this web site does not imply a negative evaluation or rating."

Whenever there is change, some will benefit and some will be hurt by it. Responsible organizations make serious efforts to become aware of the unintended disruptions their proposed changes will cause. Recognizing this puts them, and the communities they serve, in a better position to decide if the secondary consequences are worth the price; and if they are, to ameliorate some of the worst effects. For example, during the 1980's, child sponsorship became a popular and effective way to raise funds. The sponsored children benefitted, but the unsponsored and their parents justifiably became jealous and rifts developed between former friends. Knowing this, many organizations now work to make benefits more equitable.

Kathleen Parker of the *Washington Post*[1] asked, "What if saving women from cultures that treat them as chattel was in our strategic and not just moral interest?" Parker's impulse to improve the lives of Afghan women is laudable, but the notion of "saving" them is problematic and even repugnant to many women I met.

"Saving" implies that those being saved are helpless and dependent. The "saved" are victims; poor, pitiful people at a liberator's mercy. Unconscious patriarchal ideas ("We know best what you need and how to provide it") remove respect and equality from the relationship. "Saving" assumes that the rescuer has a better understanding of the sufferers' lives and the problems in their society than they. "Saving" infers that the deliverers will be around to make sure victims "stay saved"; and will still be there to pick up the pieces and take the blame for unwanted changes.

Afghan women request our support and it benefits them, their society, ourselves, and the world for us to give it. They want power to reshape their society according to their own vision, in ways that work for them, ways that won't always have immediate effects, but might have a chance for lasting ones.

Glossary

abaa Sleek and beautiful, an *abaa* is a kind of *hijab* worn mostly in Iran and western Afghanistan by modern women. Remember that Herat's summer temperatures average over 100° F (38C°).

Alahu Akbar Arabic for "God is Great."

baad Also known as *baadi*. A traditional means of resolving serious disputes among Pashtun tribes, usually by giving a young girl from the perpetrator's family to the victim's.

badal Exchange marriage. By "trading" daughters, families can avoid high bride prices.

burqa *Burqa*-like garments were brought to Afghanistan by the Moguls in the 16th or 17th century and were worn by upper class Mogul women. This fashion spread to upper-class Afghans of the time and later filtered down through the social classes. During the time of British rule, they became more common.

chador An Iranian veil. A large half-circle of cloth, its diameter is wrapped around the face and held with one hand under the chin. The *chador* covers the head and shoulders, falling all the way to the ground.

duloq Baggy homespun pants worn outdoors over pants women might wear at home.

ghee Clarified butter used as cooking oil in India.

hajj A religious journey to Mecca that Muslims who have the resources are expected to make at least once in their lives. It is one of the Five Pillars of Islam. Men who complete this pilgrimage are called *Hajis* (also *Hajjis*). Women are called *Hajais* in Afghanistan.

hijab An Arabic word popularly used to mean headscarf or veil; however those Arabic words, in the *Quran*, are *khimār* (headscarf) and *jilbaab* (loose outer garment), not *hijab*. Hijab also has a wider meaning of modesty and often refers to covering women's arms, legs, and hair.

Insha'alla An expression meaning "God willing." It is often used as a polite and politic way to say "maybe."

jerga; Loya Jerga; Wolesi Jerga Also spelled *jirga* or *jargah*. A *jerga* is a tribal assembly of elders that makes decisions by consensus. It is similar to a town meeting in the United States or a regional assembly in England, where important regional matters are addressed among the people of the area. *Loya* means grand, so a *Loya Jerga* is a grand or large assembly. The *Wolesi Jerga* is the "House of the People," or lower house of Afghanistan's Parliament.

jihad In the West, people have taken this word to mean "holy war," but in the *Quran* it refers to a struggle. There is a distinction between an internal struggle to live a moral life and the external struggle against an oppressor or persecution.

madrassa Also *madrasa*. Arabic for any educational institution. Currently in the West, the word is used to indicate an Islamic school.

maharam A husband or another male who is ineligible to marry a particular woman, such as her son, brother, father, or uncle. A woman going out of her home was required to be accompanied by a *maharam* during the Taliban era and families sometimes require them now.

masjid Arabic for "mosque." Sometimes the word is used to refer to fundamentalist clerics.

mujahid, *pl.* **mujahidin** (also *mujahideen*) Literally, people who carry out *jihad*. In Afghanistan, it refers to the Afghans who fought against the USSR. It comes from the Arabic word *jihad*. *Jihadi* is a less respectful term that, in Afghanistan, refers to *mujahidin* who, after the Soviets left, fought against each other.

mullah Also *mulla*. A Muslim man trained in religious law and doctrine. In Afghanistan it is also the title given to local clerics or mosque leaders, whether or not they have a formal Islamic education.

nazr An Arabic word meaning "an offering." In Afghanistan, it has become a social custom used to bring good luck. Sometimes it involves giving something simple like one nut or loaf of flat-bread to each woman while she makes a wish. At other times, women may cook a special dish together, especially before Now Ruz (New Year). Suraia Perlika used *nazr* as a means to gather women and spread her empowering ideas.

Quran Also spelled *Koran* and *Qur'an*. Scribes wrote down Mohammad's revelations as he gave them. These were compiled into the *Quran*, the holy book of Islam. In addition to this, Muslims also refer to the *Hadith*, a body of writings gathered from tales of the Prophet's life. Particular passages of the *Hadith* are given greater or lesser weight based on the chain of narration.

shahid Also, *shaheed*. Arabic for "martyr."

shalwar kameez Enormously wide pants gathered at the waist and topped with a knee-length tunic, worn by Pakistani and Afghan men and women.

Sharia law Islamic life is regulated by the *Shari'a* (the Way), or Islamic law. In the strict sense it is much more than law, containing prescriptions for every aspect of life, from rituals, customs, and manners to family law, including the treatment and rights of children.

Shia Also known as Shiite. One branch of Islam and also the name for its adherents.

shura Arabic for "consultation." *Shuras* are congregations of tribal elders who mediate between families in dispute. *Shuras* are believed to be the method that pre-Islamic Arabian tribes used to select leaders and make major decisions. *Shuras* are generally smaller than *jergas*. Both *shuras* and *jergas* are traditionally male; however, women are now often included in the *Loya Jergas*, and separate women's *shuras* are emerging around the country.

Sunni A branch of Islam and also the name for its adherents.

talib- *pl.* **taliban, talibs; Taliban** *Talib* means "student" in Arabic. The plural is *taliban*. Several individuals might be called *talibs,* just as "persons" is used to refer to individuals as a group in English. I use "Taliban" to refer to the organization that ruled Afghanistan from 1996 to 2001.

toshaks Cushions used for sitting and sleeping.

zina The crime of having sex outside of marriage.

Houses built into the hillsides surrounding Kabul. Flat land in the city is very expensive. The land on the hills is free, but offers no city services.

Glossary of People, Places, and Organizations

10,000 Women. A joint project of Goldman-Sachs and the Thunderbird School of Global Management that trains women in entrepreneurial skills. In Afghanistan, they are based at the American University of Afghanistan. http://www.goldmansachs.com/citizenship/10000women/index.html Also, http://www.thunderbird.edu

Afghanistan Institute of Learning (AIL). AIL works to empower Afghans by expanding their educational and health opportunities and by fostering self-reliance and community participation. http://www.afghaninstituteoflearning.org

Afghan Women's Business Council (AWBC). The mandate of AWBC is to advocate for women entrepreneurs throughout the country, thereby facilitating women's entry into the private sector. It also has training programs in business skills development and production for local markets. http://artisanconnect.net/organizations/6779/#.UNtxnm88CSo

Afghan Women's Education Center (AWEC). In addition to educating women and girls, AWEC works with street children and has recently created a school for them. These youths are very often abused and vulnerable to exploitation by terrorists and other unsavory characters. AWEC gives them a chance at a more promising future. http://www.awec.info

Afghan Women's Fund. A collective of Afghan and non-Afghan women who are committed to ensuring the human rights of Afghan women. They have a variety of projects devoted to improving women's lives and education. http://afghanwomensfund.org/index.html

Afghan Women's Network (AWN). Established in 1995, AWN is an organization where Afghan Women can share their observations and concerns and find ways to address them. It is a cornerstone of Afghanistan's fledgling women's movement. In addition to functioning as a network, AWN also undertakes its own projects around issues such as gender-based violence, youth empowerment and girls' education. http://www.afghanwomennetwork.af

Afghan Women's Writing Project (AWWP). Founded by Masha Hamilton during a 2008 trip to Afghanistan after she began to see doors closing for women she'd met on a previous trip in 2004. Masha was inspired to create

AWWP so that women could have a direct voice, unfiltered by their families or the media. You can see their powerful writing at http://www.awwproject.org Donations to provide women with netbooks are always welcome, but perhaps more important are your comments to these aspiring writers. Also needed are authors, editors, and English teachers to act as online mentors. Some of the poems and stories on the AWWP blog are delightful; others difficult to take in. All give insight into what individual Afghan women experience and how they view it. Your comments to them are like gold.

Airserv. An aviation **NGO** that operates mostly in Africa. Flight services for NGOs that Airserv used to offer in Afghanistan are now provided by Pactec. http://www.airserv.org, http://www.pactec.org/afghanistan

Aljazeera (also *Al Jazeera*)."The island." A satellite and internet channel owned by the State of Qatar that transmits in both English and Arabic. It has been praised by the Index on Censorship for avoiding censorship and broadcasting dissenting views. *Aljazeera's* Kabul office was bombed by the Americans in 2001.

al Qaeda. Also al-Qaida and al-Qa'ida. Means "the base." A designated terrorist organization comprised of a network of radical Sunni Muslims calling for global *jihad* and a strict interpretation of *Sharia* law.

All Afghan Women's Union (AAWU). Works "to strengthen people's efforts through organizing, networking, training, material products, and action advocacy." AAWU was formed in 1992 by a team of experienced activists to work for human rights and advocacy. Its mission is to help people organize, expand their capacity, equip themselves for economic self-sufficiency, and overcome various deprivations under which they live. http://blog.world-citizenship.org/wp-archive/706

The American Institute of Philanthropy (AIP), now known as Charity Watch, rates and evaluates charities to help donors make informed giving decisions. http://www.charitywatch.org

Amin, Hafizullah (1929 – 1979). After graduation from Kabul University and graduate study at Columbia University in New York, Amin worked as the principal of a teacher training college. Later, he became the strongman for the **People's Democratic Party of Afghanistan** (PDPA), led by Nur Mohammad **Taraki.** Amin helped topple President **Daoud Khan.** When Taraki became president, Amin was his deputy prime minister. In September, 1979, Amin overthrew Taraki; he himself was overthrown and killed that December.

Ayni Education International (AEI). Ayni is an ancient Peruvian word for "reciprocity." AEI focuses their school-creating efforts in the Mazar-e Sharif area. They partner with Afghan and American schools to broaden children's understanding of each other. http://aynieducation.org

Bashardost, Ramazan (1965 –). An ethnic **Hazara**, Bashardost earned Master's degrees in diplomacy and political science from Paris University and a PhD in law from Toulouse University. As an independent scholar and political activist, he is a prominent voice for human rights and against corruption. His firm stances on these issues resulted in his being fired as Planning Minister. In a 2009 bid for the presidency, he finished third in a field of 38.

Bayat Foundation provides for the needy and unlocks the potential of widows, women, children, youth and men through programs and partnerships offering quality healthcare, access to education, entrepreneurship, social justice, strengthened families, competitive sporting events, and cultural preservation. http://www.bayatfoundation.org

Canadian Women for Afghan Women (CW4AW). Focuses its efforts on securing human rights for Afghan women and girls; on education, including teacher training; and on creating mini-libraries. http://www.cw4wafghan.ca

Catholic Relief Services (CRS). Helps people racked by war, poverty and drought. They work in agriculture, water and sanitation, women's livelihoods, emergency response, and education. Their community-based schools, with classes held in village buildings or tents, demonstrate a practical way to bring education to remote areas. http://crs.org/countries/afghanistan

Church World Service (CWS). An organization of ecumenical Christians who "reach out to neighbors in need near and far – not with a hand out, but a hand up." They do not proselytize; in fact, all of their staff in Afghanistan are Muslim.

Danish Committee for Aid to Afghan Refugees (DACAAR). A non-governmental, non-profit, non-political, humanitarian organization that focuses on long-term sustainable development of water and sanitation services, particularly in rural communities. It is committed to sustainable, Afghan-led, and Afghan-produced projects. http://www.dacaar.org

Dostom, Abdul Rashid (1954 –). An **Uzbek** commander educated in the USSR. He fought as an ally of the Soviets against the *mujahidin* until joining the rebels in 1992 to help them capture Kabul. After the departure of the Soviets, he joined forces with **Massoud** and the **Northern Alliance** to fight **Hekmatyar**, but later joined with Hekmatyar to fight against **Rabbani**. When the Taliban came to power, Dostom joined Rabbani to fight them. A ruthless and brutal warlord, he was accused of leading a massacre of hundreds of *talibs* by stuffing them into shipping containers without food or water in the stifling summer heat.

Farrokhzad, Forugh (1935 – 1967). Forugh, an Iranian poet, attended school until age 16, dropping out to marry for love and escape her stern father. She divorced two years later to follow her independent life and her calling as a poet. She once said, "If I have pursued poetry and art, it has not been as hobby or amusement. I consider poetry and art my whole life." Forugh spoke her mind freely and engaged in a number of affairs. As a result, she faced strong negative social pressures. She was a dramatic example of individualism and courage among the Iranian intelligentsia and on the literary scene. She died in a car crash.

Halo Trust. A non-political, non-religious British NGO specializing in the removal of landmines and the hazardous debris of war. http://www.halotrust.org

Haqqani, Jalaluddin (1950 –). Patriarch of the **Haqqani Network**, Jalaluddin fought ruthlessly with the *mujahidin* against the USSR. As a *mujahid*, Jalaluddin received support from the CIA and Pakistan's Inter-Services Intelligence to fight the Soviets. Due to Jalaluddin's ill health, his son, Sirajuddin, has taken over the day-to-day operations. Siraj is reported to be even more brutal than his father and to be seeking closer ties with other terrorist organizations.

Haqqani Network. An insurgent group started by Jalaluddin **Haqqani** and consisting of various members of the Haqqani clan. They are loosely allied with the Taliban and **al Qaeda** and are a formidable terrorist group.

Hazara. An ethnic group making up nine percent of the population of Afghanistan. Historians claim that they come from the Xinjiang region of northwestern China and are descendants of the followers of Genghis Khan and other central Asians. Their first language is Dari and they are mostly Shia.

Hekmatyar, Gulbuddin (1947 –). Studied engineering at Kabul University and became a pro-Soviet militant in the **PDPA**. He was reputed to have thrown acid in the faces of unveiled women in the 1960s. A few years after graduation, he became Islamized while in prison for murder. During the Soviet war, Hekmatyar and his party, Hesb-e Islami, received the majority of US and Saudi funding. Unwilling to compromise in building a new Afghan government once the Soviets left, he was largely responsible for Afghanistan's descent into civil war. Indeed, he was responsible for most of the damage to Kabul. In his fight against the Taliban, he joined forces at different times with former foes Rabbani and **Dostam**. He was designated a "global terrorist" in 2003 by the US State Department. In March 2010, he delivered a

15-point peace proposal to the **Karzai** government. Both Hekmatyar and the Taliban claimed responsibility for the 2011 attacks on the Intercontinental Hotel and the US Embassy in Kabul.

Institute for the Economic Empowerment of Women (IEEW) focuses on educating, mentoring and coaching women to develop entrepreneurial skills that will help them start and grow a business. See also, Peace Through Business, their premier program.

International Midwife Assistance (IMA). Established and operated the Community Midwife Training Program in Afghanistan from 2004 until 2006. Currently, the midwife training program is run by the Aga Khan Development Network. IMA now provides similar services in Uganda. http://www.midwife-assist.org

International Rescue Committee (IRC). The IRC responds to the world's worst humanitarian crises and helps people survive and rebuild their lives. Founded in 1933 at the request of Albert Einstein, the IRC offers lifesaving care and life-changing assistance to refugees forced to flee from war or disaster. In 1988, they began work in Afghanistan. http://www.rescue.org/irc-afghanistan

Inter-Services Intelligence (ISI). Pakistan's secret police.

Ka'aba. A cube shaped building in Mecca that Muslims circumambulate as part of the rituals of the *hajj*. The Ka'aba is the most sacred site in Islam.

Karmal, Babrak (1929 – 1996). Karmal became involved in Marxist political activities while a student at Kabul University. After graduating in law, he became a founding member of the **PDPA** and served in the National Assembly. When the PDPA split, he became a member of the more moderate Parcham faction and was soon "exiled" by Taraki (of the Khalq faction), becoming Ambassador to Czechoslovakia. When the Soviets invaded Afghanistan, Karmal was brought back to become President. He was replaced by **Najibullah** in 1986. Karmal died in Moscow of liver disease, the only Afghan communist leader to die of natural causes.

Karzai, Hamid (1957 –). President and Chairman of Afghanistan's Transitional Administration. He was elected to the presidency in 2004, and again in a contested election in 2009. He has a Master's degree in political science and speaks five languages.

KGB. The USSR's Committee for State Security was the intelligence, internal security, and secret police arm of the Soviet state.

Glossary of People

Khan, Amanullah (1892 – 1962). Crowned King of Afghanistan after the assassination of his father, Habibullah Khan. He led a surprise attack against the British in 1919, beginning the third Anglo-Afghan War and leading his country to independence in 1921. He modernized the nation, creating roads, hospitals, and schools. Upon his return from a European tour, he accelerated reforms, including the unveiling of women, which helped lead to his overthrow in 1929. He died in exile in Zurich.

Khan, Mohammad Daoud (1909 – 1978). First cousin of King **Zahir Shah**, he was educated in France and rose through the ranks as Governor, then Commander of the Kabul Army Corps, Minister of Defense, Interior Minister, and later Prime Minister (1953 – 1963). In July, 1973, he seized the throne while Zahir was in Italy for health treatments, establishing the Democratic Republic of Afghanistan. His socialist, land reform, and modernization policies angered *mullahs* and rural elites. His attempts to unite the Pakistani and Afghan Pashtuns in Afghanistan would have meant taking land from newly-formed Pakistan. The prospect of having more Pashtuns in the country worried minority groups. For all these reasons, this effort was doomed to failure. Daoud's attempt to distance himself from his Soviet patrons resulted in his assassination in 1978.

Leprosy Control (LEPCO). A German NGO originally founded to find and treat leprosy patients. They have expanded their Afghan services to include tuberculosis, now their main focus there. http://www.lepco.de

Massoud, Ahmad Shah (1953 – 2001). Known as "The Lion of Panshir," Massoud was the **Tajik** leader of the Northern Alliance and a brilliant commander. Two *talibs* posing as reporters exploded themselves in his presence, killing him two days before 9/11.

Medica Mondiale (MM). A German NGO that works for women's rights around the world. In 2011, MM Afghanistan became an independent Afghan NGO, although it still receives support from the parent organization. http://www.medicamondiale.org/projekte/afghanistan/?L=1

Médecins Sans Frontières (MSF), aka **Doctors Without Borders**. An excellent organization that provides medical care in rural Afghanistan and around the world. They do not take sides in areas of conflict. In June 2004, five of their staff were killed in Badghis Province and they withdrew from Afghanistan, but returned in 2009. http://www.msf.org

Mohseni, Ayatollah Asif (1935 –). A **Pashtun** Shia born in Kandahar, he founded the Islamic Movement of Afghanistan in 1978 which played an important role in the anti-communist resistance. He fought with the Northern Alliance against the Taliban. Mohseni is the owner of Tamadon ("civilization") TV, a privately owned station. The night before the protest against the Shia Personal Status Law, the station broadcast a message that advised people to prevent their family members from participating.

Mojaddidi, Professor Sibghatullah (1925 –). A moderate *mujahidin* leader who fought the USSR. After the Soviets withdrew, he was the first president of the new Islamic Republic of Afghanistan, stepping down after two months as the power-sharing agreement dictated.

Najibullah, Mohammad Ahmadzai (1947 – 1996). Also called Najib. Former head of the Afghan secret police until the USSR installed him as President of the Democratic Republic of Afghanistan. He ran the country from 1986 until 1992, two years after the Soviet Army left. As he was losing power, he offered to step down in favor of a transitional government, but the *mujahidin* leaders weren't interested and his regime collapsed. When the *mujahidin* took over Kabul, he fled to sanctuary in the United Nations compound. As the Taliban approached Kabul, he refused several offers of help to escape, believing that the *talibs* wouldn't harm him due to their shared ethnic background. The Taliban castrated and beat him, dragged him behind a truck, and then hanged him from a traffic barricade.

Non-Governmental Organization (NGO). A legally constituted organization independent of any form of government. NGOs operate both nationally and internationally, as both for-profit and non-profit corporations. Some receive government contracts, others, like Doctors without Borders and Oxfam, refuse them.

Northern Alliance. A confederation of various commanders including Dostom, Rabbani, and Massoud, who fought against each other during the civil war after the Soviets left but came together in 1992 to fight the Taliban. Dostom, especially, is accused of war crimes, including massacres. With the help of the US and its allies, the Northern Alliance drove the Taliban into Pakistan in late 2001. Of the three commanders listed above, only Dostom remains alive. Currently, he and other Northern Alliance commanders are preparing to take up arms against the Taliban again when US troops leave in 2014.

Omar, Mullah Mohammad (c. 1959 –). Fed up with the widespread corruption during the civil war, Mullah Omar led a small militia to rescue two youths who had been kidnapped and raped by a local militia commander. That led to the formation of the Taliban and Mullah Omar's position as their spiritual leader. He was the head of state from 1996 – 2001. An introverted and secretive man, his current whereabouts are unknown; in fact it is uncertain whether he is alive.

Glossary of People

Our Journey to Smile. The Afghan Peace Volunteers are a grassroots group of ordinary, multi-ethnic Afghans seeking a life of non-violence, the unity of all people, equality, and self-reliance. They seek non-military solutions for Afghanistan and do not work for the benefit of any political group or religion. http://ourjourneytosmile.com/blog/

Pashtun. Also rendered as: Pushtuns, Pakhtuns, Pukhtuns or Pathans and known as ethnic Afghans. The largest ethnic group in Afghanistan at just under half the population, their language, Pashtu, is the second language of Afghanistan.

Peace Through Business (PTB). A program of the Institute for Economic Empowerment of Women (IEEW). Their mission is to empower women economically, socially, and politically, thereby helping to cultivate peace. They focus on developing leadership and helping women leaders develop as entrepreneurs. http://www.ieew.org/programs

People's Democratic Party of Afghanistan (PDPA). A communist party established in 1965. The PDPA deposed Daoud, replacing him with Mohammad Taraki. The PDPA divided into rival factions, the most powerful being the Khalqs and the Parchams.

Red Crescent. The name the Red Cross uses in Muslim countries. The Red Cross was founded by Jean-Henry Dunant in 1863 to assist those wounded in war. The name was changed in 1983 to include Red Crescent.

Revolutionary Association of Women of Afghanistan (RAWA). A group of highly dedicated women who run schools, clinics, and other projects for women. They operated secret schools during the Taliban and continue to do so. http://www.rawa.org

Rabbani, Professor Burhanuddin. (1940 – 2011). A *mujahidin* leader who in 1993 became the second president of the *Mujahidin* government. The country disintegrated into civil war shortly afterwards. In 2011, he worked to facilitate contacts with the Taliban while head of the Karzai government's peace council. Rabbani was assassinated in September, 2011.

Save the Children Federation (SCF). Focuses on child protection, emergency relief and recovery, health and education initiatives in their Afghan programs. http://www.savethechildren.org/site/c.8rKLIXMGIpI4E/b.6150517/k.EAA2/Afghanistan_Humanitarian_Aid_for_Children.htm

Sayaf, Ustad Abdul Rab Rasul (1964 –). Received a degree in religion from Kabul University and a Master's degree from Al-Azhar University in Cairo, Egypt. Sayaf rose to prominence in the war against Soviet occupation and had a close relationship with Osama bin Laden. Some say he invited bin Laden into Afghanistan and that together, they established a network of militant training camps. Sayaf joined the Northern Alliance to fight the Taliban but was suspected of arranging the false interview in which Massoud was assassinated. In 2003, he was elected to the Constitutional *Loya Jerga* and to the Parliament in 2005. He called for an amnesty for former *mujahidin* to prevent them (and himself) from being charged with war crimes.

School of Leadership, Afghanistan (SOLA). Ted Achilles founded SOLA to help educated, English-speaking potential leaders, especially women, gain access and scholarships to US Ivy League universities. With their top-notch educations, SOLA's students are eager to contribute to rebuilding their country. http://www.sola-afghanistan.org

Shuhada Organization. Founded in 1989 by Sima Simar, Afghanistan's first Minister of Women's Affairs. Shuhada is a social business enterprise dedicated to the welfare and progress of Afghans, particularly women and girls. http://www.shuhada.org.af

Solace for the Children. A US nonprofit that brings Afghans to the US for medical treatments too complex to be performed in their own country. http://www.s4tc.org

The Swedish Committee for Afghanistan. The Swedish Committee has been working in Afghanistan for 30 years. Their programs include education, health, support to persons with disabilities, and rural development. They mostly operate in the eastern half of the country. http://www.swedishcommittee.org

Tajik. An ethnic group making up approximately one-quarter of the Afghan population and most of the population of neighboring Tajikistan. They trace their roots to ancient Iranian civilizations. Dari is often their first language. "Tajik" comes from a Turkish word meaning "non-Turk."

Taraki, Nur Mohammad (1917 – 1979). Helped found the PDPA in 1963. When the party split, he led the more radical Khalq faction. With help from the Soviets, he overthrew Daoud Khan and succeeded him as president and prime minister. He was killed during **Amin's** coup in 1979.

The United States Agency for International Development (USAID). Started under President John F. Kennedy to "further America's foreign policy interests in expanding democracy and free markets while also extending a helping hand to people struggling to make a better life, recover from a disaster or striving to live in a free and democratic country." http://www.usaid.gov

Uzbek. A Turkish ethnic group comprising nine percent of the Afghan population and most of the population of neighboring Uzbekistan. They came into Central Asia and Afghanistan as late as the 13th century CE. Uzbeki is often their first language.

Women for Afghan Women (WAW). A women's human rights organization based in Kabul and New York. It was founded in April 2001, six months before 9/11, and since then has advocated for the rights of Afghan women and built programming to secure, protect, and advance Afghan women's human rights, both in New York and across Afghanistan. http://www.womenforafghanwomen.org

Young Women 4 Change (YW4C). A program that seeks to change old perceptions of women and give them the education, skills, and opportunities to accomplish their goals. They've established an internet café, Sar Gul Café, in Kabul and use the space for various activities and to help women network. http://www.youngwomenforchange.org

Zahir Shah (1915 – 2007). The last King of Afghanistan. He reigned from 1933 –1973, when his throne was usurped by his cousin, Daoud. Zahir Shah returned from exile in 2002 to open the *Loya Jerga* that chose the interim government, and was given the title "Father of the Nation." He died in July, 2007, after a long illness. The word "shah" means "king" in Dari, but Tajwar and others who referred to him in English always called him "King Zahir Shah."

Bibliography

Albinati, Edoardo; Howard Curtis, Trans. *Coming Back: Diary of a Mission in Afghanistan.* London: Hesperus Press Ltd. 2003.

    Mr. Albinati spent four months of 2002 in Afghanistan helping the UNHCR with the repatriation of returning refugees. This book of personal observations chronicles the efforts he and others made to help with repatriation. The book presents a picture of Afghanistan just after the Taliban left and gives insights into the workings of aid efforts.

Ansary, Mir Tamim. *East of New York, West of Kabul.* London: Macmillan, 2003.

    Written by an Afghan exile who had an American mother. The most interesting parts tell about growing up bicultural in Afghanistan. The chapter titled "Unintended Consequences" gives an Afghan perspective about American aid on the Helmand River Project during the 1950s.

Ansary, Mir Tamim, and Yalda Asmatey. *Snapshots: This Afghan-American.* San Francisco: Kajaki Press, 2008.

    This anthology, written by young Afghan-Americans is a first step towards bringing their little-known community, with its roots in Afghan history and culture, into wider view. This first generation of Afghan-Americans has their own story to tell, both as part of and distinct from other refugee communities in America.

Ansary, Mir Tamim. *The Widow's Husband.* San Rafael, CA: Numina Press, 2009.

    This engrossing story, which takes place during the British occupation of Kabul (1841), gives insights into rural Afghan society as well showing parallels with current events.

Ansary, Mir Tamim. *Destiny Disrupted: A History of the World Through Islamic Eyes.* New York, NY: Public Affairs, 2009.

    Ansary's lighthearted prose and lively style make enjoyable reading of this complex topic. Through this alternate perspective, not only do we gain an understanding critical to comprehension of current events, but we also acquire insight into how events were interpreted by people when they occurred. Ansary's even-handed sympathy to all sides and his clear, concise depiction of events and their importance make this book invaluable to historical understanding.

Ansary, Mir Tamim. *Games without Rules: The Often Interrupted History of Afghanistan.* New York, NY: PublicAffairs™, 2012.

Games without Rules is much more than a history of Afghanistan over the past several centuries. Ansary draws instructive parallels between historical, subsequent, and current events. Through his detailed observations the reader is given refreshing insights into his complex country and it's current situation.

Ayub, Awista. *However Tall the Mountain: A Dream, Eight Girls and a Journalist.* New York, NY: Hyperion Books, 2009.

Ayub emigrated to the US when she was two. As an adult, she founded the Afghan Youth Sports Exchange to bring Afghan girls to the US for training. Her book chronicles her struggles as she takes on this endeavor, as well as the lives of the eight athletes in the first exchange group.

Badkhen, Anna. *Peace Meals: Candy-Wrapped Kalashnikovs and Other War Stories.* New York, NY: Free Press, 2010.

Intrepid Russian journalist Badkhen describes shocking violence and hardship in war-torn Afghanistan, as well as stories of inspiring humanity and everyday life. Recipes for common Afghan dishes end each chapter.

Benard, Cheryl. *Veiled Courage: Inside the Afghan Women's Resistance.* NY: Broadway Books, 2002.

This book provides an understanding of RAWA and its activities within the historical and social context of Afghanistan from the 1970s through 2002. Stories and analysis convey a good understanding of and deep respect for the organization and its brave members.

Bick, Barbara. *Walking the Precipice: Witness to the Rise of the Taliban in Afghanistan.* New York: NY: Feminist Press at the City University of New York, 2009.

Bick traveled to Afghanistan three times: in 1999 in the company of a pro-Soviet woman; in 2001 with some feminist activists; and in 2003 to attend a conference for the Declaration of the Essential Rights of Afghan Women. She passed away in 2009.

Brodsky, Anne. *With All Our Strength: The Revolutionary Association of the Women of Afghanistan.* NY: Routeledge, 2003.

Brodsky had in-depth access to RAWA and visited their operations in Afghanistan and Pakistan both before and after 9/11. This scholarly work is filled with stories of individual women and astute analysis of the organization and the political context wherein it operates.

Chayes, Sarah. *The Punishment of Virtue: Inside Afghanistan after the Taliban.* New York, NY: Penguin Press, 2006.

Chayes was a National Public Radio (NPR) reporter from 1997 – 2002. She quit her job reporting on Afghanistan to work for Afghans for a Civil Society and later founded a NGO, Arghand Cooperative. This book explores the current situation in terms of her experience living in Kandahar and is grounded in a history of the area. This is one of the most important books I've read yet on Afghanistan for its cultural, as well as political understanding of the country and general US foreign policy. Written as an inquiry into the assassination of the Kabul Chief of Police, it's a fascinating read.

Coll, Steve. *Ghost Wars: The Secret History of the CIA, Afghanistan and bin Laden from the Soviet Invasion to September 10, 2001.* New York, NY: Penguin Press, 2004.
A very detailed account of the relationship among the CIA, the Mujahidin, Al Qaeda, and the Taliban between the invasion of the Soviet Union in 1979 and the assassination of Massoud in Sept. 2001.

Delloye, Isabelle. *Women of Afghanistan.* St. Paul, MN: Ruminator Books, 2003.
Isabelle lived and worked as a teacher in Afghanistan from 1974 until December 1979 and made a return trip as a journalist during the Taliban rule. The stories in this book transcend time and politics. Although many took place before the recent wars, the issues they raise are still current. Isabelle's commentary and observations about Afghan cultural practices make this a useful and fascinating book.

Elliot, Jason. *An Unexpected Light: Travels in Afghanistan.* New York, NY: Picador, 1999.
Elliot, a British journalist, fought with the *mujahidin* against the Soviets and later returned to Afghanistan just before the Taliban took over. The book is part adventure story, part history, and part travelogue. It gives good insight into the male Afghan mindset, as well as illuminates the physical and cultural geography of the regions through which he traveled.

Ewans, Martin. *Afghanistan, a Short History of its People and Politics.* New York, NY: HarperCollins, 2002.
The history of Afghanistan from its earliest times until after the fall of the Taliban is examined by Ewans, a former Head of Chancery in Kabul. He weighs the lessons of history to provide a frank look at Afghanistan's prospects in the immense task of political and economic reconstruction.

Fitzgerald, Paul, and Elizabeth Gould. *Invisible History: Afghanistan's Untold Story.* San Francisco: City Lights Books, 2009.
This comprehensive and probing analysis of American involvement in Afghanistan gives a fresh perspective in this very well-documented volume. A must-read for those wanting to understand Afghanistan today.

Hafvenstein, Joel. *Opium Season: A Year on the Afghan Frontier.* Guilford, CT: The Lyons Press, 2007.
Hafvenstein tells of his year in Helmand Province directing Chemonics' "Work for Hire" efforts to stem opium production. He soon found himself caught up in the deadly intrigues of drug lords and the Taliban. The book gives important insights into the character of Afghans in that part of the country and

the internal workings of international development.

Hosseini, Khaled. *The Kite Runner.* New York, NY: Riverhead Books, 2003.
Hosseini gives a vivid and engaging glimpse of the culture and customs of Afghan society in this story of betrayal and redemption. This very personal story of dealing with violence speaks to each of us, transcending time and culture.

Hosseini, Khaled. *A Thousand Splendid Suns.* New York, NY: Riverhead Books, 2007.
Here are the stories of two women, each forced into an unwanted marriage by circumstances, and their unlikely friendship. This book really gives one a feel for the lives of many Afghan women.

Hosseini, Khaled. *And the Mountains Echoed.* New York, NY: Riverhead Books, 2013.
As with his previous books, Hosseini's gift in painting pictures with words gives insight into complex human relationships and Afghan culture, even even as the characters are living in Western countries. The story feels credible and real.

Jones, Ann. *Kabul in Winter: Life without Peace in Afghanistan.* New York, NY: Metropolitan, 2006.
Jones went to Afghanistan in 2002 to train teachers and worked there until 2005. This book sheds light on the dysfunctional prison system, NGO-run schools, and the thinking of their Afghan participants, while offering insights into how humanitarian aid works.

Joya, Malalai, with Derrick O'Keefe. *A Woman Among Warlords: The Extraordinary Story of an Afghan Who Dared to Raise Her Voice.* New York, NY: Scribner, 2009.
Joya stood up in front of the Constitutional Loya Jerga to ask the world how Afghanistan could have a democracy when there were warlords and criminals in the government. The book tells the story of Malalai's remarkable life and her efforts to promote women's rights. Born in southwestern Afghanistan, she offers a perspective much different from that of Kabuli women.

Kargar, Zarguna. *Dear Zari.* London: Random House, 2011.
Kargar left Afghanistan in 1994 to live in London. In 2005, the BBC offered her a position with a new program they were developing, *The Afghan Women's Hour.* She traveled back to Afghanistan and found local reporters to collect the stories of women from around the country. Those fascinating stories and her own narrative and commentary fill this book.

King, Dedie; Judith Inglese, Ill. *I See the Sun in Afghanistan.* Hardwick, MA: Satya House Publications, 2011.
This delightful children's book tells the story of a day in the life of an Afghan

girl living in Bamyan. The book, written in both English and Dari, rings true to my experiences there and is a great introduction to Afghanistan for young children. *I See the Sun in Afghanistan* is part of a series that includes China, Nepal, and Russia.

Klaits, Alex, and Gulchin Klaits. *Love and War in Afghanistan.* New York, NY: Seven Stories Press, 2005.
  Love and War gives voice to a dozen Afghans who lived in and around the northern province of Kunduz from the time of the Soviet War through 2005. Interviewees, both men and women, with their varying situations and viewpoints, broaden our understanding of "life on the ground" among the different players and survivors during the wars. One of the stories is of an ex-Soviet soldier captured by the *mujahidin* who settled in Kunduz after the war. Fascinating.

Koofi, Fawzia. *The Favored Daughter: One Woman's Fight to Lead Afghanistan into the Future.* New York, NY: Palgrave Macmillan, 2012.
  Koofi's autobiography tells of her life during the Afghan wars and her struggles to survive as a widow raising her two daughters. Her commitment to her country is courageous and admirable as is her presidential candidacy. Some say she is ill prepared to run a country such as Afghaistan, but her contribution lies in just putting herself out there to change Afghan people's (men as well as women's) mindsets about women's capability.

Kristof, Nicholas D., and Sheryl Wudunn. *Half the Sky: Turning Oppression into Opportunity for Women Worldwide.* New York, NY: Alfred Knopf, Random House, 2009.
  This book includes insightful chapters on women in Afghanistan and Pakistan who make important changes in their country. An eye-opening and inspiring look into the lives and situations of women, and more importantly, a guide to ways to help.

Lamb, Christina. *The Sewing Circles of Herat: A Personal Voyage through Afghanistan.* New York, NY: HarperCollins, 2002.
  Lamb, a British foreign correspondent, spent extensive time in Pakistan and Afghanistan during the late 1980s. She returned there in 2002 after the fall of the Taliban to find out what had happened to the people she had met as a young graduate. This book contains some surprising interviews and interesting insight into the effect of war on individuals, mostly in Herat. It also contains a good bibliography.

Latifa, with Shékéba Hachemi. *My Forbidden Face: Growing up under the Taliban: A Young Woman's Story.* New York, NY: Hyperion, 2001.
  This book is written from the perspective of a 16-year-old and is suitable

for young readers. It portrays Latifa as a young woman to whom women in the West can easily relate because her (pre-Taliban) life, hopes, and dreams are so similar to theirs. *My Forbidden Face* gives a real feeling for life under the Taliban. There is also a brief chronology of Afghan history.

Lemmon, Gayle Tzemach. *The Dressmaker of Khair Khana: Five Sisters, One Remarkable Family, and the Woman Who Risked Everything to Keep Them Safe.* New York, NY: HarperCollins, 2011.

Even more interesting than the spellbinding story is the detailed description of Kabul under the Taliban and the intimate portrayal of the lives of Kamila and her sisters. This book reads like a swift-paced novel, but the characters are real people and the book completes their stories with an update on where they are now.

Magnus, Ralph H., and Eden Naby. *Afghanistan: Mullah, Marx, and Mujahid.* Boulder, CO: Westview Press, 2000.

An excellent textbook about the geopolitics that gave rise to the Taliban, this book offers a good historical perspective on the country. It has a detailed timeline and brief biographies of modern rulers.

Pasha, Kamran. *Mother of the Believers, A Novel of the Birth of Islam.* New York, NY: Washington Square Press, 2009.

Meticulously researched, this expansive novel tells the story of the birth of Islam from the Prophet's fourth wife, Aisha's, point of view. *Mother* is the fascinating story of a young girl as she develops into a teacher, political leader, and warrior. An enjoyable, interesting way to learn about the origins of Islam.

Pazira, Nelofer. *A Bed of Red Flowers: In Search of My Afghanistan.* New York, NY: Free Press, 2005.

Afghanistan's history comes to life in this story of Nelofer's experiences and resistance activities during the Soviet war. She was saddened to leave her friend behind when her family evacuated, so decades later, she returned to find her. The film "Kandahar" is based on this book.

Rashid, Ahmed. *Taliban: Militant Islam, Oil and Fundamentalism in Central Asia.* New Haven, CT: Yale University Press, 2001.

A chapter titled "Heroin and the Taliban Economy" and the section on oil and pipelines make this book important for understanding the economy of the Taliban era. The book also includes extensive notes, a bibliography, a chronology, and tables of pipeline information.

Rashid, Ahmed. *Descent into Chaos: The United States and the Failure of Nation Building in Pakistan, Afghanistan, and Central Asia.* New York, NY: Viking Penguin, 2008.

Utilizing his connections in very high and very low places, this extremely well-documented book offers a panoramic view along with detailed nuances that give insight into the many reasons for the current situation.

Rostami-Povey, Elaheh. *Afghan Women: Identity and Invasion.* London: Zed Books, 2007.

This scholarly work, using stories from Rostami-Povey's interviews, shows how Afghan women have fought repression within Afghanistan and in their diaspora. Insights gained from her diverse subjects help challenge assumptions and stereotypes and place Afghan women's struggle for equality in the light of post-conflict development in Afghanistan.

Seierstad, Åsne; Ingrid Christophersen, Trans. *The Bookseller of Kabul.* New York, NY: Back Bay Books, 2004.

After six weeks spent with the commandos of the Northern Alliance, Åsne went to Kabul, where she met a bookseller. He invited her to live with his family for three months during the spring when the Taliban took its flight. This fascinating book gives an intimate description of an Afghan household and the life of one family.

Sadeed, Suraya, with Damien Lewis. *Forbidden Lessons in a Kabul Guesthouse: The True Story of a Woman Who Risked Everything to Bring Hope to Afghanistan.* New York, NY: Hyperion Books, 2011.

Forbidden Lessons tells the story of an extraordinarily brave Afghan-American woman who began raising money and delivering aid during the Afghan civil war and continued during the Taliban and afterwards. The first-hand account of her struggles to deliver aid during those times is compelling and enlightening.

Stewart, Rory. *The Places In Between.* Olando, FL: Harcourt, Inc., 2004.

Rory Stewart walked from Herat in western Afghanistan to Kabul, its capital. This book chronicles his journey along with his insights and observations as he stayed with villagers along his route. It's a view of Afghanistan that we seldom see.

Stewart, Rory, and Gerald Knaus. *Can Intervention Work?* New York, NY: W.W. Norton and Company, 2011.

These two experts on the interventions in Kosovo and Afghanistan compare lessons from each. They show how both liberal imperialist and neoconservative dogmas have led us astray in our endeavors to improve situations around the world and offer their own suggestions.

Women in Jaroo Kashan village enjoy a lunch celebrating
the first birthday of the village midwife's son

Reading Group Questions

Who was your favorite woman in the book and why?

How is she both like you and different? What from your own experience helps connect you with the women in the book?

How was your experience different? How has it been the same? What advice might you give this woman? What advice might she give you?

If you could spend a day showing this woman your life as a Westerner, what would you most want her to see? Are there aspects of your life you would rather she not see?

In what ways might the stories you read in this book affect your life?

What issues in your own life are similar to those faced by Afghan women?

Several of the women mentioned "giving themselves hope" in hard times. How do you give yourself hope? What are the positive and negative effects of this process?

What do you think about this statement by Marzia: "In 20 or 25 years, they [youth] and their children will make Afghanistan a different country. This is my main hope."

Anisa's sister said, "If you really want to be the person you say you want to be, and if you want to repay Dad for all his hard work, then you have to forget about discrimination. You have to study even harder. Instead of being in second place, you have to be first. You have to get more involved in school activities."

Anisa told me, "After that, I became more active outside of class and my grades were only 100s. It really made me proud and that made people discriminate against me less." What do you think about this? Does having pride make people discriminate less against someone?

If you were in Hador's position, would you pay a bribe to lower your prison sentence?

If you were the prison matron, with an extended family to support, and were required to facilitate prostitution in the prison, what would you do?

Communalism vs. individualism is a major difference between Afghan and American cultures. Given that, what is the best way to support Afghan women: to select promising women leaders and empower them through education, employment, and overseas education? Or to focus on empowering the family, including increasing employment opportunities for men, the traditional breadwinners, and education for boys that would include human rights as prescribed in Islam? What other ideas do you have on how to support Afghan women, in addition to those listed here?

What does women's empowerment mean and what might it look like in places lacking electricity, potable water, and nearby schools?

What can be done to impact the 40% rate of male unemployment?

What are some positive aspects of generally negative events and negative aspects of generally positive developments in Afghanistan? For example, the Soviet war, the Taliban rule, or women's education and empowerment.

What are some of the unintended consequences, both positive and negative, of American intervention and military aid? Of humanitarian aid?

In Afghan development, is it better to focus on large scale projects such as roads, water, and electric plants; or small scale projects that help women run businesses, kids attend school, or farmers become more productive?

Women have been the focus of much of the aid that has poured into Afghanistan. What effects does this have on men, also uneducated and unemployed, who have been largely ignored? How can aid be structured to meet the needs of society at large?

What are Afghan women's different viewpoints regarding the current war and foreign troops, and with which do you agree? If you were a sequestered, uneducated, rural woman living in a war zone, would your opinion differ? If you were an educated, employed Afghan woman living in Kabul, what might you think?

Both "Peggy's Story" and several stories of women who had lived outside Afghanistan discuss the impact of foreign travel on how one sees the world. Have you traveled internationally? If so, did it change your outlook at all? How?

If you haven't traveled abroad, did reading this book make you more or less interested in the idea? If you could travel to any foreign country, which one(s) might you choose to visit?

Has anyone in your family, or your friends' families, served in Afghanistan, either in the military, as a contractor, or as an aid worker? Have you talked with them about their experiences? What do they have to say? Are their stories different from those in this book, and if so, how?

If you have served or worked in Afghanistan, have you gotten any new insights from this book? Discuss.

Wool Spinner

Acknowledgements

This book never would have happened without the loving encouragement of my husband, Bill Kelsey. Bill has provided support of every kind since first telling me about the reception where the idea for the Afghan Women's Project came to me.

I am also grateful for:

❋ people and organizations both in Afghanistan and the US who gave help and guidance all along the way, from providing connections and logistics to bouncing ideas around with me and guiding me through the labyrinth of publication. Among them are: Shakila H., Ted Achilles, Henry Friedman, Airserv, Susan Violente, Vic Getz, Vicki Flaugher, Stephanie Barko, and Estephania LeBaron. Dave Miller spent countless hours helping me sharpen and improve the manuscript and it is immeasurably better for his help.

❋ my translators, Najis M., Shakilla S., Shakila H., Nargis, Mary, and Fatemeh.

❋ the many friends of the Afghan Women's Project, who offered money, support, connections, and invited me to speak to their groups.

❋ D'Ann Johnson and Alan Pogue, who opened their home and gallery to the touring Afghan women who inspired my project, and later opened their gallery to my photographs.

❋ my early readers: Paula Travis, Alice Embree, Nancy Simons, Bernice Hecker, Kathy Kravitz, Lynda Berman, Penny Fordham, Diane Potter, Kristin Johnson, Paulette Delahoussaye, and Lanaye Geiser.

❋ unending patience and dedication from my editors: Aimée Loft, who cut the manuscript down to size and shaped it from the perspective of a young woman; Mariann Garner-Wizard, whose editing skills helped sharpen my ideas and text into a coherent, consistent document; Debra L. Winegarten, my eagle-eyed proofreader; and from Stacy Klawunn, my flexible and creative book designer and typographer. Mayapriya Long of Bookwrites designed the beautiful cover. My long-time friend and publicist, Stephanie Barko, has been a steady source of advice, encouragement, and promotion.

● my daughters, Petra and Danielle, who "held down the fort" while I was off on my journeys or sequestered in my writing efforts.

● and always my parents, Harry and Phyllis Fry who laid the foundation of who I am, and who, overcoming their parental fears, have given their loving support to my choices and journeys.

● Financial support for the book came from: Mark Scholmann, Evette Babich, Paul Thornton, Thuong Dang, Jack Cheevers, Amanda Winters, Lois Dvorak, Nancy Simons, The Debster, Margaret L. Wade, Juli Fellows, Connie Frisbee Houde, Brenda Machala, Ajay, Petra Kelsey, Peg Runnels, Tura Campanella Cook, Charlie Jackson, Leslie McCullough, Mariann Wizard, Diane Potter and Bill Kelsey.

I especially thank all of the Afghan women who allowed me to talk with and photograph them and who encouraged me in my project, whether or not their stories appear in this book. I wish for each of them, and their daughters and sons, lives of peace and plenty, education, dignity, and opportunity.

Notes

Preface

[1] "Settlements in Afghanistan with less than 100 houses number over 10,000 and those with 100 to 250 houses number about 1000. There are 53 urban centers that range in size from 2500 to 25,000 people. In the smaller villages there are no schools, no stores, nor any representative of the government. Each village has three sources of authority within it: the malik (village headman), the mirab (master of the water distribution), and the mullah (teacher of Islamic laws). Commonly a khan (large landowner) will control the whole village by assuming the role of both malik and mirab." http://www.afghanistans.com/information/people/WayofLife.htm

[2] Lessing, D. *The Wind Blows Away our Words*. New York, NY: Vintage Books, 1987. p 153.

[3] Dari is a dialect of Farsi, the national language of Iran. Ancient Persian empires controlled parts of Afghanistan for centuries and when Afghanistan and Persia (now Iran) separated, Dari was born. The major differences between the two languages are the accent and some words and expressions. Anything written in Farsi would be easily intelligible to a Dari speaker and vice versa.

[4] American Heritage College Dictionary, 4th Edition, Boston, MA: Houghton Mifflin, 2002.

Sana

[1] The Advocacy Committee of Persons with Disabilities (ACSF) works with the Afghanistan National Association for the Deaf, The Community Center for the Disabled, All Afghan Women Disabled Union, Afghanistan Independent Human Rights Commission, Handicap International, and the Afghan National Association for the Blind. http://www.acsf.af/English/Advocacy.html

History & Geography

[1] http://www.allempires.com/forum/forum_posts.asp?TID=14222

[2] Malalai, daughter of a village shepherd, joined her father and fiancée on the battlefield on July 27th, 1880 to fight against the British. She and other Afghan women helped tend the wounded and brought water and spare weapons. As the soldiers were losing morale, Malalai took off her veil and shouted, "Young Love! If you do not fall at the battle of Maiwand, by God, someone is saving you as a symbol of shame." When one of the leading flag bearers was killed, she took up his flag but was soon shot. Some legends say this happened on her wedding day. The Afghan's decisive victory in this important battle turned her into a national folk hero.

[3] The origins of the ethnic groups, especially the Hazaras, is a delicate subject. Historically, rival groups have attempted to disenfranchise the Hazaras by saying that since they are descendants of Genghis Khan's soldiers, the land they own was usurped and so isn't really theirs. Since most of the land currently held by the different ethnic groups was captured at some point in history, and since the Mongol migration happened some 800 years ago, the discussion is moot except for the heavy baggage it carries.

[4] Dupree L. *Afghanistan*. London: Oxford University Press, 2002, pp. 255-413.

[5] Zoroaster, known as Zarathusti in Dari, founded Zoroastrianism sometime between 1200-1500 BCE and died in Balkh, the seat of his religion. http://www.zoroastrianism. cc/universal_religion.html. Other sources date his life anywhere from 8000 BCE to 258 years before Alexander the Great conquered Persia.

[6] Rumi's full name is Maulana Muhammed Khudawandagar Jalaluddin Rumi al Balkhi (1207-1273). A great spiritual master, poetic genius, and the founder of the Mawlawi Sufi order. He was born in Balkh Province, but Wakhsh, the reputed town of his birth, is now in Tajikistan. Some scholars say he was born in the city of Balkh. Differing researchers put his age between 7 and 12 when he and his father began their migrations, ending in up in Konya, Anatolia (now Turkey); see Rumi Network, http://www.rumi.net/about_rumi_main.htm and History of Islam, http://historyofislam.com/contents/the-classical-period/maulana-rumi When his father died in 1231, Rumi succeeded him as a professor of religious sciences and head of a madrassa. Rumi's friendship with Sufi mystic Shams-e Tabrizi led him into Islamic mysticism, and when Shams disappeared, in his love and grief, Rumi poured out a tide of lyric poems for which he is renowned today. His epitaph reads, "When we are dead, seek not our tomb in the earth, but find it in the hearts of men."

[7] Textile Research Center, Hogewoerd 164, 2311 HW Leiden, UK. http://www.trc-leiden.nl

[8] Ansary T. Destiny Disrupted. New York: Public Affairs, 2009. p. 236.

[9] Afghanistan Forest Information and Data, http://rainforests.mongabay.com/deforestation/2000/Afghanistan.htm

[10] The most seriously endangered are the goitered gazelle, leopard, snow leopard, markor goat, and Bactrian deer. Afghanistan is also home to over 380 species of birds, with more than 200 breeding there. Flamingo and other aquatic fowl breed in the lake areas south and east of Ghazni. Ducks and partridges were also common, but all birds are hunted widely, and therefore are becoming scarce, including the endangered Siberian crane.

[11] Polo, Yule, Cordier. *The Travels of Marco Polo*. Mineola, NY: Dover Publications, 1923. "Then there are sheep here as big as asses; and their tails are so large and fat, that one tail shall weigh some 30 pounds. They are fine fat beasts, and afford capital mutton."

[12] International Bird of Mystery, http://www.wcs.org/new-and-noteworthy/warbler-of-the-wakhan.aspx

[13] En Derin, http://www.en-derin.com/artworks/afghanistan-in-the-1950s-and-1960s

[14] Morrison Knudson was founded in 1905 and positioned itself as a major dam builder throughout the United States. Its projects included the Deadwood Dam, 1929-30; the Hoover Dam, 1931-35; and the Grand Coulee Dam, 1941. In all, Morrison Knudsen built over 150 dams. The company was acquired by *URS Corporation* of *San Francisco* in November 2007.

[15] http://www.institute-for-afghan-studies.org/Foreign%20Affairs/us-afghan/helmand_0.htm

[16] Ansary T. *West of Kabul , East of New York*. New York: Picador, 2002, p. 83.

[17] Brzezinski Z. CIA Helped Afghan Mujahideen Before 1979 Soviet Intervention: Agence France-Presse. January 13, 1998. Also: "Brzezinski said, 'We didn't push the Russians to intervene, but we knowingly increased the probability that they would. Now,' he told US President Carter in 1979, 'We can give the USSR its Vietnam War.'" Dreyfuss R. Devil's Game. New York: Metropolitan Books, 2005, p. 265.

[18] Examples of this may be found in Klaits and Klaits' Love and War in Afghanistan. New York: Seven Stories Press, 2005.

[19] Amstutz JB. *Afghanistan: The First Five Years of Soviet Occupation.* Washington, DC: National Defense University Press, 1986.

[20] A person who believes in political Islam.

[21] Because this aid was coming through Pakistan, it was filtered through the interests of the Pakistani Inter-Services Intelligence (ISI), Pakistan's secret police.

[22] Rashid A. *Taliban*. New Haven: Yale University Press, 2001, p. 25.

[23] Mullah Omar was one of four like-minded *mullahs* who were disturbed by the excesses of the warlords who were fighting each other. They chose Mullah Omar as the "first among equals". Ibid., pp. 22-23

[24] Ibid., p. 29

[25] *Madrassa* is Arabic for any type of educational institution. Both religious and secular madrassas were prominent throughout the Islamic world in the eleventh century. Female scholars played an important role even though their numbers rarely rose above one percent. The Mongol sack of Baghdad in 1258 CE ended the inclusion of women. The number of *madrassas* expanded greatly during the 1980s under Pakistani President Zia ul-Haq, and several were used as indoctrination and training centers for jihadists. These were mainly financed by Saudi Arabia. Only a small minority of *madrassas* in Pakistan promote violent jihad. Rather than fighting non-Muslims, the curriculum in most *madrassas* focuses on Islamic studies. This includes the proper length of beards, correct practice of rituals, and opposition to un-Islamic (to Sunnis) practices, such as worshiping at saints' graves. Other madrassas are simply large Islamic schools where three-fourths of the curriculum is in subjects other than Islam. Still, graduates of all of these schools have the requisite fundamentalist beliefs to be attracted to the Taliban army. The US also played an important role in harnessing madrassas for holy war. Part of US support for the Afghan jihad against the Soviets included producing some notably bloodthirsty *madrassa* textbooks, "filled," according to a Washington Post report, "with

violent images and militant Islamic teachings." When the Taliban came to power, these textbooks were distributed for use in their schools as well. A full report on these textbooks, produced by the US Agency for International Development (USAID) with CIA financing, can be found on the Washington Post web site. Stephens J, Ottaway DB. From US, the ABC's of Jihad. Washington Post, March 23, 2002. http://www. washingtonpost .com/ac2/wp-dyn/A5339-2002Mar22?language=printer.

[26] In 1998, Iran and the Taliban were on the verge of war after the Taliban "slaughtered hundreds of Shiites, including nine Iranian diplomats, in Mazar-e-Sharif, Afghanistan." Rapprochement between the two foes began in January, 2000. Joscelyn T. Iran and the Taliban, Allies against America. The Long War Journal. July 28, 2009. http://www. longwarjournal.org/archives/2009/07/iran_and_the_taliban.php#ixzz1rw4mV3QG

[27] United Nations. Press conference on Afghanistan opium survey 2004 (Press release). November 18, 2004. http://www.unodc.org/pdf/afg/afghanistan_opium_ survey_2004.pdf

[28] Rashid A. Op. cit., p. 120. Throughout the 1980s "an immense narcotics trade had developed under the legitimizing umbrella of the CIA-ISI covert supply line to the Afghan mujahidin."

Peggy's Story

[1] Alan Pogue directs the Center for Documentary Photography and is a gifted and dedicated human rights photographer. http://www.documentaryphotographs.com

[2] Mohammad Reza Pahlavi (1919-1980) ruled Iran from 1941 until he was overthrown in 1979.

[3] Rostami-Povey, E. Afghan Women: Identity and Invasion. Zed Books New York, NY p. 11.

[4] After her husband, Shah Rukh Mirza, youngest son of Tamerlane, died, Ghoharshad ruled the Timurad dynasty through her grandson for 10 years until her execution in 1457 at age 80. http://www.helium.com/items/1926370-timurids-queen-gawhar-shad-afghanistan For more on Herat, see my blog post: Herat Parts 1 and 2 http:// www.kelseys.net/blog/page/2

[5] Mary Moffat Livingstone was the wife of David Livingstone, of "Dr. Livingstone, I presume" fame, renowned Scottish medical missionary and explorer. He walked across Africa from Luanda, Angola to Quelimane while Mary was sailing from Scotland to meet him at the mouth of the Zambezi River. They sailed upriver together but she died of malaria in the early stages of their journey, at the age of 41. Mary was a very strong, interesting person. See Healey E., Wives of Fame (London: Sidgwick and Jackson. 1986) and Forster M., Good Wives? Mary, Fanny, Jennie and Me, 1845-2001 (London: Chatto & Windus. 2001).

[6] Joia Jitahidi. The Executive Coach. http://www.amusingworld.com

[7] In Afghanistan as well as Mozambique and other developing countries, many foreigners and most organizations hired unarmed guards whose main job was to act

as a filter for solicitors and guests, and to be a presence against would-be intruders. These guards also had ancillary duties such as gardening, washing cars, and fetching items from the market. With the resurgence of attacks, guards in Afghanistan hired by institutions, especially high profile groups, are increasingly armed.

[8] **Global Exchange** is an international human rights organization dedicated to promoting social, economic and environmental justice since 1988. The "reality tours" they offer in various parts of the world are "experiential educational excursions which give participants connections with local people and an understanding of issues they face." Their Afghan team in Kabul was excellent. http://www.globalexchange.org

[9] Two famed Buddha statues that were blown up by the Taliban sat within a wall of man-made caves that once housed several thousand Buddhist monks. The space including and between the two Buddha grottoes is now a World Heritage Site. On both sides of that area, the caves are used for animal and human housing. For images see my blog post: Bamyan Province, part 1. http://www.kelseys.net/blog/page/2

[10] The Silk Road isn't one road but a network of interlinking trade routes connecting Asia with the Mediterranean and Europe. Marco Polo walked the part of it that crossed the Wakhan Corridor, but not this part that went in front of the wall of Buddhas.

Artists

[1] The 2006 film *Girls on the Air* by Valentina Monti focuses on the station's founder, Humaira Habib.

[2] Nordland, R. *Working to Help a Haven for Afghan Women Blossom* New York Times June 20, 2010 http://www.nytimes.com/2010/06/21/world/asia/21kabul.html?pagewanted=all Also: there are lovely photographs of the newly rehabilitated Women's Garden here. http://www.nytimes.com/slideshow/2010/06/20/world/asia/KABUL.html?ref=asia

[3] See Elaha perform here: http://www.youtube.com/watch?v=xkiNOZplou8 and here: http://www.youtube.com/watch?v=scwT9JbPUX4&feature=related

[4] Forugh Farrokhzad http://www.forughfarrokhzad.org

[5] See the chapter Welayat Prison.

[6] This national dish consists of rice mounded over chunks of mutton and topped with shredded carrots, nuts and raisins. Much as I would have liked, I didn't partake of the fresh salad and peppers, a self-imposed restriction that kept me healthy for the entire trip.

Islam

[1] Mapping the Global Muslim Population http://www.pewforum.org/mapping-the-global-muslim-population.aspx

[2] Nazeer A. *Islam in Persia.* http://historyofislam.com/contents/the-classical-period/islam-in-persia/

[3] Christian children in the West have been told many inaccurate tales about Islam, including that "conversion by the sword" was widely enforced. These, like frightening stories told to Muslim children about Christians, mostly have their origin in the mutual atrocities of the Crusades.

[4] Ebo Stone. A stone in Mecca that represents evil. As part of the hajj, pilgrims participate in the ritual of Stoning the Devil by throwing pebbles at the Ebo Stone.

[5] Afghan Women Writer's Project blog. http://www.awwproject.org/2010/02/the-cemetery-of-my-identity/

Women's Rights

[1] Sharia law. Also Shari'a. Islamic life is regulated by the Shari'a (the Way), or Islamic law. In the strict sense it is much more than law, containing prescriptions for every aspect of life, from rituals, customs, and manners to family law, including the treatment and rights of children. It must be noted that domestic violence runs contrary to many interpretations of Sharia law. Unfortunately, in Afghanistan, perspectives that emphasize equality between the sexes are silenced or ignored. The Quran contains numerous verses implying that domestic abuse is unacceptable in the eyes of the Prophet and that joint decision-making and peace within the household are central to a full embracing of Islam. (See Quranic verses 3:159 and 30:21.) Nijhowne, D., Oates, L. "Living with Violence: A National Report of Domestic Abuse in Afghanistan" Global Rights: Partners for Justice March, 2008. http://www.globalrights.org/site/DocServer/final_DVR_JUNE_16.pdf?docID=9803

[2] The Afghan Women Lawyers Council, the Afghan Women Judges' Association, Afghan Women Lawyers and Professional Association, and the Afghan Civil Society Forum are supported by the United Nations Development Fund for Women (UNIFEM) to support women's leadership and participation in the reconstruction of Afghanistan.

[3] The Shia Personal Status Law is also referred to as the Shia Family Law and the Shia Law in Afghanistan, and as the Marital Rape Law in the West. Human Rights Watch says that the law directly contravenes rights provided under the Afghan Constitution, banning any kind of discrimination and distinction between citizens of Afghanistan. Article 22 states that men and women "have equal rights and duties before the law." The law also contravenes the Convention on the Elimination of All Forms of Discrimination against Women, to which Afghanistan is a party. http://www.hrw.org/news/2009/08/13/afghanistan-law-curbing-women-s-rights-takes-effect

[4] In the cities, courts would use parts of the civil law, as Shinkai says, but in the countryside, where local shuras take on the role of the court system, they would use traditional law.

[5] I visited this beautiful mosque, high school, and university complex. The exquisite architecture, immaculately pruned gardens, well-appointed dorms, thousand-person-capacity mosque, large library, cutting-edge technology, and sports fields offer a peaceful respite from the poverty, dirt, and chaos of Kabul streets. During our tour,

the university president talked about their ecumenical course offerings, with studies in all of the world religions. I was impressed. It wasn't until after I talked with Shinkai and a few others that I learned this is Mr. Mohseni's mosque, and the study of world religions there is from the perspective of their inferiority to Islam.

[6] Other informants, such as Soroya, told me the age is seven for boys and nine for girls. This may be a recent change in the law.

[7] Recipe for a Protest, http://awwproject.org/?s=recipe+for+a+protest. The document has been edited for this book.

[8] Nijhowne, D., Oates, L., op. cit. http://www.globalrights.org/site/DocServer/final_DVR_JUNE_16.pdf?docID=9803. This research is unique in many respects. It is one of the first to report on domestic violence throughout Afghanistan based on samples of women representative of its ethnic and geographic diversity. This study is also one of the first to gather data from surveys with women at the household level, rather than relying on secondary sources, such as records of reported violence at police stations or hospitals.

[9] Ibid.

[10] Sponsored by Arzu. "Arzu" means "hope" in Dari. http://www.arzustudiohope.org

[11] This is an example of "honor killing" – murdering women for damaging their family's perceived honor, even if that damage is merely suspected. In Afghanistan, where women's virtue symbolizes much of the honor of the family, honor killing is seen as a means of restoring pride to the family and stability to society at large. Fathers, brothers, husbands or other family members who kill for honor are following the customs of their culture. Murder, including honor killing, is illegal in Afghanistan, but isn't often prosecuted because it is sanctioned by custom. Although prevalent in Islamic communities, there is nothing in the Quran that justifies honor killings.

RAWA

[1] Brodsky, A. *With All Our Strength*. New York: Routledge, 2003.

[2] You can see horrific footage of a woman's assassination by the Taliban on RAWA's website, and also how to invite a RAWA member to speak to your group: http://www.rawa.org

[3] Support Association for the Women of Afghanistan (SAWA): http://www.sawansw.org.au

Welayat Prison

[1] To take a picture with this camera, the photographer made an exposure by removing the lens cap, counting the time, then replacing the lens cap. Inside the box were trays of developer, wash, and fixer. Once the paper negative developed, it was placed on a stand attached to the camera and photographed to create the positive. The process

took about 10 minutes. The picture I had made in 2003 is now very faded.

[2] The wands look like giant dental mirrors and allow visual checks beneath vehicles to detect any explosives wired there.

[3] Women for Afghan Women (WAW) rehabilitated the newly-painted rooms I saw and has done a lot of other work to make the lives of the prisoners easier. They run seven women's shelters around the country that include family guidance centers, a children of prisoners' support center, and other facilities. http://www.womenforafghanwomen. org

[4] Jones A. *Kabul in Winter: Life Without Peace in Afghanistan*. New York, NY: Metropolitan Books, 2006.

[5] I asked this because while Bill and I were in Burma (Mayanmar), we met Sai, a man who had spent about ten years as a political prisoner. There were four political prisoners in his cell, including a doctor and an engineer. By the time they were released, Sai had acquired much of their knowledge. They had passed the time by teaching each other what they knew. I wondered if this sort of thing went on with the women at Welayat. I found that it did, but only to a small degree. These women didn't have the fervor of political prisoners; in fact, many struggled with depression. Many were traumatized by what had happened and what might yet await them. Also, many were preoccupied about their families outside of prison and perhaps wondering who had caused them to be in prison, and why.

Education

[1] Hansen M. "Soviet Era Textbooks Still Controversial." The Associated Press, The JournalStar.com. September 23, 2007. http://journalstar.com/special-section/news/article_4968e56a-c346-5a18-9798-2b78c5544b58.html

[2] This is Suraia Perlika's organization. You will find more about it in the chapter about her.

[3] The ISAF were taken over by NATO in 2003.

[4] An illustration of this is found in a conversation that Rory Stewart and some old Afghan hands had with Richard Holbrooke, UN special representative for Afghanistan and Pakistan, 2009-2010. Holbrooke stated, "Surely you agree that it is ridiculous to attempt to eradicate opium poppies." But a Harvard fellow who had been working on counter-narcotics policy during the Taliban, replied, "Well, it depends on where you are doing it..." And he launched into an explanation of the various situations and scenarios in differing locales that might respond differently to certain strategies. Localized solutions can often succeed where blanket ones fail. Stewart R., Knaus G. Can Intervention Work? New York: W.W. Norton & Company, 2010, pp.81-83.

[5] The currency of Afghanistan is designated by the symbol "A" for Afghani.

[6] Partlow J. "Afghan widows form community on Kabul hill." Washington Post. August 14, 2011. http://www.washingtonpost.com/world/asia-pacific/afghan-widows-form-community-on-kabul-hill/2011/08/02/gIQA35KtFJ_story.html

Horigal

[1] Afghanistan is one of the most heavily mined countries in the world. According to the Organization for Mine Clearance and Afghan Rehabilitation, (OMAR), "Estimates suggest that around ten people every day are being injured or killed by landmines or unexploded ordinance (UXO)." http://www.mineclearance.org/ Other organizations involved in Afghan landmine education and clearance include: UN Mine Action Centre for Afghanistan (UNMACA) http://www.un.org/apps/news/story.asp?NewsID=29515&Cr=unmaca&Cr1; and Halo Trust, http://www.halotrust.org

Women in Business

[1] Afghan Women's Business Council. http://www.unifem.org/afghanistan/prog/CEED/activities/AWBC.html

[2] Crisps are similar to US-style potato or corn chips except the material is ground into a paste and shaped before being baked.

[3] Aghan Women's Empowerment Grants program. http://kabul.usembassy.gov/awe_2011.html

Women's Health Care Workers

[1] Bartlett, L., MD, Mawji, S., MPH, Whitehead, S., MD, Crouse, C., MSc, Dalil, S., MD, Ionete, D., MB, Salama, P., MD and the Afghan Maternal Mortality Study Team. "Where giving birth is a forecast of death: maternal mortality in four districts of Afghanistan, 1999-2002." The Lancet. March 5, 2005; 365 (9462):864–870. http://www.thelancet.com/journals/lancet/article/PIIS0140-6736(05)71044-8/abstract

[2] The National Midwifery Education Program in Afghanistan: Training Women and Saving Lives. http://www.cfr.org/afghanistan/national-midwifery-education-program-afghanistan-training-women-saving-lives/p25260

[3] International Midwife Assistance operated the Community Midwife Training Program in Afghanistan from 2004 until 2006. Currently, the midwife training program is run by the Agha Khan Development Network. IMA is now providing similar services in Uganda. http://www.akdn.org/afghanistan and http://www.midwifeassist.org

[4] According to Medicinenet.com, eclampsia is a dangerous condition of pregnant women with symptoms including high blood pressure and protein in the urine. It sometimes leads to seizures. Pre-eclampsia, which is sometimes asymptomatic, can develop into full blown eclampsia without treatment. ViTamim deficiency and poor nutrition play a big role in this and many other pregnancy issues. http://www.medicinenet.com/pregnancy_preeclampsia_and_eclampsia/article.htm

[5] Cartwright-Jones, C. Neonatal henna and bilirubin levels. The Henna Page. http://www.hennapage.com/henna/encyclopedia/medical/neonatal.html

[6] Rubin, A. "Burning Desperation: Why Did You Burn Yourself?" New York Times, November, 7, 2010.http://www.rawa.org/temp/runews/2010/11/17/burning-desperation-why-did-you-burn-yourselfo.html

[7] Ibid.

[8] Rubin, A. "For Afghan wives, a desperate, fiery way out." New York Times, November 7, 2010. http://www.nytimes.com/2010/11/08/world/asia/08burn.html?pagewanted=all

[9] Garcia, J.M. "Abusive Afghan Husbands Want this Woman Dead." Mother Jones. January/February, 2011. http://motherjones.com/politics/2011/01/self-immolation-afghanistan-maria-bashir-herat?page=1

[10] Quoted in: O'Donnell, L. "Desperation Drives Abused Afghan Women to Death by Fire." AFP. September 27, 2010.

http://www.google.com/hostednews/afp/article/ALeqM5jnfbboHmBAwkh2YVMOf6olV4faDA?docId=CNG.08c83b13d2be2980df3ec18ebf2dd1d5.51

[11] Ibid.

[12] ___. "Suicide rate soars among Afghan women." Xinhua. Kabul, July 31, 2010. http://news.xinhuanet.com/english2010/world/2010-07/31/c_13424261.htm

[13] Quoted in: O'Donnell, L. Op. cit.

[14] Smith, D. "Between Choice and Force: Marriage Practices in Afghanistan." In: Heath J, Zahedi A, eds. Land of the Unconquerable: The Lives of Contemporary Afghan Women. Berkeley and Los Angeles, CA: University of California Press, 2011, pp. 162-174.

[15] Exchange marriage occurs between two families, both with a daughter and a man wanting marriage, who agree to trade daughters and thus avoid the high bride prices. When the groom has no say in the matter he often takes out his displeasure on his bride.

[16] TrustLaw, http://www.trust.org/trustlaw/blogs/the-word-on-women/afghan-tribal-elders-ban-an-abusive-tradition-for-women-in-khost-province-what-it-means-for-women-across-afghanistan

Elderly

[1] The World Bank. http://data.worldbank.org/country/afghanistan

Parliamentary Women

[1] The Bonn Agreement (officially called the Agreement on Provisional Arrangements

in Afghanistan Pending the Re-Establishment of Permanent Government Institutions) was created to set up a transitional government in Afghanistan after the fall of the Taliban government.

[2] Malalai was schooled in the RAWA feminist and activist philosophy, and although privately she is a RAWA supporter, she has distanced herself from them for her own and the group's protection.

[3] http://opawc.org/index.php

[4] Joya., M, O'Keefe., D. *A Woman Among Warlords: The Extraordinary Story of an Afghan Who Dared to Raise Her Voice.* New York: Scribner, 2009.

[5] Defense Committee for Malalai Joya. http://www.malalaijoya.com/dcmj

[6] Literacy is not a requirement to become a Member of Afghanistan's Parliament.

[7] By "tested warlords," she means the commanders who proved their lack of concern for their country during their fights against each other for personal power in the civil war.

[8] Joya, M., Op. cit, pp. 213, 217.

[9] The London Conference of 2006 produced *The Afghanistan Compact* establishing the framework for international cooperation with Afghanistan for the following five years. http://www.nato.int/isaf/docu/epub/pdf/afghanistan_compact.pdf

Refugees

[1] The Bayat Foundation, started by Afghans living in the US, provides a variety of programs to aid people throughout Afghanistan. http://www.bayatfoundation.org/index.html

Returnees

[1] Branden, N. The Six Pillars of Self-Esteem. New York: Bantam, 1994.

Tajwar Kakar

[1] Night letters were the primary means of mass communication for the resistance. Tajwar led a team that wrote and distributed these letters after curfew by tossing them over house-compound walls. In Afghanistan, all houses lie within walled compounds that contain outbuildings such as a privy, storage buildings, and secondary houses for servants or extended family members.

[2] May Day is International Worker's Day, and was celebrated in Kabul with parades of Soviet soldiers and military equipment.

[3] See Lessing, D. *The Wind Blows Away our Words.* New York, NY: Vintage Books 1987.

[4] It's a 12-hour drive when the roads and driving conditions are good.

[5] "They" is likely Afghan communists, but it could also have included warlords, bandits, or others taking advantage of the chaos.

[6] Peshawar and Quetta are two conservative Pakistani cities near the Afghanistan border. Peshawar alone was hosting 4,000,000 Afghan refugees at the time, some in camps outside the city, some living on their own resources in houses and apartments.

[7] Islam allows a number of things that Afghan and especially Pashtun traditions might forbid such as a girl or woman's right to study, work, and go out alone. The *mullahs* she talked with understand this and would have allowed those and perhaps other things.

[8] What Tajwar means here is that when the *mujahidin* were ridding their country of the Soviet invaders, it was a "holy war" in their eyes. When the seven leaders began fighting against each other to win the country for themselves, they were "selling the *jihad*."

[9] The UN's Disarmament, Demobilization and Reintegration (DDR) program was launched in April, 2003, by the UN Development Program and has reportedly been successful in removing most of the heavy weaponry of the recognized militias. However, there are weaknesses, like the 1870 unofficial militias that lie outside the DDR mandate. The Karzai government and its international supporters have been partially complicit in maintaining the power of these militia commanders. The US-led coalition has relied on such commanders in its operations against al Qaeda and the Taliban, empowering US local allies militarily and economically at the expense of central government. The UN began Disbandment of Illegal Armed Groups (DIAG) in 2005. http://www.undp.org.af/whoweare/undpinafghanistan/Projects/psl/prj_anbp.htm

[10] "Hajai Sultana." Tajwar went on the *hajj* before she returned to Afghanistan to start the Omid School, so she is called *hajai*, the female form of *haji*. As mentioned earlier in the chapter, Sultana means queen, and some *mujahidin* leaders had called her Sultana while they were fighting the Soviets. It is a title of utmost respect.

[11] Tajwar ran in the September, 2010 election after all, but didn't win.

Suraia Perlika

[1] See Kakar, M. Afghanistan: *The Soviet Invasion and the Afghan Response, 1979-1982*. Berkeley and Los Angeles, CA: University of California Press, 1997.

[2] See Martin, E. *Afghanistan: A Short History of Its People and Politics*. New York: Harper Collins, 2002. p. 251.

[3] Death Tolls for the Major Wars and Atrocities of the Twentieth Century. http://necrometrics.com/20c1m.htm#Afghanistan

[4] King, L. "Afghan Women Break Barriers in a Male Bastion: The Army." September 25, 2010. Los Angeles Times. http://articles.latimes.com/2010/sep/25/world/la-fg-afghan-army-women-20100925

The Taliban

[1] Gross, T., Rubin A. "Growing Violence Clouds Afghanistan's Future." Fresh Air, National Public Radio member station WHYY (Boston, MA). September 8, 2011.

[2] From my interview with Professor Akhram on March 1, 2010. The National Independant (sic) Peace and Reconciliation Commission's website is: http://www.pts.af

[3] Cohen, T. "Taliban factions compete for credit in CIA bombing deaths." CNN US, January 3, 2010. http://articles.cnn.com/2010-01-03/us/cia.bombing.claims_1_pakistani-taliban-baitullah-mehsud-hakimullah-mehsud?_s=PM:US

[4] Shinkai is using the term "mafia" in a generic sense meaning organized crime. There are many different organized crime groups in Afghanistan. See "Drug Trafficking and the Development of Organized Crime in Post-Taliban Afghanistan." http://siteresources.worldbank.org/SOUTHASIAEXT/Resources/Publications/448813-1164651372704/UNDC_Ch7.pdf

[5] Hafvenstein, J. *Opium Season*. Connecticut: Lyon's Press, 2007.

[6] Chemonics is an international development company headquartered in Washington, DC. http://www.chemonics.com/Pages/Home.aspx

[7] Baker, A. "What happens when we leave Afghanistan" Time Magazine. July 29, 2010.

[8] Khoshnood, Z. "The end of a tradition." Afghanistan Today. January 5, 2011. http://www.afghanistan-today.org/article/?id=105

[9] International Crisis Group. http://www.crisisgroup.org

[10] Rondeaux, C. "Reconsidering reconciliation in Afghanistan." Foreign Policy Magazine. September 21, 2011. http://afpak.foreignpolicy.com/posts/2011/09/21/reconsidering_reconciliation_in_afghanistan

Youth

[1] Index Mundi. Afghanistan Demographics Profile 2012. http://www.indexmundi.com/afghanistan/demographics_profile.html

[2] Mohib, L. and Mohib, M. "Can Civil Society Save Afghanistan?" Foreign Policy. August 16, 2012. http://afpak.foreignpolicy.com/posts/2012/08/16/can_civil_society_save_afghanistan

[3] Youth, Exchange and Study Program. http://exchanges.state.gov/youth/programs/yes.html

[4] Arghandiwal, M. "Afghan Social Media War Steps up with New Campaign." Reuters. July 22, 2012. http://www.reuters.com/article/2012/07/22/net-us-afghanistan-media-idUSBRE86L08P20120722

[5] Strand A. and Suhrke A. Refugees in Iran: From Refugee Emergency to Migration Management. Oslo: Chr. Michelsen Institute and the International Peace Research Institute. June 16, 2004. http://www.cmi.no/pdf/?file=/afghanistan/doc/CMI-PRIO-AfghanRefugeesInIran.pdf

Frequently Asked Questions

[1] The Mini Mobile Children's Circus (MMCC) teaches children and youth how to juggle, rollerblade, do acrobatics and perform for school children. When I rode the bus with them to a performance, the kids laughed and joked, and didn't seem at all nervous about being onstage. MMCC has two shifts of training. Children must attend school either morning or afternoon in order to qualify for the program. http://mmccinternational.org/pages/about.htm See also: http://www.clownswithoutborders.net/countries/afghanistan http://www.nostrings.org.uk http://skateistan.org

[2] **Rostom-Povey, E.** *Afghan Women Identity and Invasion*. London: Zed Books, 2007.

[3] **Brodsky, A.** *With All Our Strength*. New York: Routledge, 2003. pp. 162-179.

Epilogue

[1] **Parker, K.** "Women Aren't Pet Rocks." Washington Post, April 1, 2011.

Index

CPSIA information can be obtained at www.ICGtesting.com
Printed in the USA
LVOW08s1951121213

365049LV00006B/601/P

9 780985 750206